INKSTONE
PAINTINGS AND POEMS

Published 2022 by Page Addie Press. United Kingdom
Inkstone. Paintings and Poems Hanoi. Copyright© All rights reserved, Bruce Blanshard and Susan Blanshard

ISBN: 978-1-7397780-0-2 paperback

A CIP record for this book is available from the British Library,

BLANSHARD & BLANSHARD

INKSTONE
PAINTINGS AND POEMS

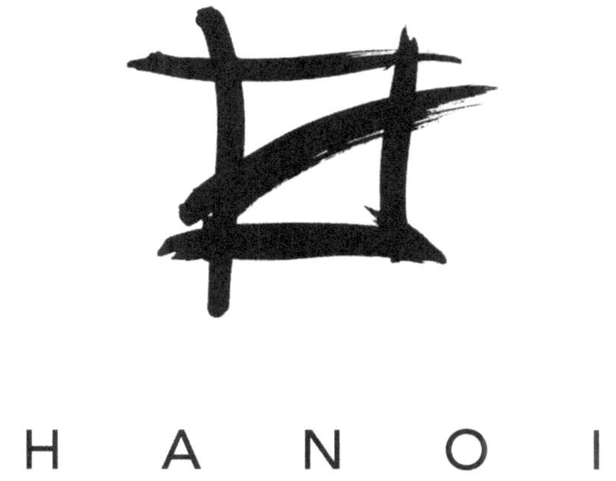

HANOI

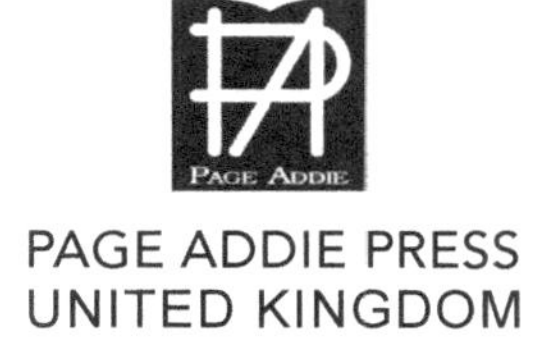

PAGE ADDIE PRESS
UNITED KINGDOM

CONTENTS

In a foreign
landscape,
we are ghosts
entering
night's

séance

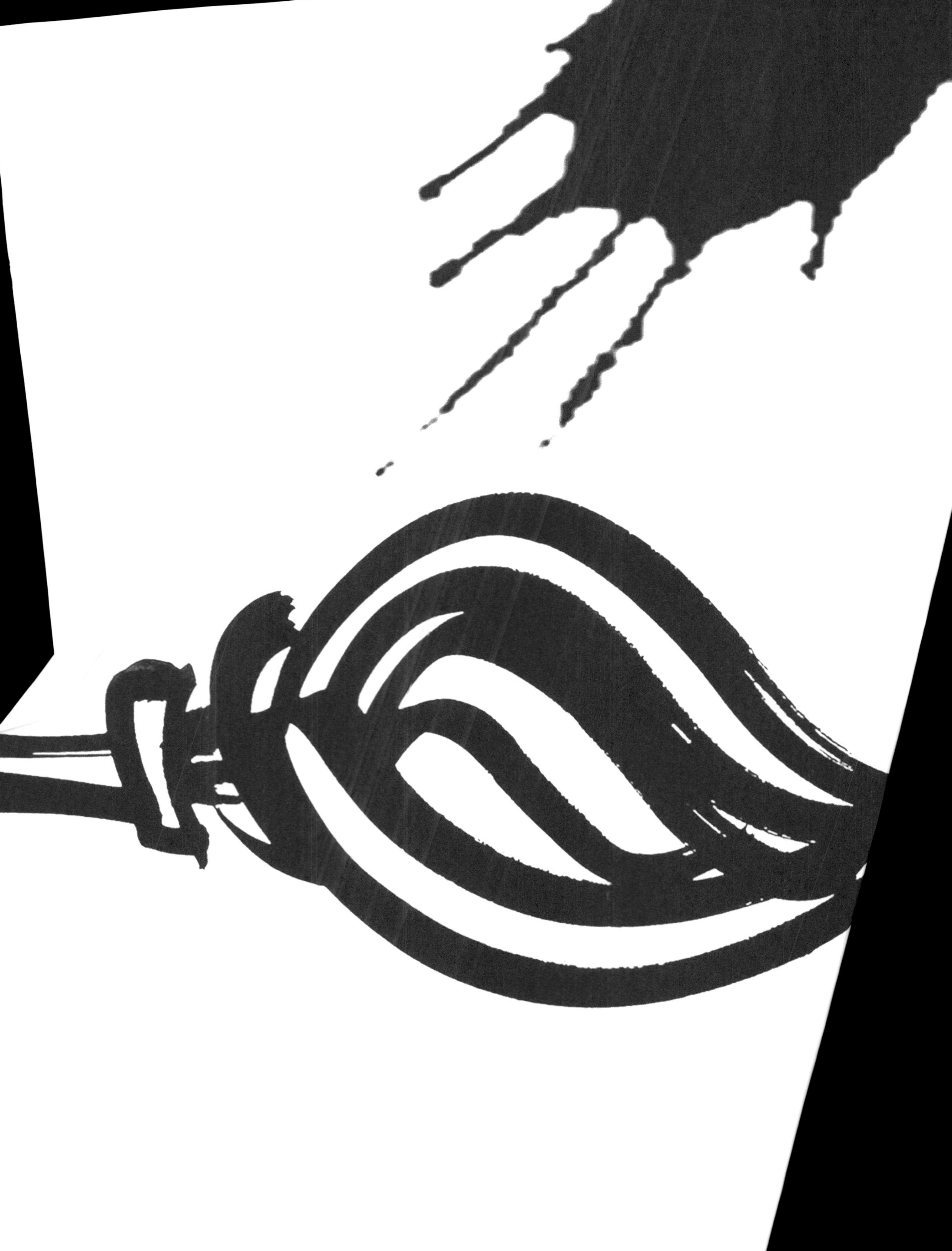

NOCTURNES

In the morning of altered ways
white blossoms lasting longer
if I return, to you, my lover
the fragrance will be stronger

whatever is loved, becomes a blessing
brings in morning, as milk
mixes with ashes, for alms
as the pearl-bowl is lowered

whatever exists in a place, and so on
a place on grave mound found
a long line of otherworld ghosts
gather winter sedge in timely mist

each face with familiar features exist
in former times more than beautiful
The Lovely Ones, wild and licentious
decline with the seasons, to become
n auspicious collection of bones
t under the old moon, I saw it happen
gh I wish, not to grow old
omen's faces, gone centuries pale

e reflection in the mirror
-own orphaned shadow.

THE MONKS' GARDEN

At Ho Bo De Lake House
people come to pray for fortune
where bamboo grows, orchids open
a lotus is that, and lucky as well

there, fountain of moss and brick
beyond this, across the mist flowers
Temple Monks' left or fled, gone --
open, the lacquer gate

and gone, vanished silent
a thousand prayers come undone
it was strange emptiness, left eerie silence
as an untended garden outgrows its despondency

yesterday, a drop of dew, sylvan by nature
handful of spice, incense or ashes, to catch
the slightest puff of prevalent wind
still gold-winged dragonflies appear a whisper
blossoms of apricot, peach gold and silver
on the same tree, defying verdant alchemy

we came here, in the same garden
trees appear far and hazy
and forsake; branch, twig, leaves, the flesh
lucid seed, into a garden of floating light
between mirage and ghost --
just where we chance to belong
there falls an ever-after-shadow.

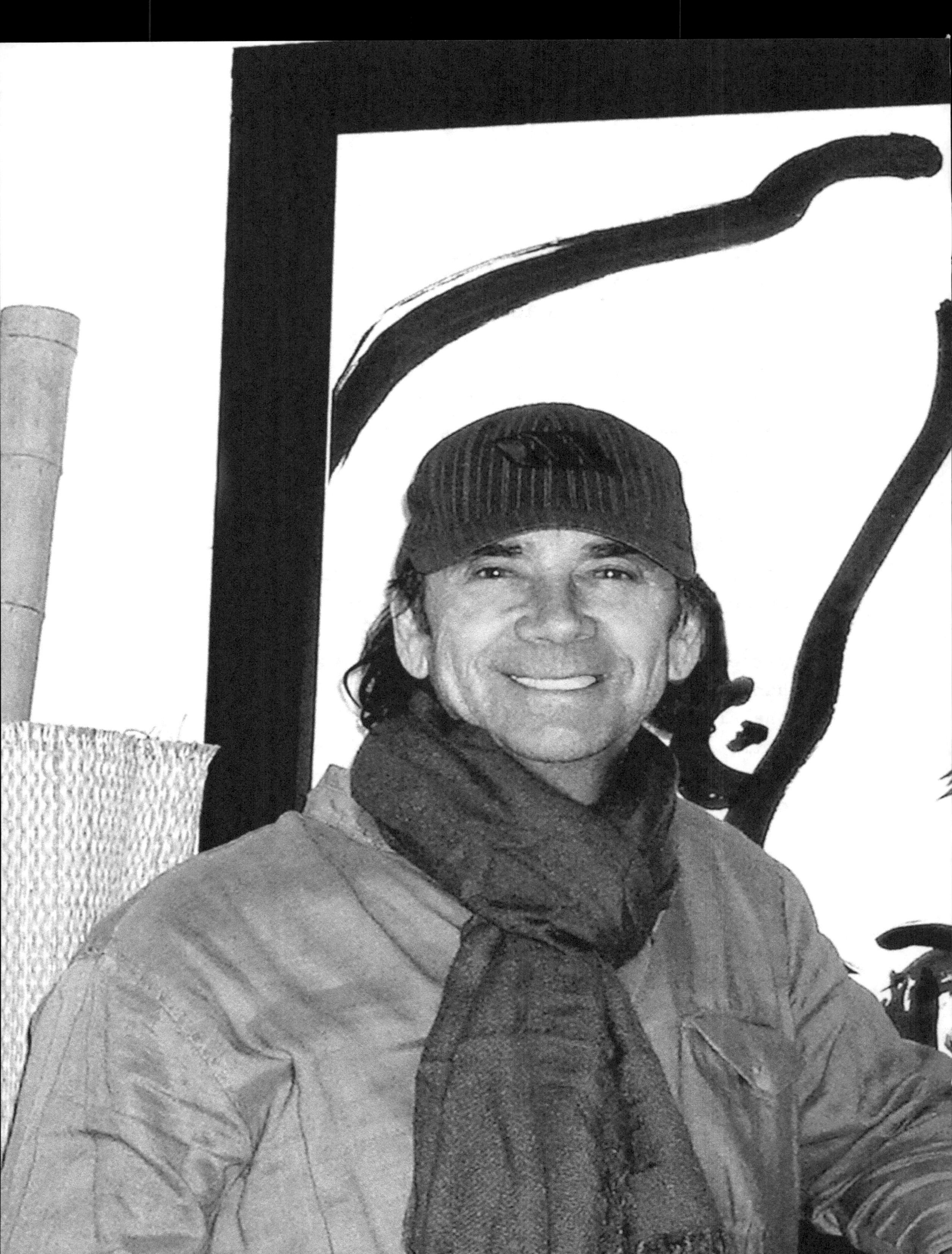

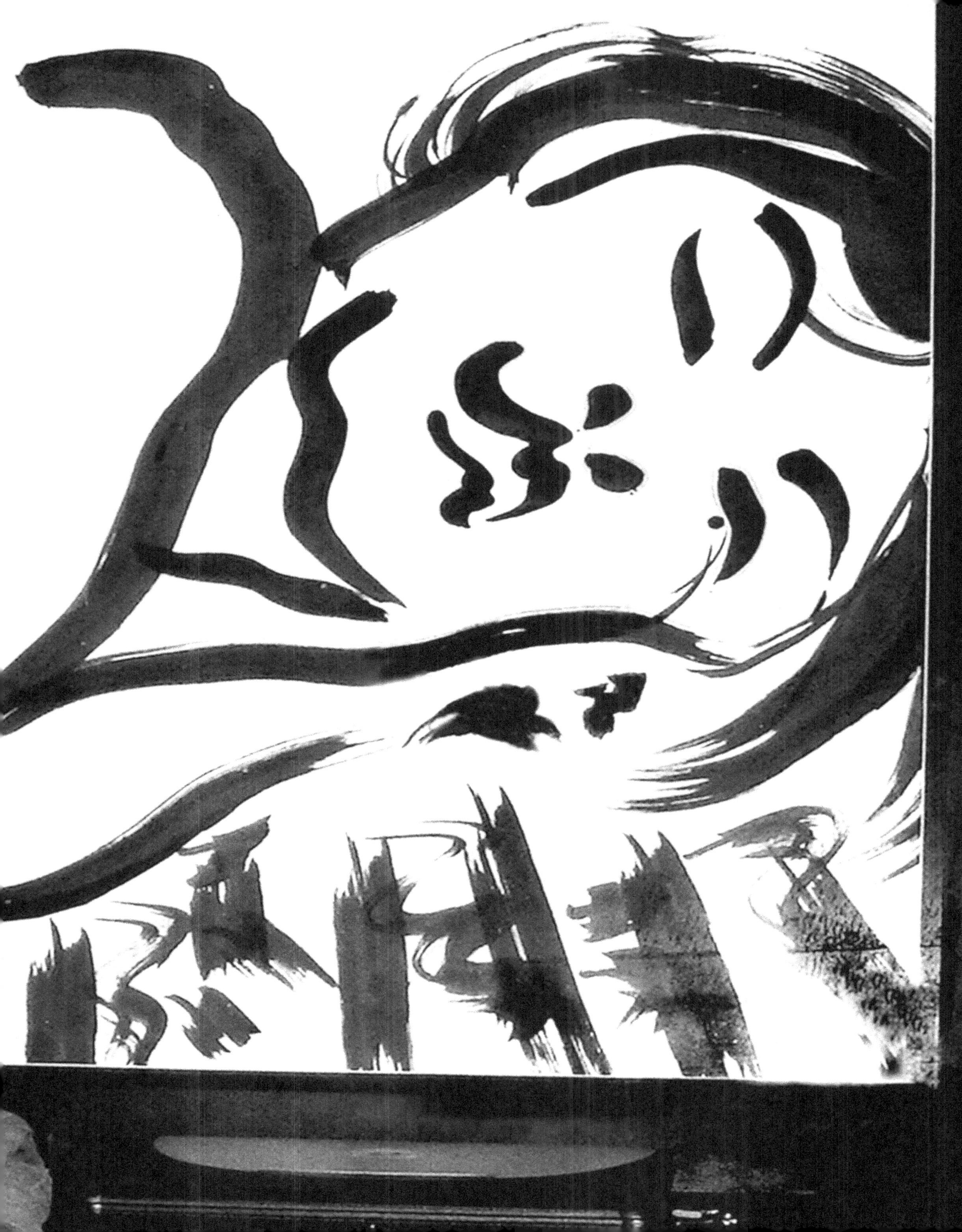

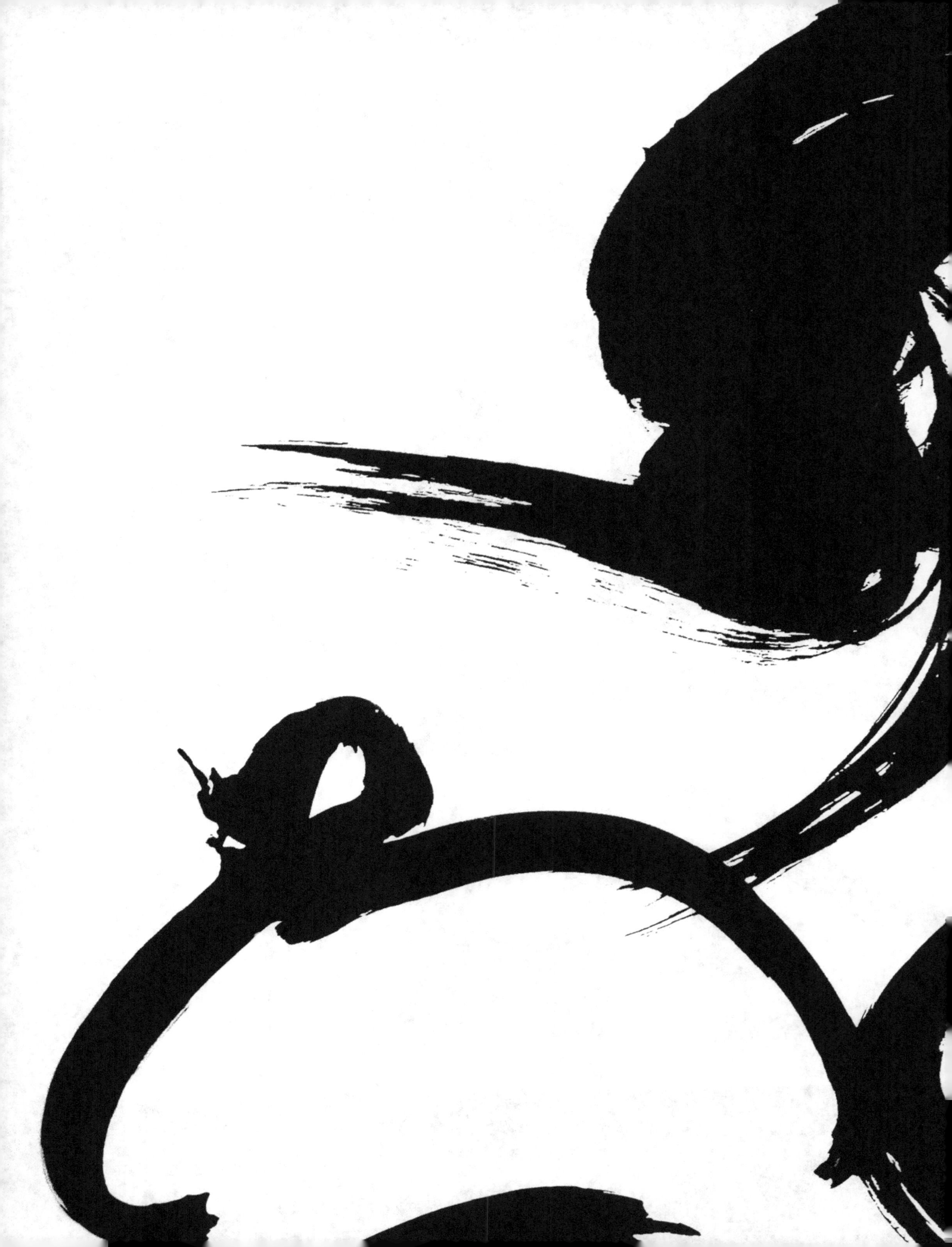

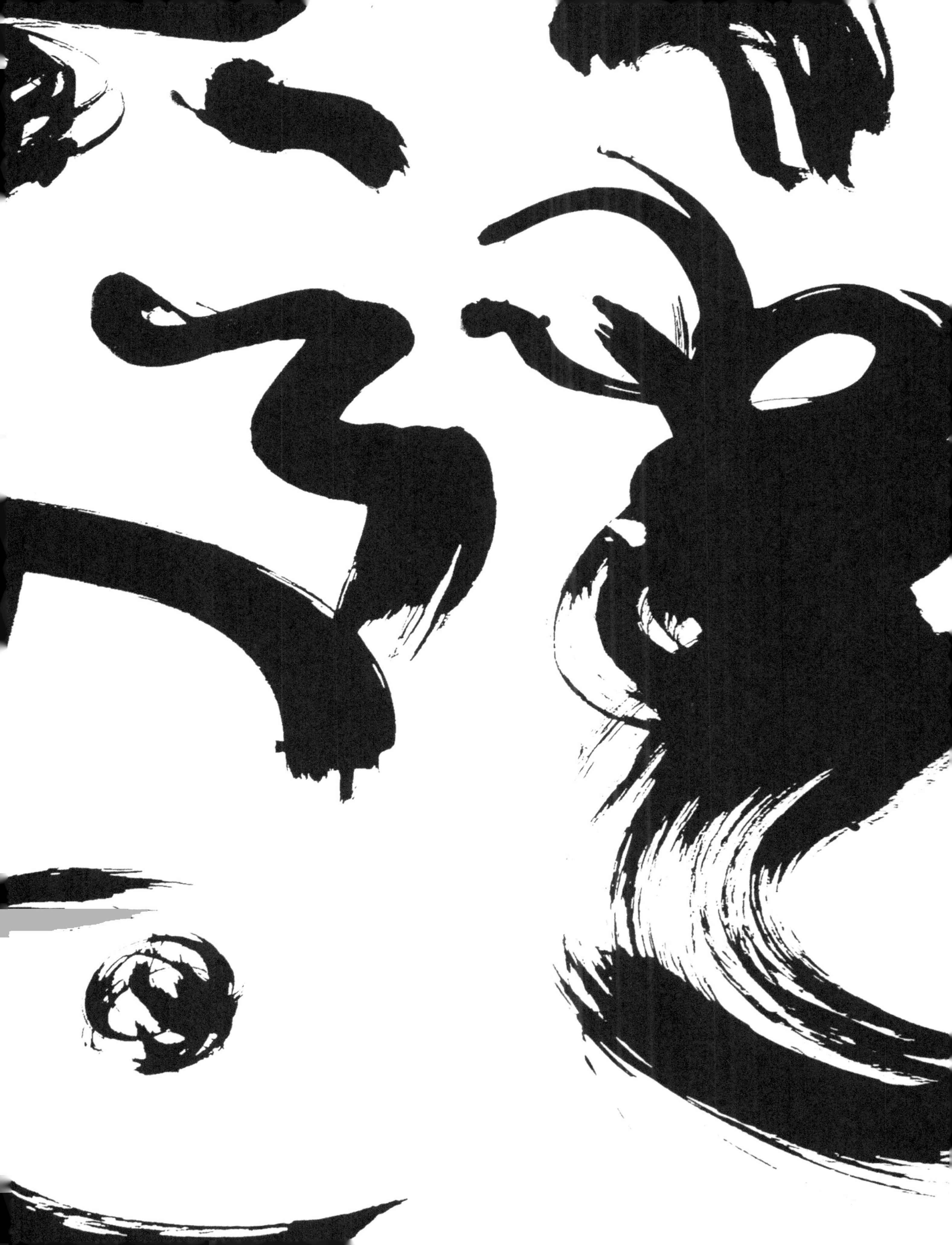

THE CROSSING

One bridge over The Red River
Gustave Eiffel's second masterpiece
reaches up and over mosses and grasses

a simple house in north village-yard
light rain remains on the light dust
all old streets, alleys, walls, stones

all ways, of clay tile roofs, home
there is no summer in cast-iron roses
we are housed between earth and sky

one season, the river floods
one season, the river goes dry

now, when you come to the bridge
we must make separation
and go out through thousand miles
cross the river of dead iron-grass

how smoke-flowers blurred over the river
splitting our world to fragments.

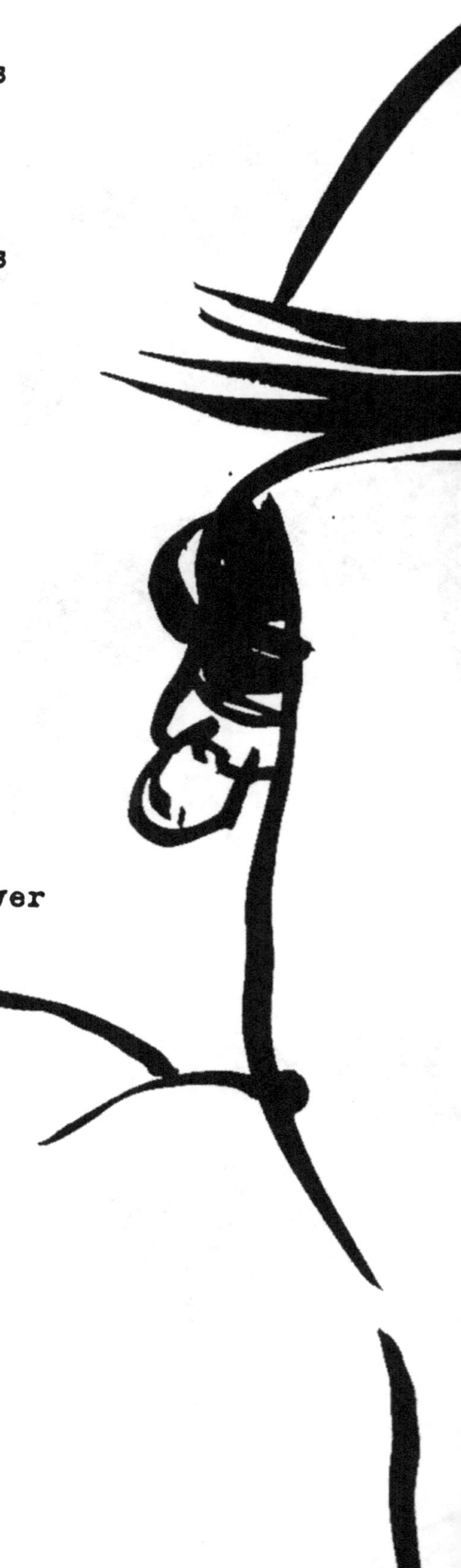

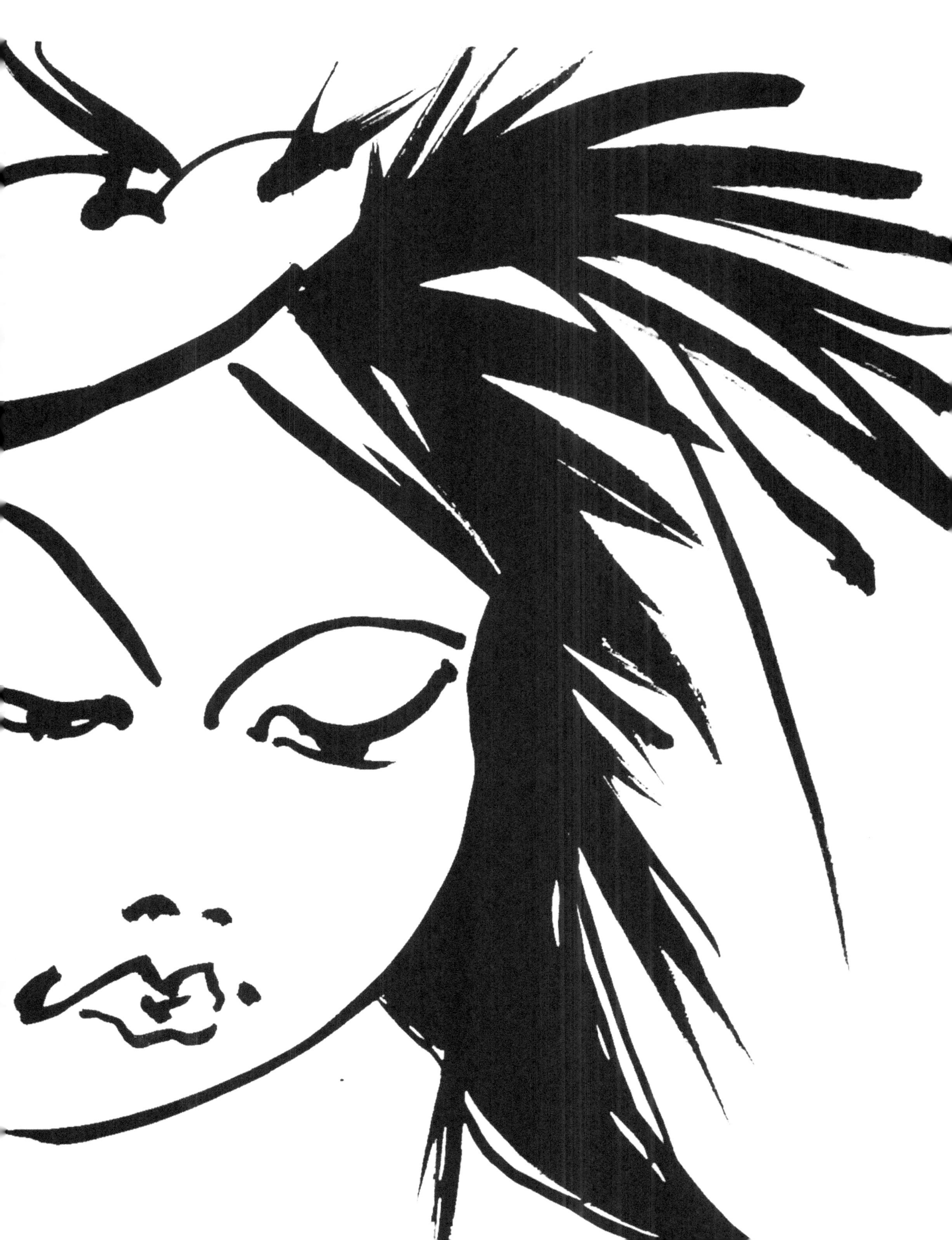

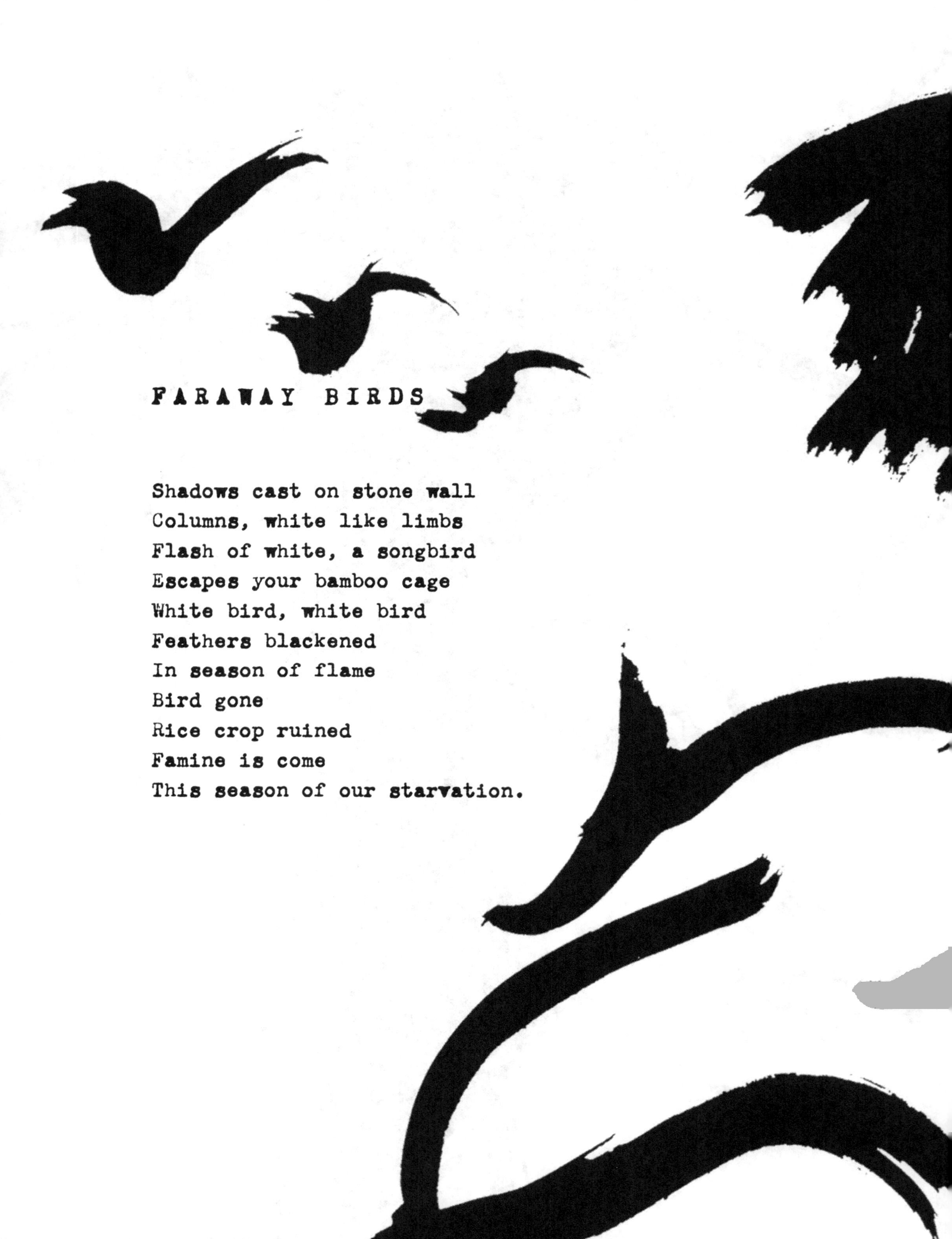

FARAWAY BIRDS

Shadows cast on stone wall
Columns, white like limbs
Flash of white, a songbird
Escapes your bamboo cage
White bird, white bird
Feathers blackened
In season of flame
Bird gone
Rice crop ruined
Famine is come
This season of our starvation.

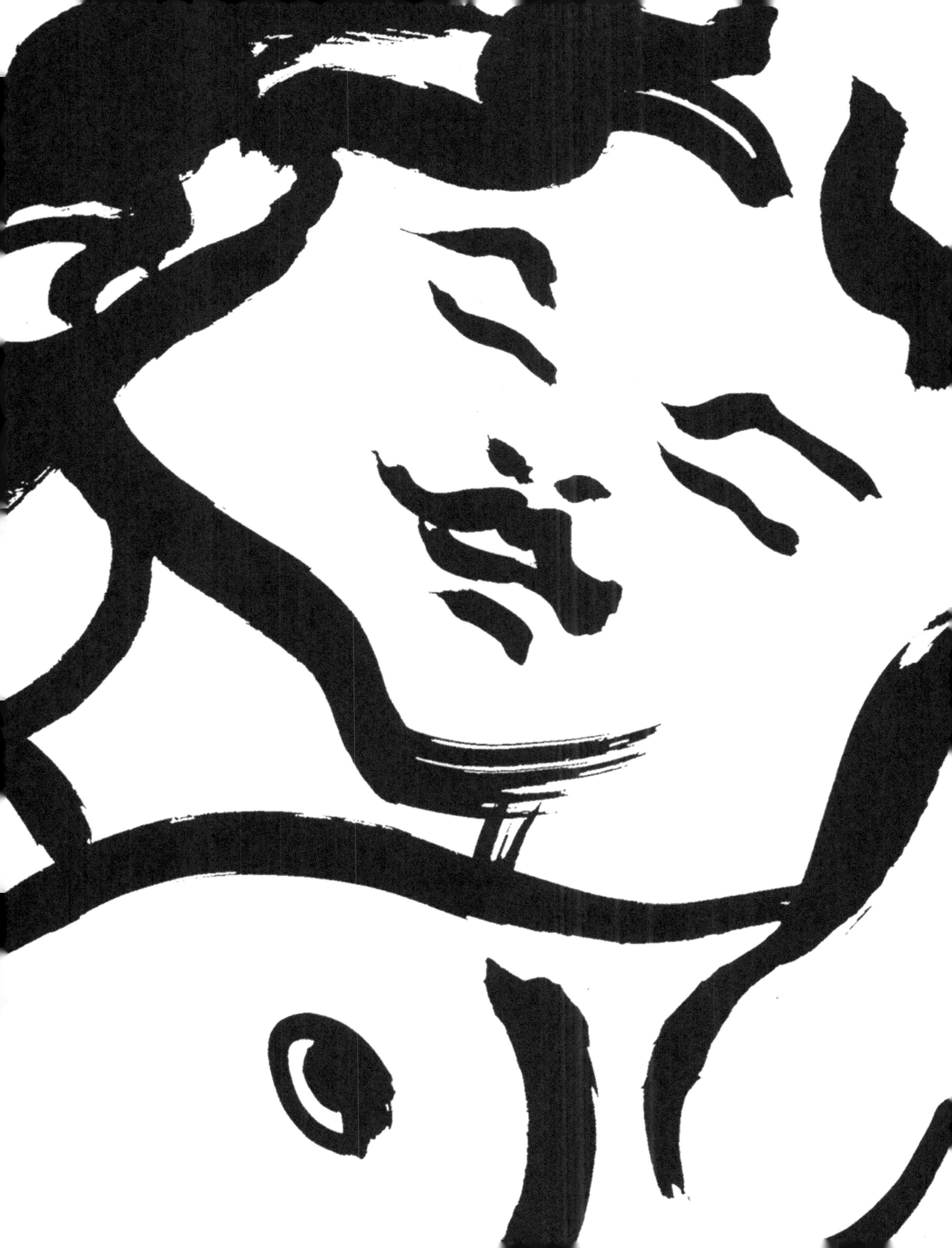

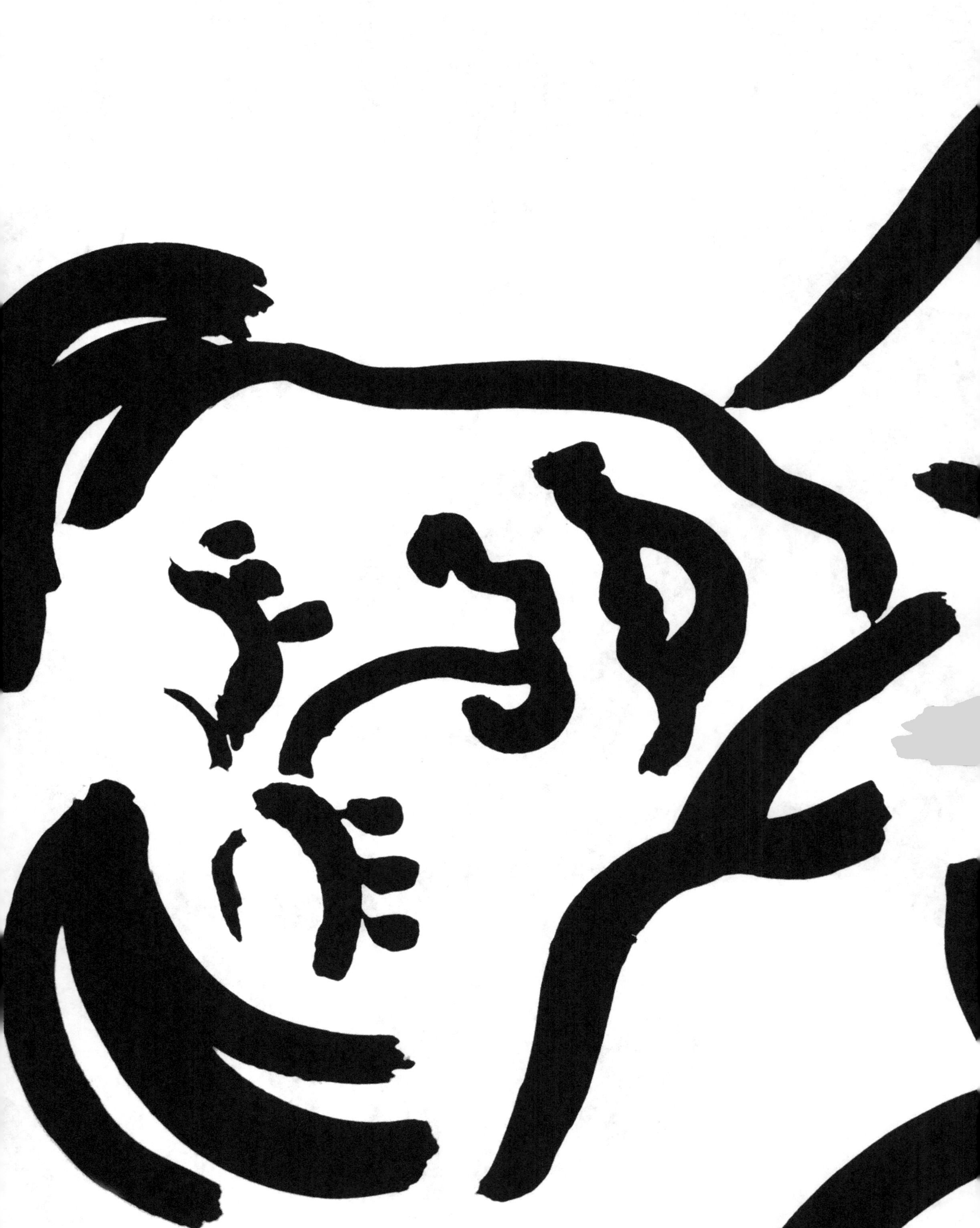

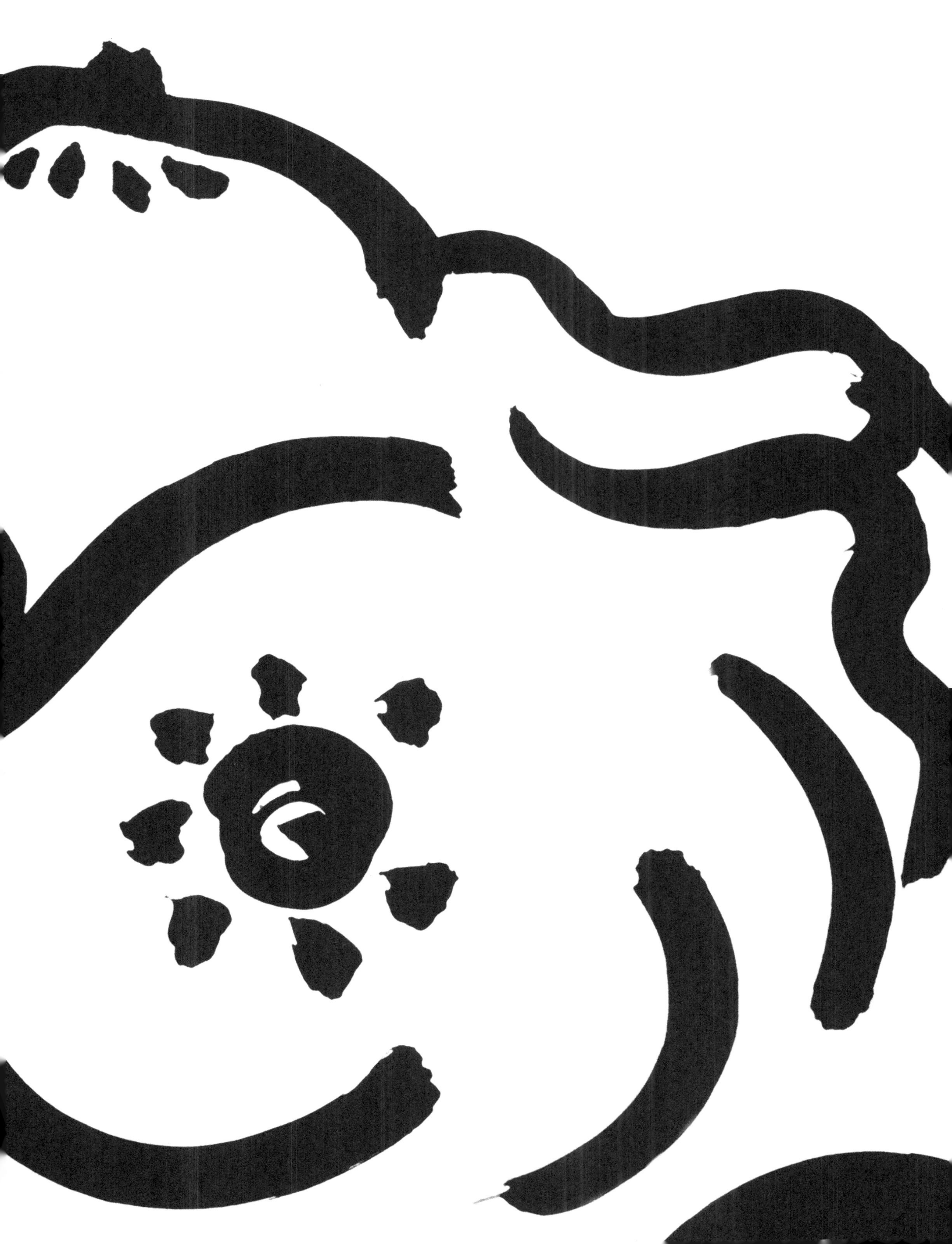

SLEEPING MAT

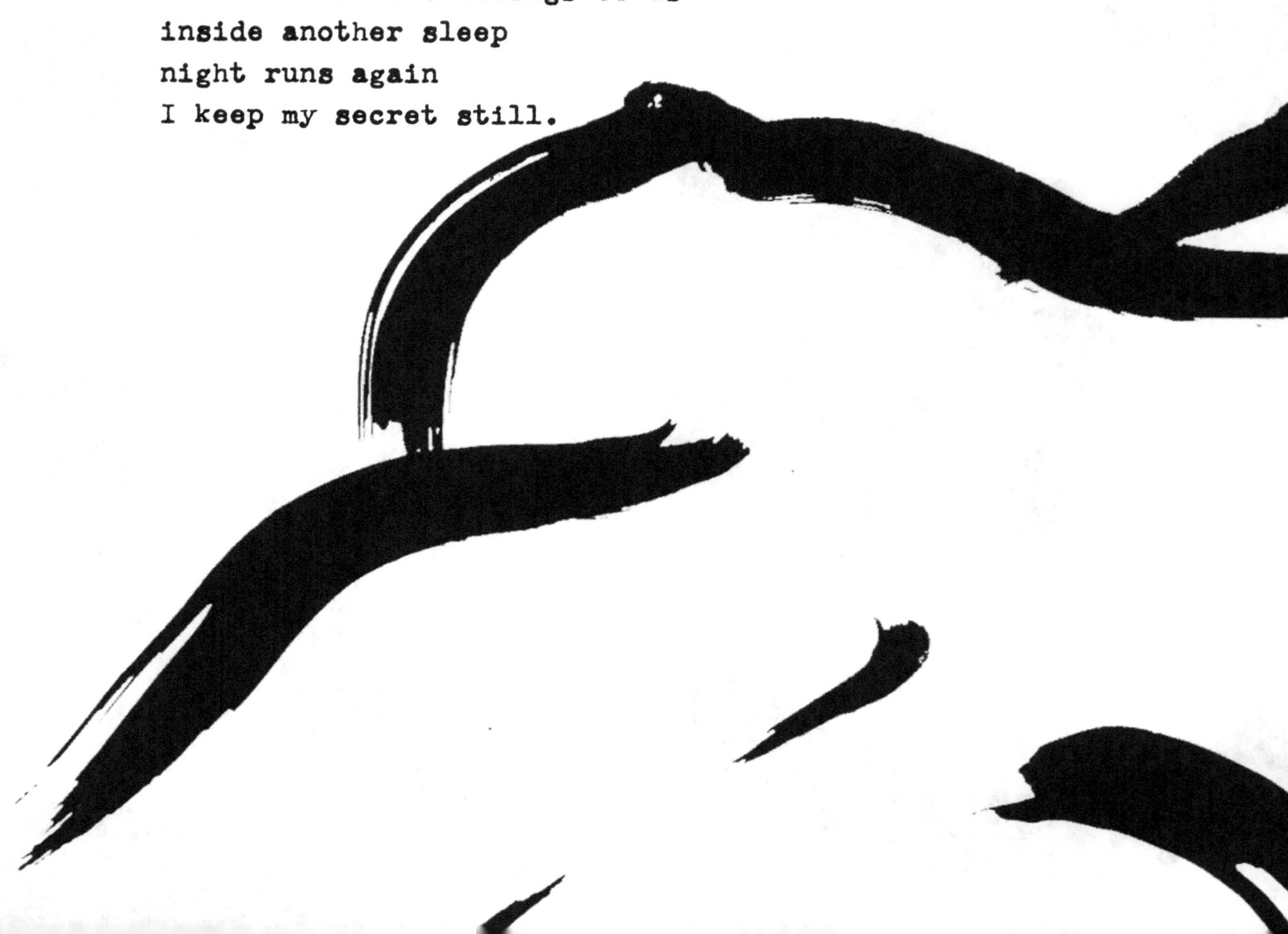

But now -- scent of summer
the heart longs
for a simple four-mat room:

I find myself falling
deep into your beautiful words
blurring my senses to everything
your voice magnetic
and all that is inside
I see the dream
between the words
saying yes
the remains of life we keep
all we have left belongs to us
inside another sleep
night runs again
I keep my secret still.

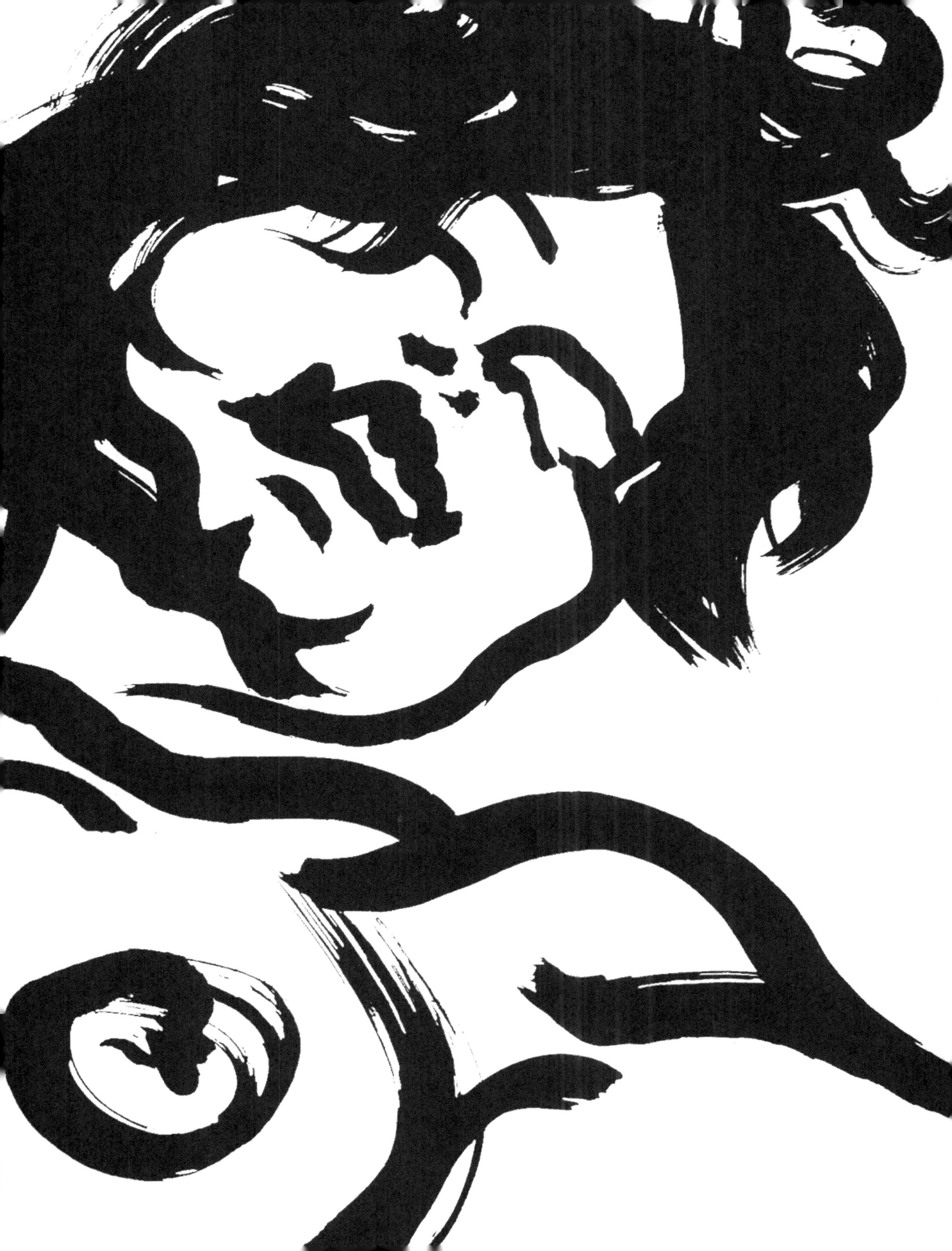

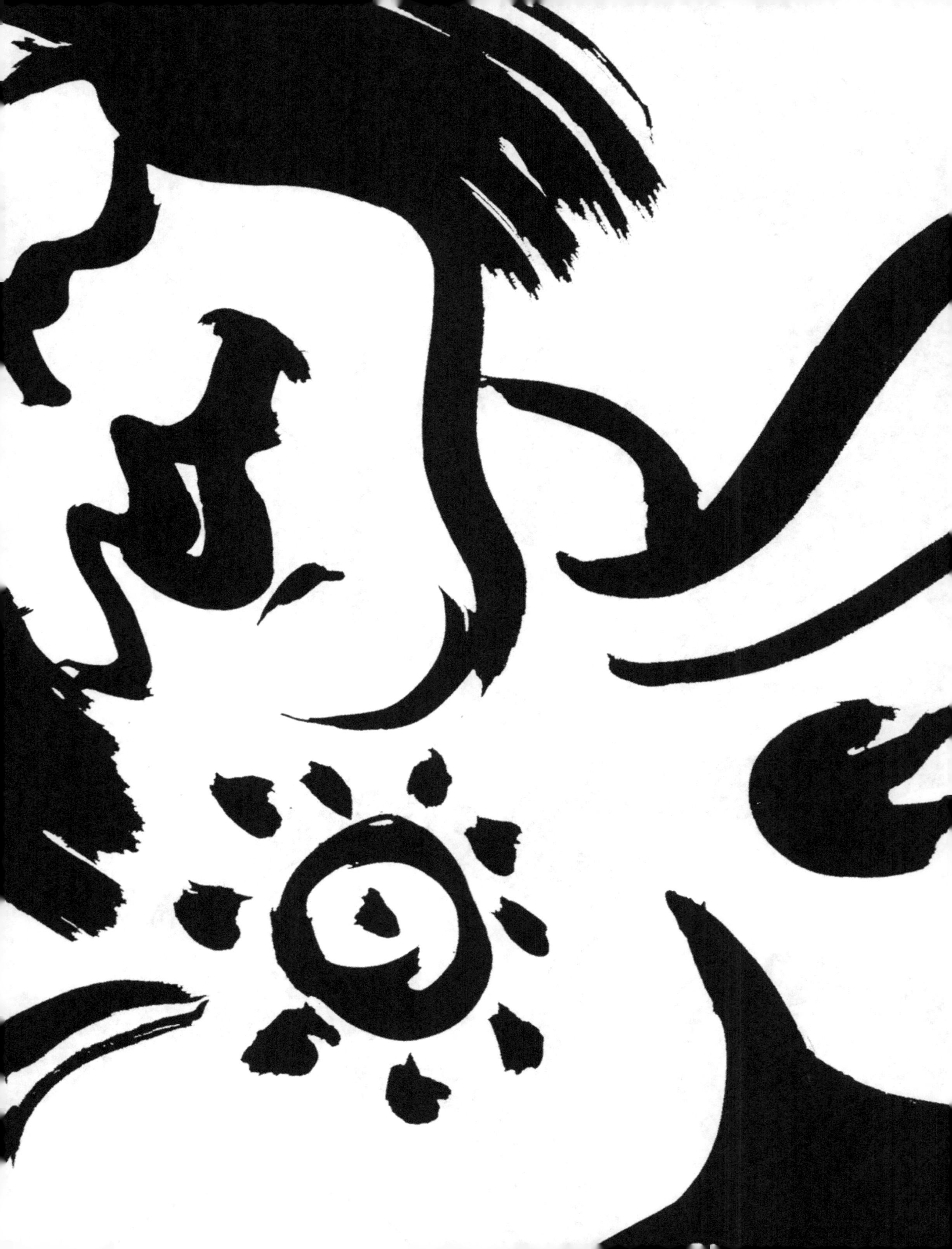

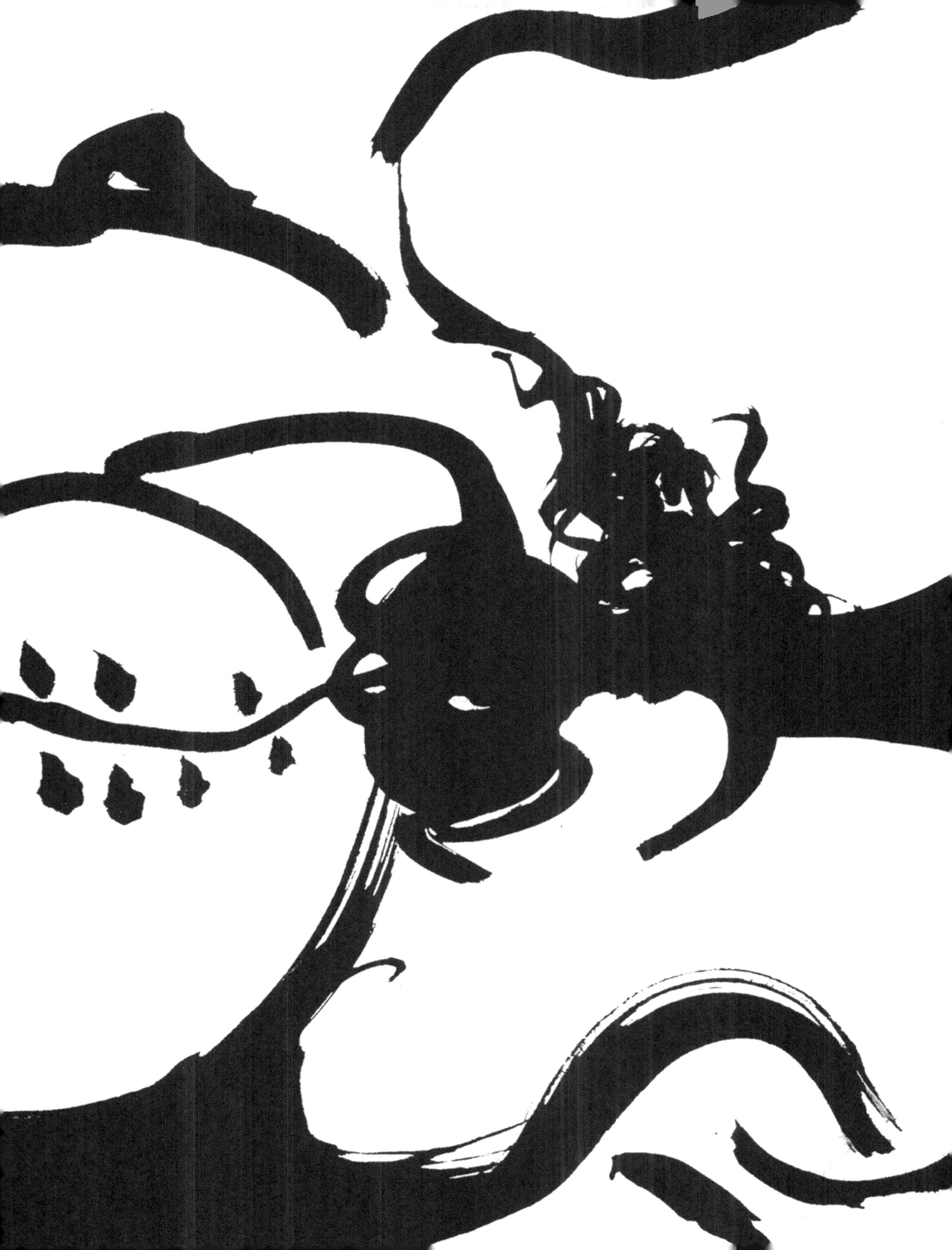

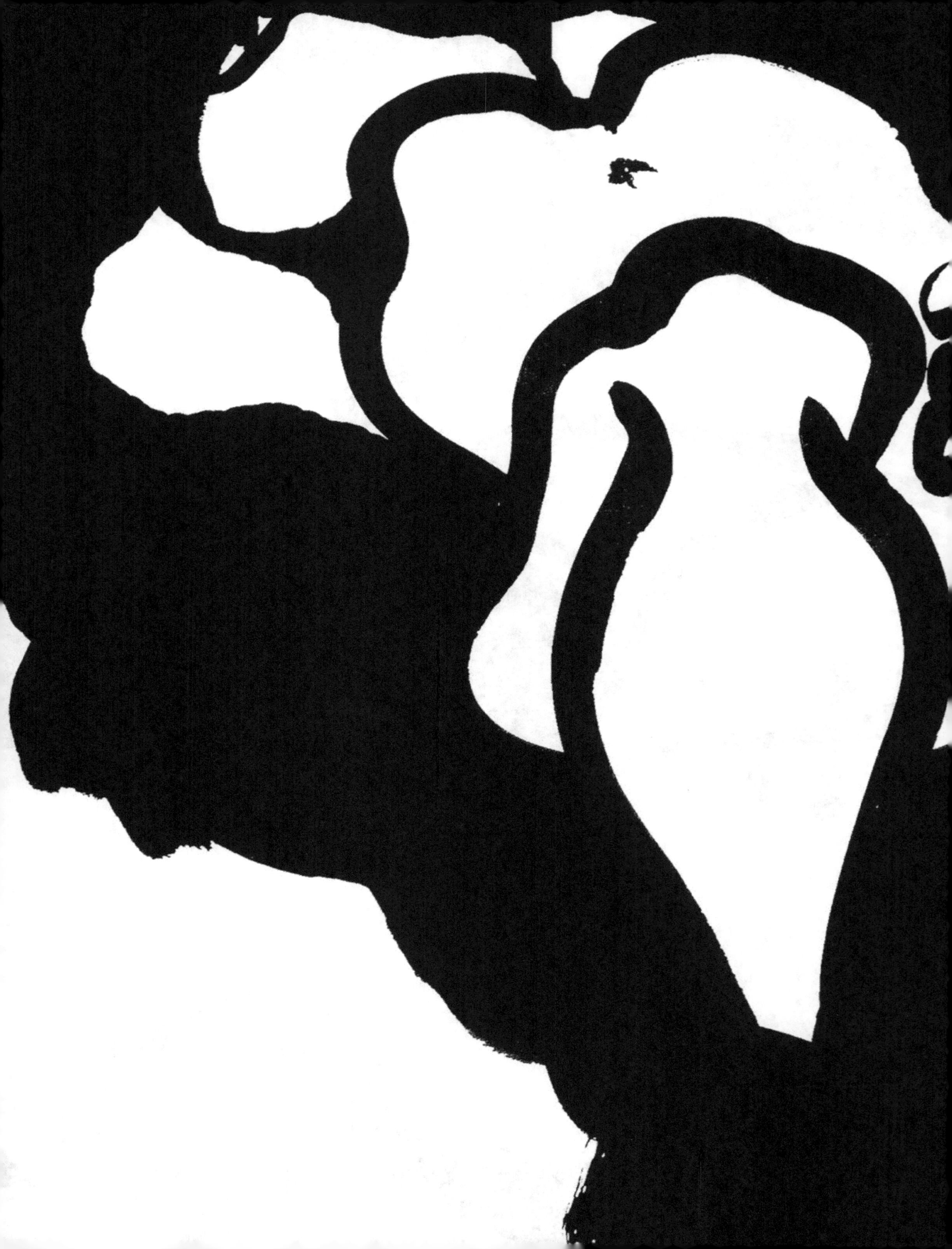

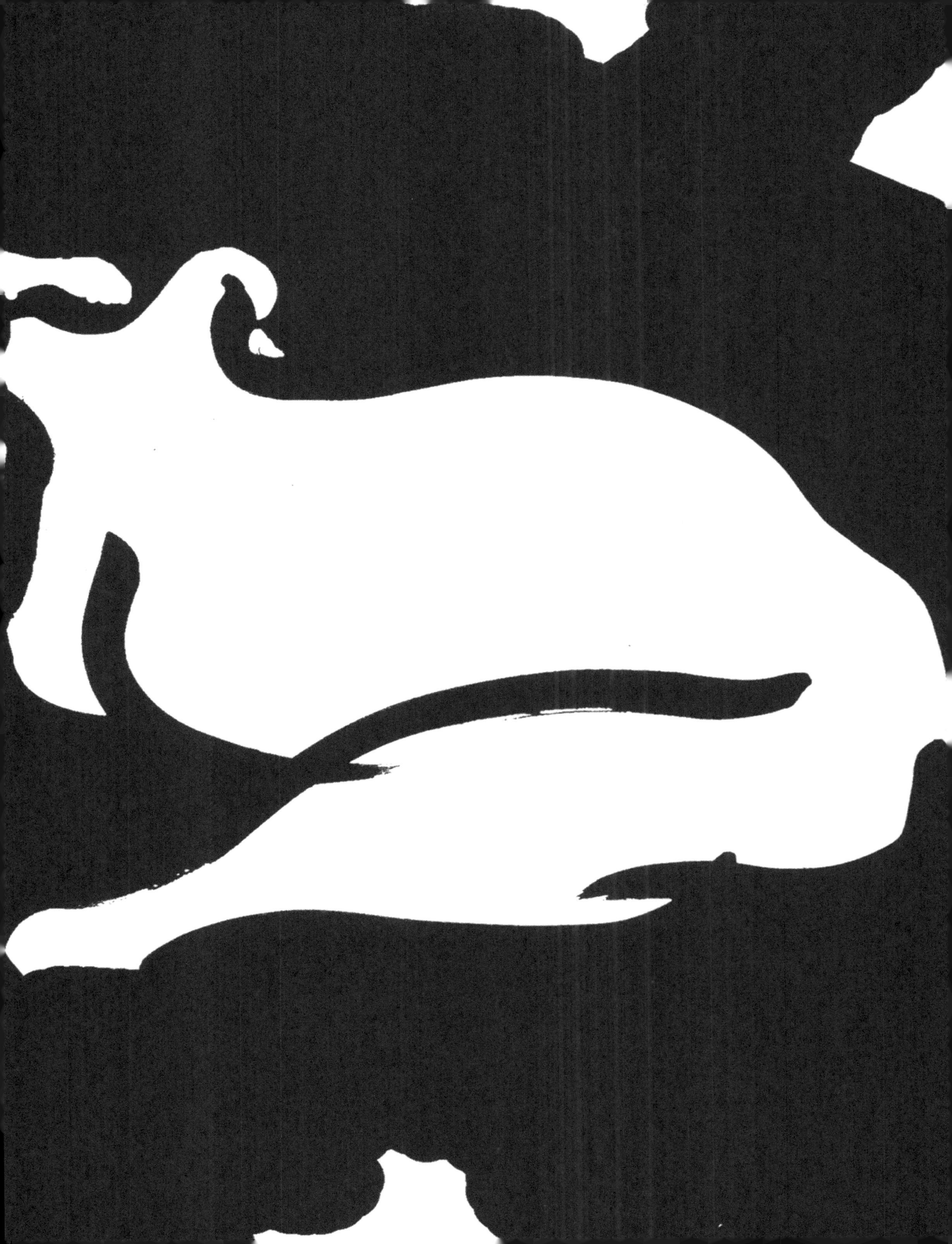

O U T   O F   S I G H T

Now that your road is mine
its unlimited length of dust
the blinding plains of night
to keep your eyes from my face

rare stones, blue fires of fate
the exact moment hypnotized
I have absorbed the thirsty core
and what is more

I have already described
the muscle and bone of raw feeling,
the reason I undress in a hurry
and cannot leave this Lover

love of the road the blinding arias
stitched with sand and dust
saying yes, lead me to your body
by simple branch of yew tree

and the filigree of night
held the ancient coin
the blackened one they toss back
and it lands on the road
the face looking up
the same as the night
all silver bells --
my sight is yours.

THE WATER CLOCK

It was in the season of eternity

Fishing in auspicious light
in blackened boat of buffalo dung
painted *fish-hawk* on the prow
strong in water, not afraid of wind
our oars bend endless water --
memory makes me remember
the lake wears more than one face

We catch fish east of The Temple
by evening, trap carp in west estuary
set our net where tide is deepest
like silk awash in the stream
among the drifting duckweed

Raindrops drip like newborn pearls
from green velvet leaves of longevity
and carp with golden scales
as large as our hands, as we passed
turns pond golden, pure and mystical

By the time misted rain falls, incarnadine
incense from the far pagoda
borrow sandalwood for sweetest dusk
you and I watch smoke-wisps through sky
and before incense turns to ashes -- prayers begin

Through and through, you understood by my heart
wild herons come with the season, as fragments
painted on a wedding screen.

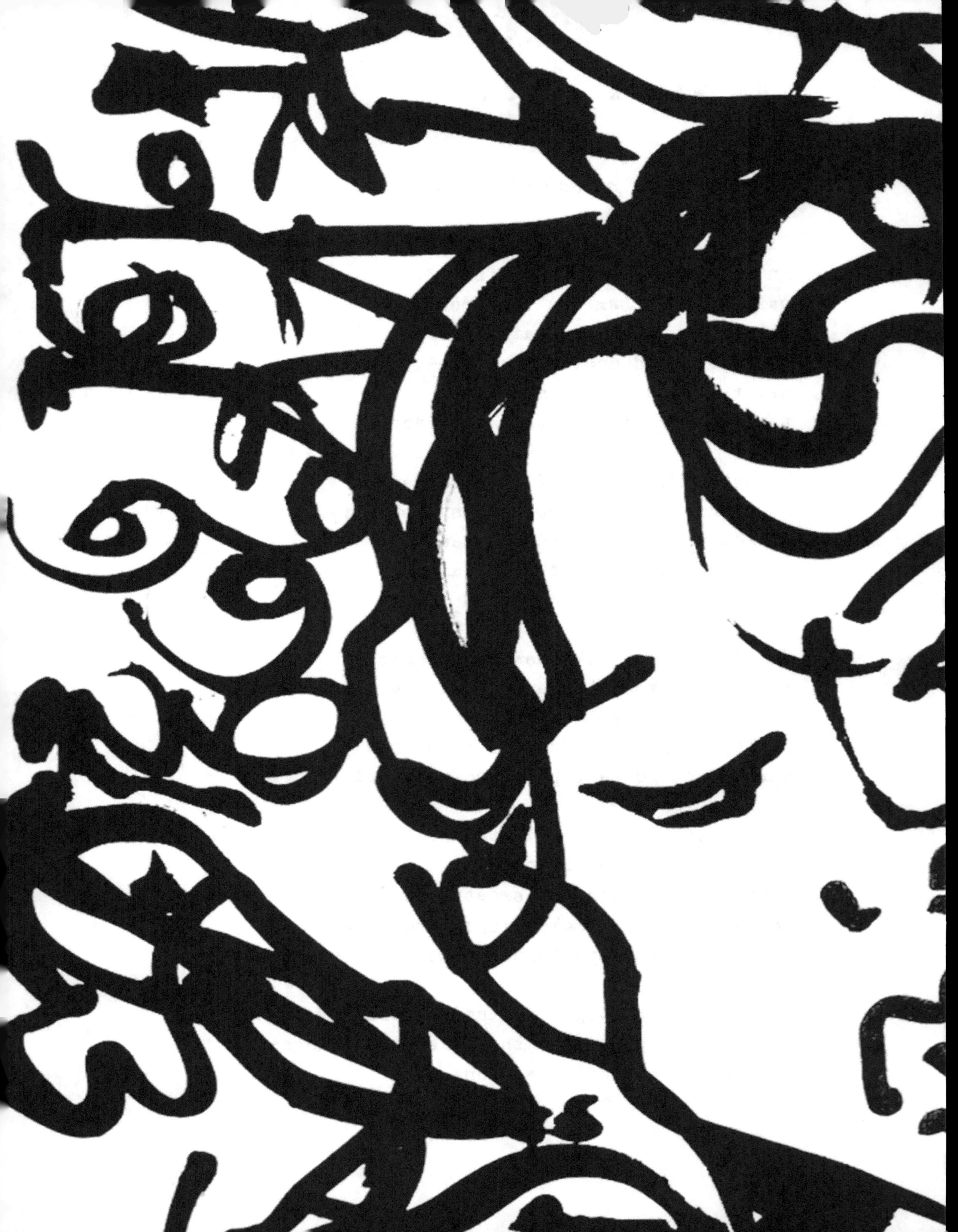

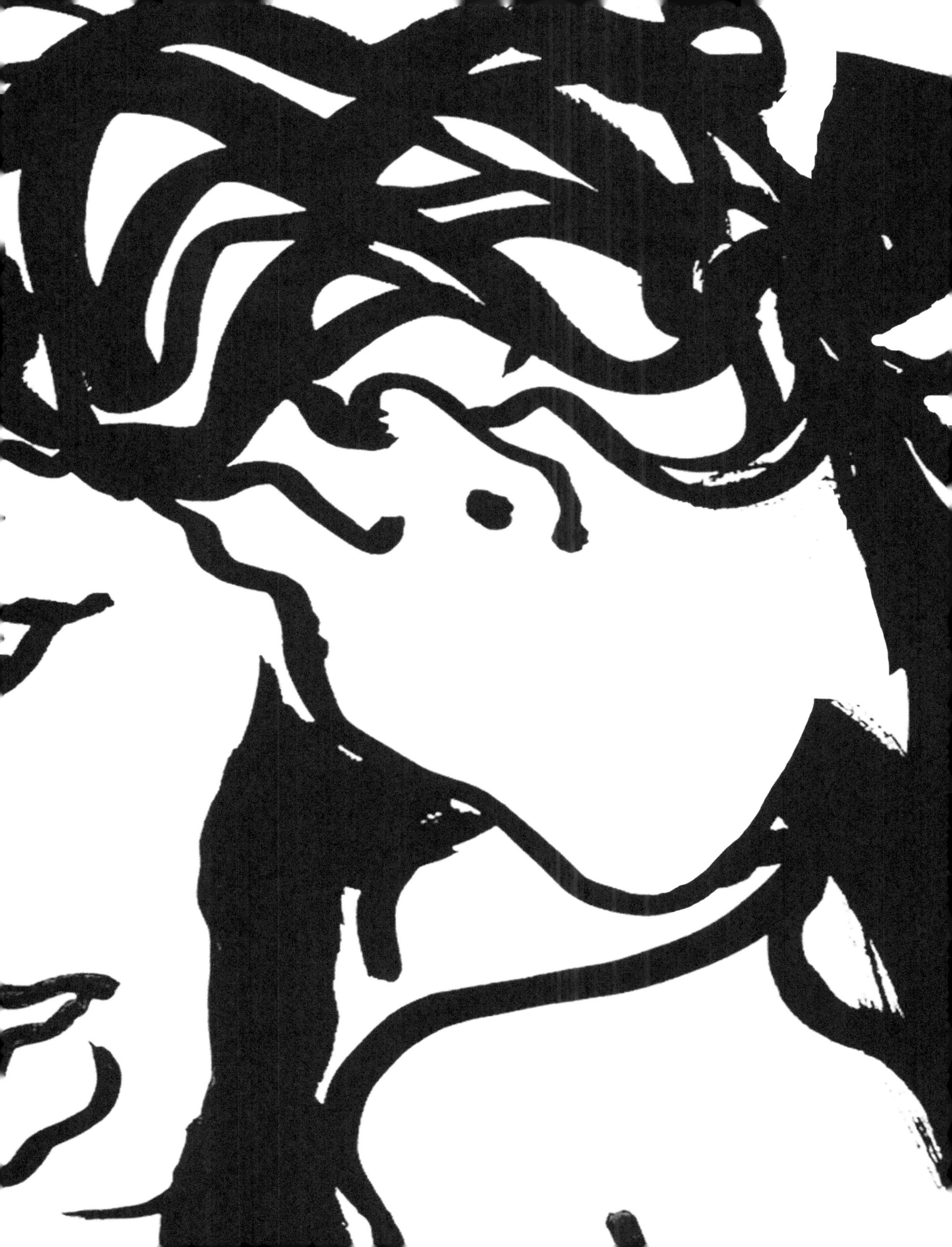

THE MEMORY GARDEN

In dreams a butterfly -- still, seeking blossoms

A place of refuge is not complete
without a perpetual ally, to ask
is it better to be friends with Kings'
or with the butterflies

Nothing belongs to us, impossible this
request for a bit of earth, bequeath
I was only an ordinary gardener
and they wouldn't take it from a gardener

I lift my hand to a butterfly in the blossom
I found it myself, by chance
after a thousand things forgotten
I count everything I know, so

The butterfly effect changes margins
dissolves and vanishes in a moment
the garden becomes a kind of kingdom
in a leaf, a tiny boat

Two years of prayer has transformed
small sculptures and marble carvings
in merciful garden, a thousand years pass
it will be the making of us, you will see

Calligraphy straight as hanging needles
like lightning flashing or falling rocks
and infinite marks around raindrops
some as clouds possibilities

There are seven ponds of pink lotus
it will be the saving of us, you will see
seven bridges over winsome water
when a thousand crane-birds fly
how the dead are carried directionally

Near or far in the eye of memory
something hidden in what you see
until the mind wakes with a question
still an insider in my own garden --
you should know that lovers are still here

I have looked at the rubric
why couldn't I have found this before?
you the butterfly -- I, Basho's dreaming heart.

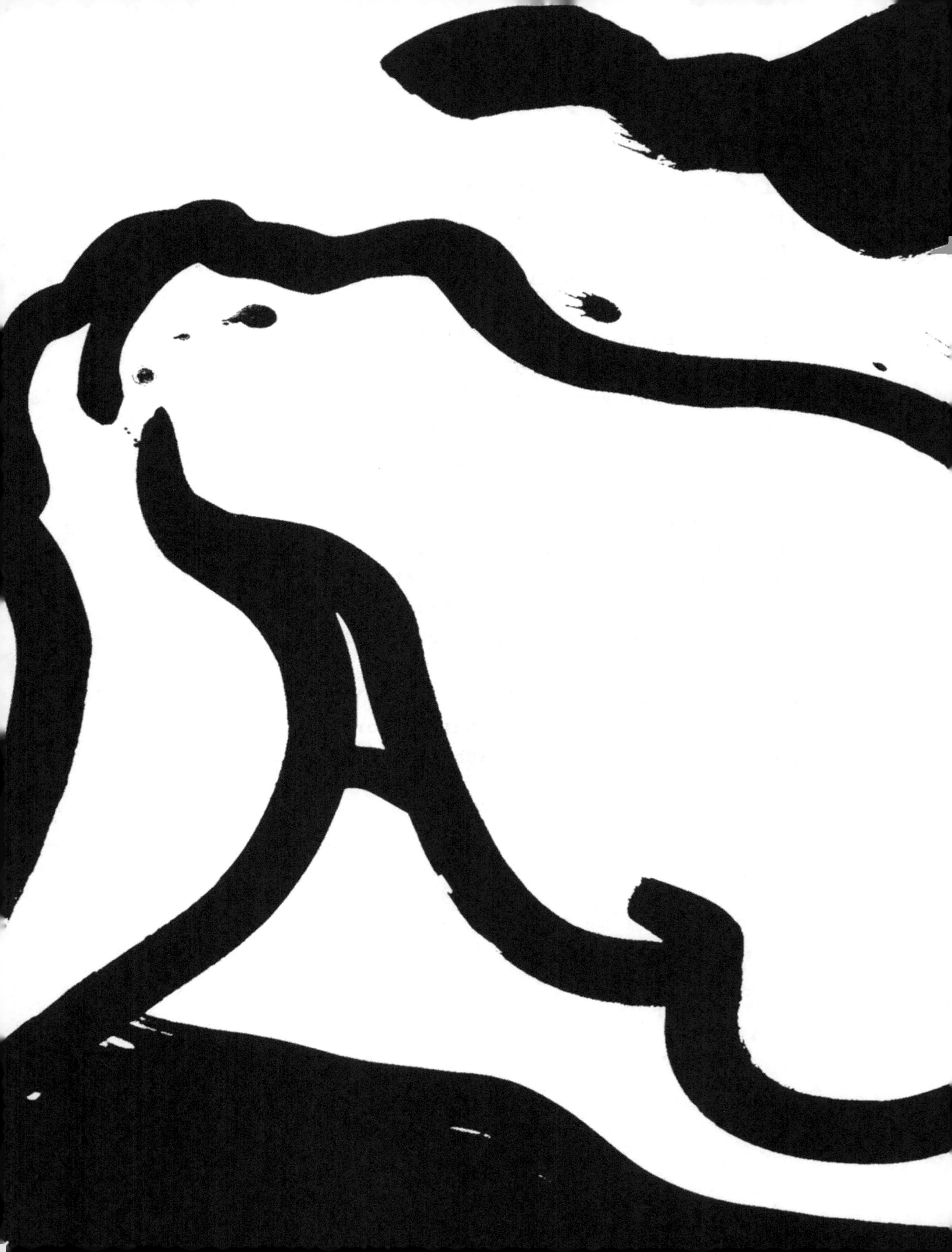

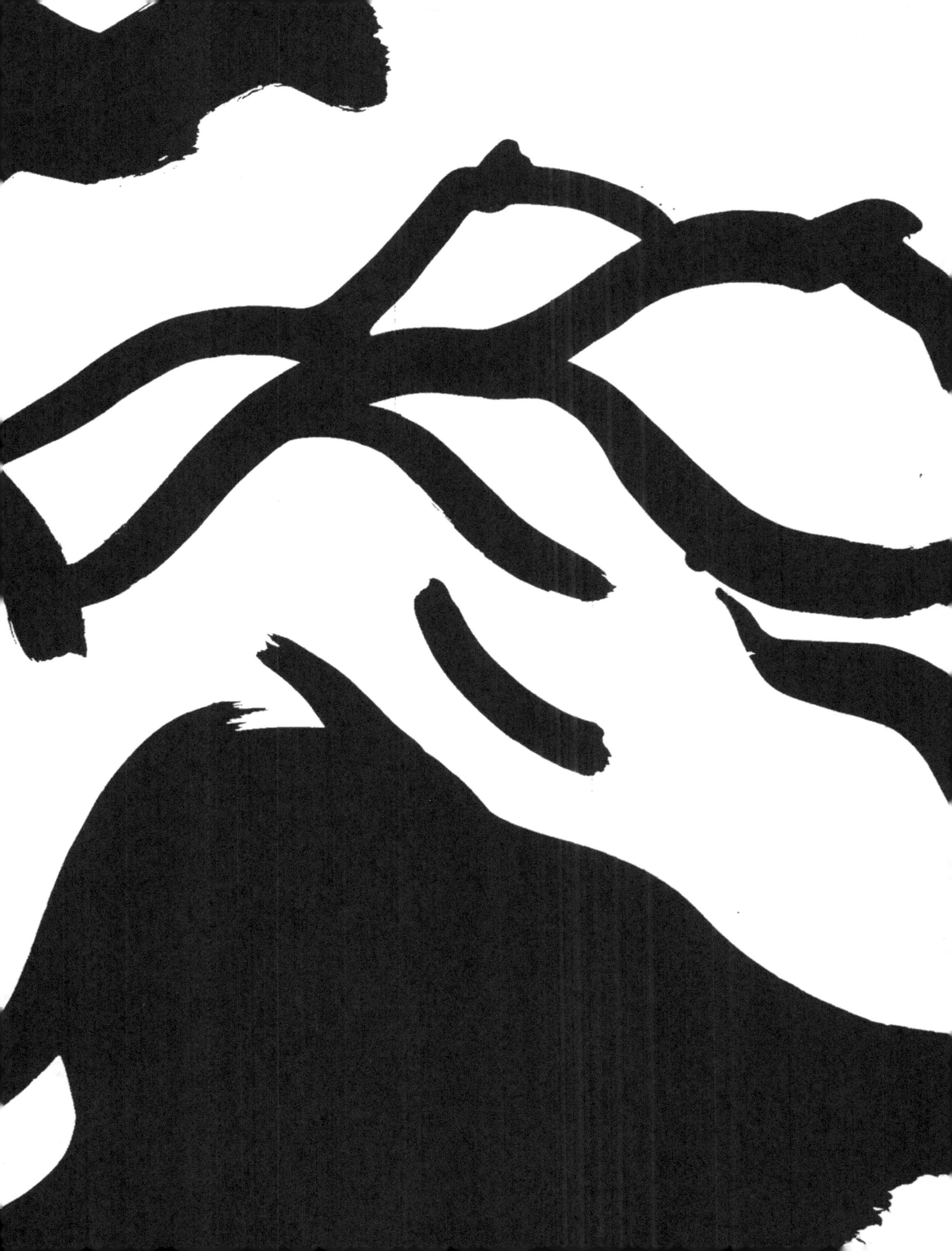

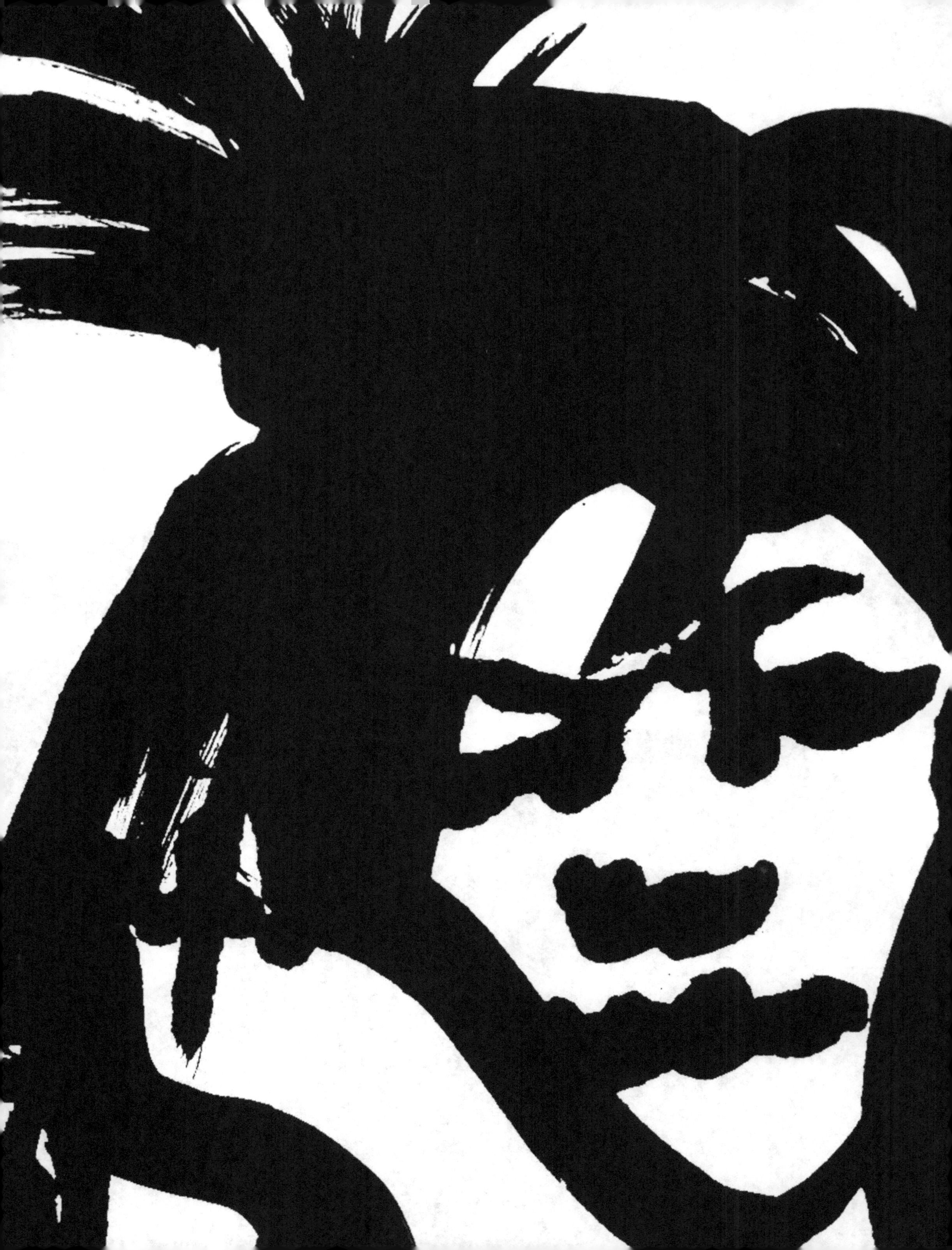

BO DE LAKE HOUSE

It is the season of crimson persimmon
birth of lunar moon, red and beautiful
like a sun-burned peach, gone ripe after rain

just a place for night sky to hook one moon
above the lake, more than single memory
seeds a thought of quantum destinies

there is dynasty, a touch of dragon that they swear
there is a feeling, luck resembles, to mark a new year
there is a surface, singular and simple, *I have seen it*

and here like temple lantern all the moons are circles
there is song and reminiscence, looked and overlooked
any chancy moment, either it works, or it doesn't

the hardest thing, to weep in wind
or write a word in rain or sand, simply to be
to those who interfere with perfect histories

words worn-out, more than the oldest moon
lost in translation, or trifled hours
it's a re-arrangement by *The Printmaker*

now, last cooking fire gone out in the old streets
much as horoscope's prediction, reckoning days
Master Dragon-Tamer has fled the world

years once lived by the flag's crude cloth
they remain, forever foreigners here
close the door on belonging
and pass back the key.

THE SLEEPERS

In a foreign landscape we are ghosts;
Entering the nights séance
Capture what is still unaccounted
Immigration beads, flags of paper
Still swathed in wax seal and twine
They speak to us through documents and deeds
In dust there are everlasting notes
You smell them on the old streets
One explosion after another
To draw you out of existence
I show you blood on my lip

                    but, this dried quickly

Resembles salt of memory and desire
You were my promise
Lips that gave everything
As your mouth moving across my body
And warmth presiding over
How we gathered our child
Second pilgrim of cold: enter dead land
As they send mysterious chill
Some shelter stolen one morning
Some you hide, others hate you
Use you until they change us
Like gentle gunpowder
The black, exists so you can taste it
Just a bowl of burned rice
Or was it *The Cave* offering a place
In the silent stones
To sleep on the rough earth
Pulling the ground around you
What does it mean to sleep --
like a dog without a blanket.

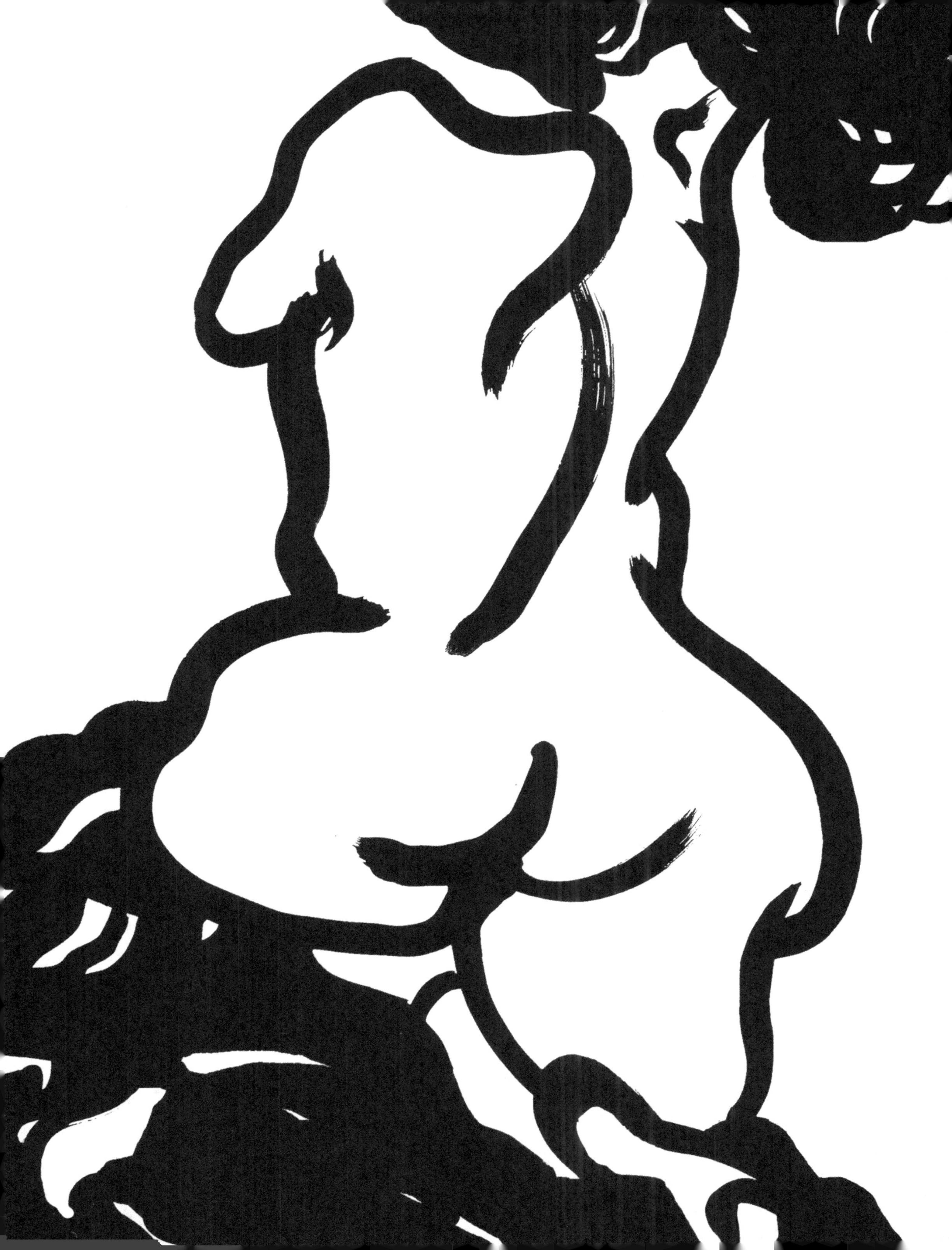

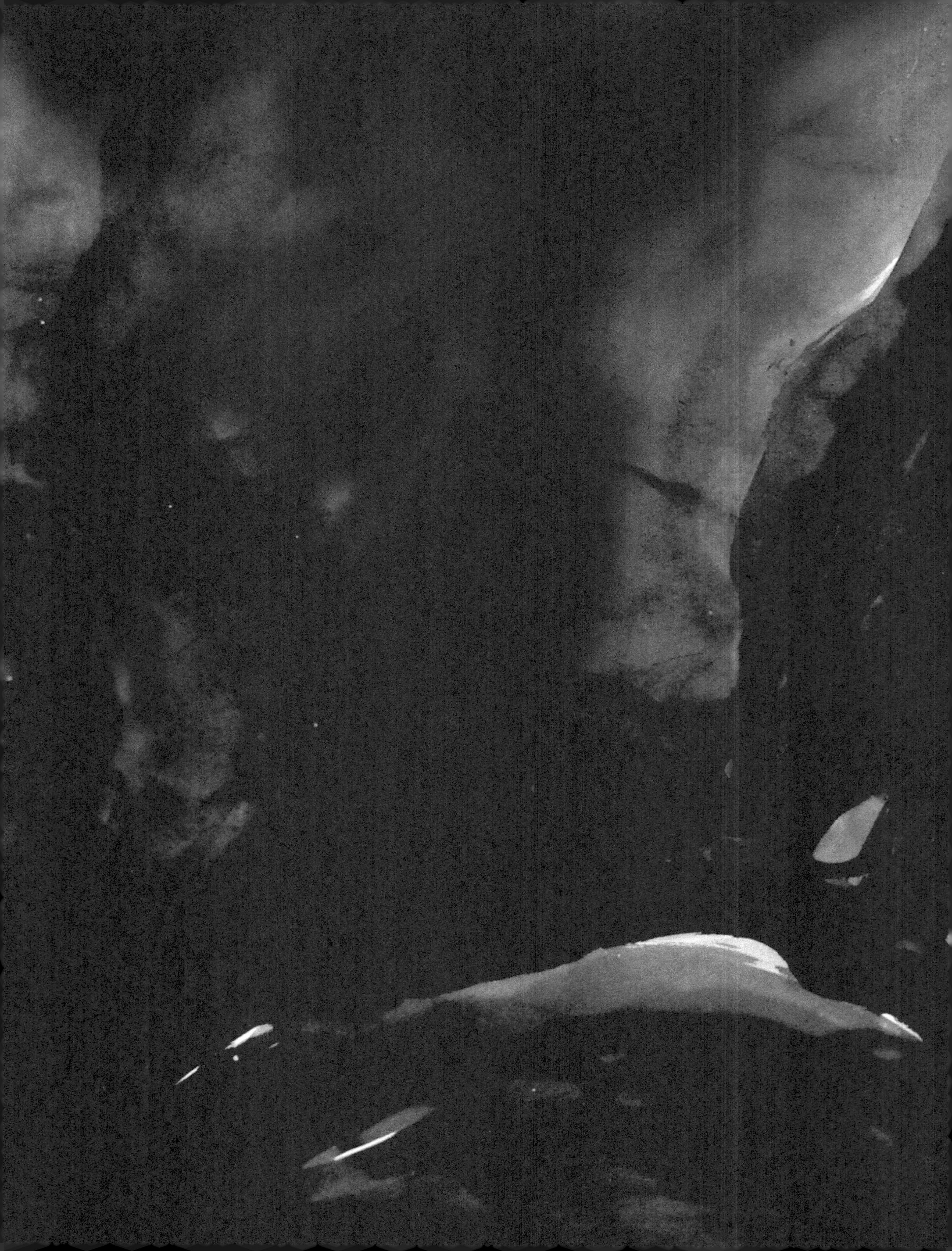

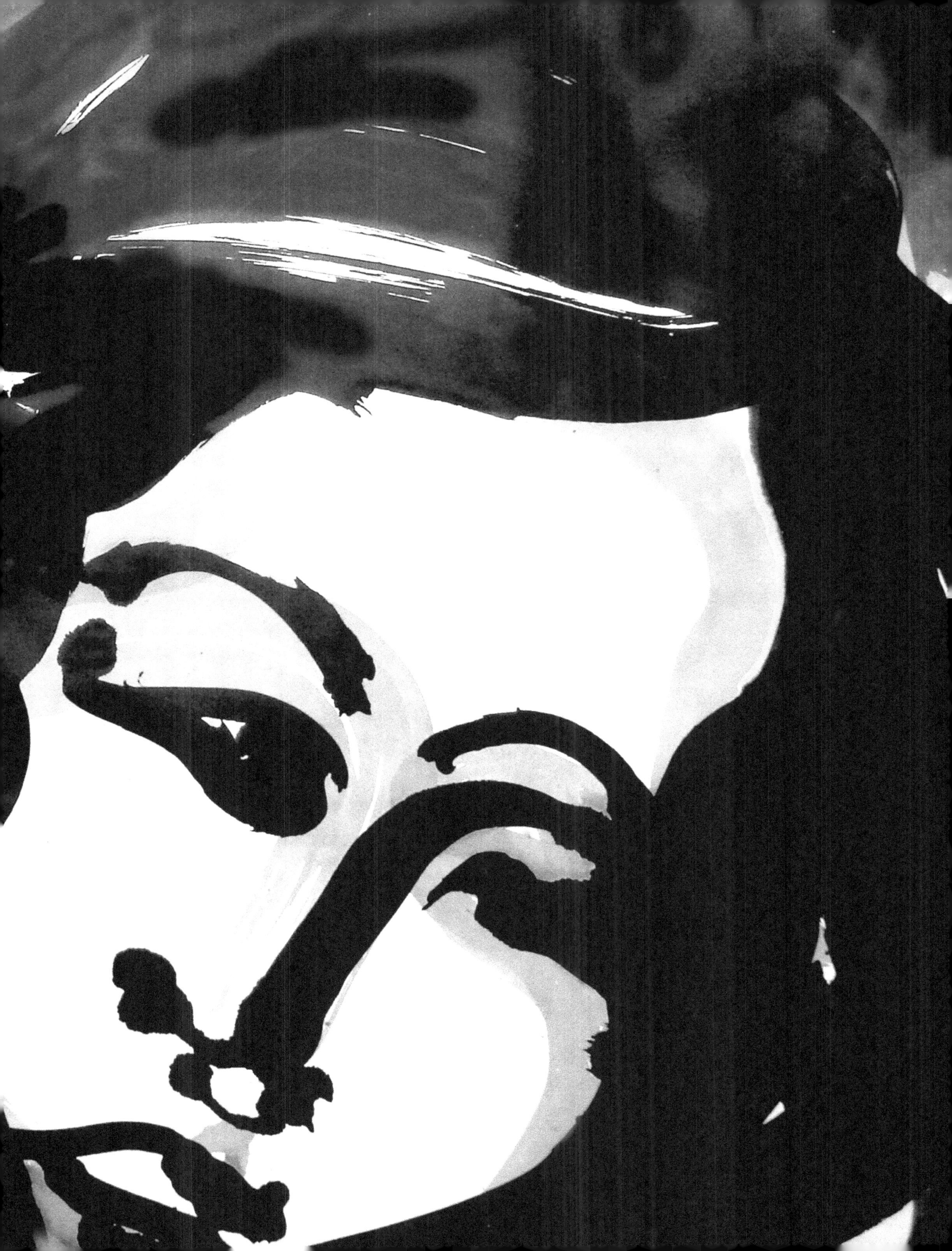

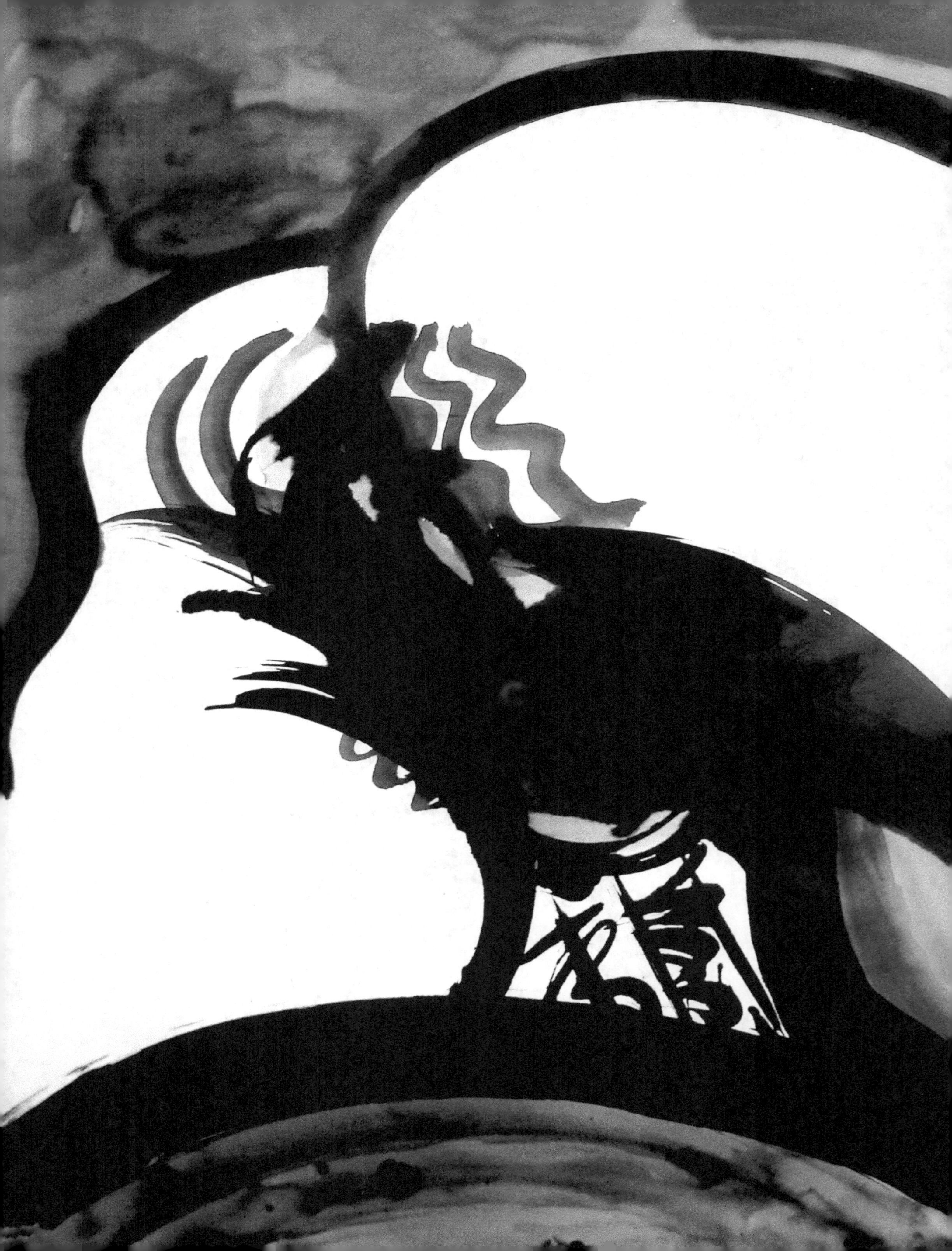

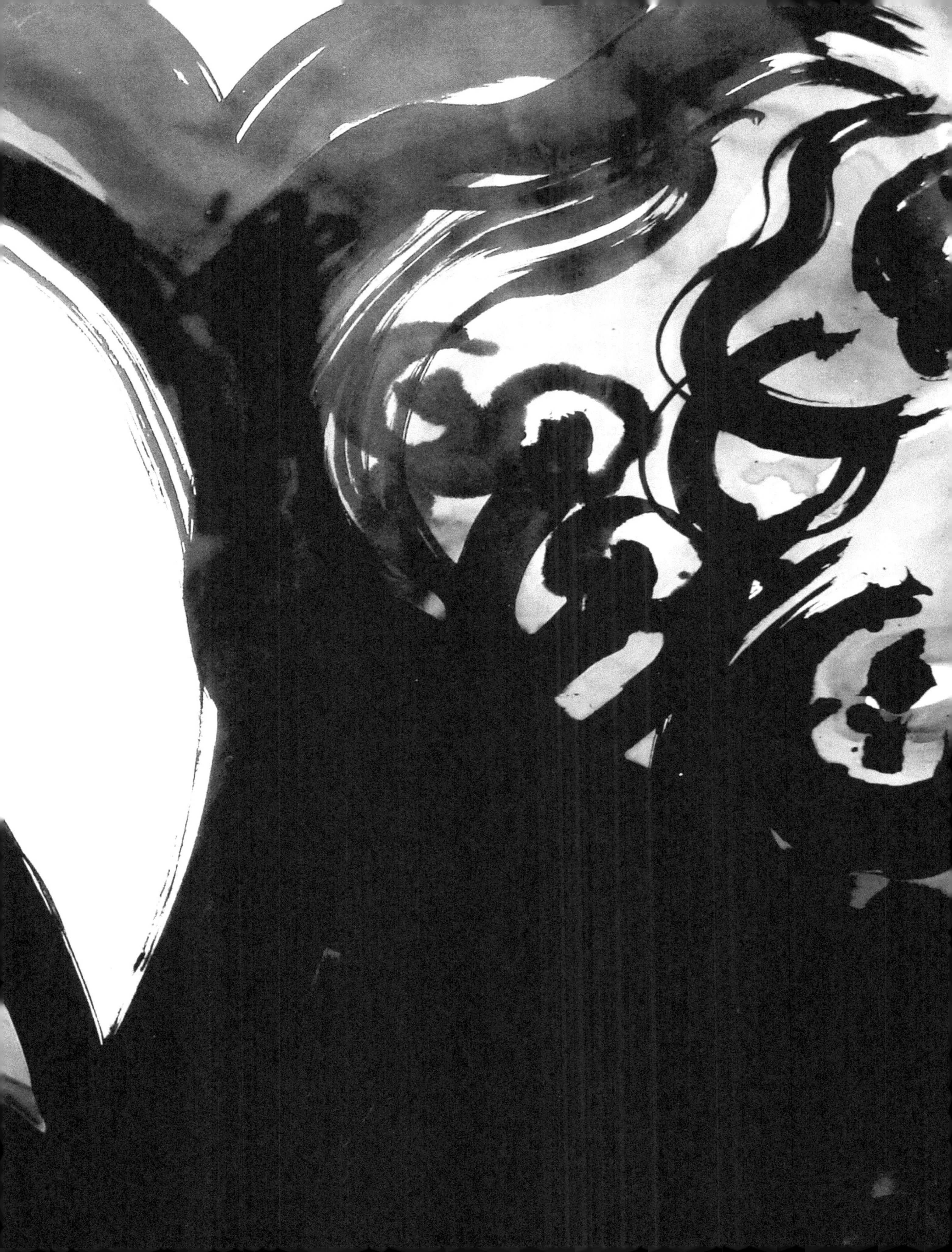

NIGHT ROSES

When the window is open to the garden

Lights of near-by houses were out
and the room was all silent
a thought of blue moon, slanting over sea
the night, soldiers broke the garden's filigree
conspirators under darkness, in the fold

trod over bones, search influential wealth
ransack gold and precious embroideries
broke familial estate taboo, by pen or gun
all that was corruptible became confused
as wild bees in a smokescreen

what if, the foreigner brings their own troubles
what if, the visionary Saints have given
the shrouds, carried beneath tired arms
two by twos, one by one, the regrets
gather histories, perpetual momentum
like a prayer, a hymn, a charter for the rich
blood-fortune accumulated, is dispossessed

it is like entering a cold grave's desolate void
leave richness, and warmth of material ways
dangerous legacy, they always say
do not carry valuables from older days
do not talk of more than tomorrow
hide-away from where you came
to live like an imposter: for only empty shame
please, send a letter, an invitation back again.

SONG BIRDS

East of our Art Deco apartment
Faded colonial architecture, high wall
Consulate buildings on embassy row
Splendid trees with enameled plaques
Identify the cardinal Latin names
Perhaps, the glories of avenues and park

Morning, a thousand songbirds
In a flight of city's compass
And return a hundred times
In the mahogany and aspen trees
High branches, splendid feathered canvas

Swallows fly home, ducks wing south
Bird-hunters' take them from us
Songbirds safe from no one
Birds flew to higher branches,
Do you hear the feathers drop?

Sunday, it was -- a day of entrapment
They trap them with a little honey
They trap birds for a little money
At the market, doves and orioles
Captured, like oriental culprits.

Soon there will be no other singer
A broken lock, flash of yellow
Forgive the ones that do not sing
Long and drawn out, sad as sorrow
In order to release tomorrows.

BONE JAR

Everywhere earthenware honey pots

Some choose to fill the myriad hives
with lotus honey and wax from joyful bees
therefore this sweetness and light
for familiar bones to be kept perfectly

but now, when told where ghosts have gone
only the bamboo flute, its fipple song
for the mourners, as the river rises
and the forever lanterns are lit wisely

the year of the rat passes
before the Golden Ox
the year of the dog and cat
and year of bee, long before that

They were always there
the honeybees that follows
an echo of pollen left behind
who tells the rest with pleasure.

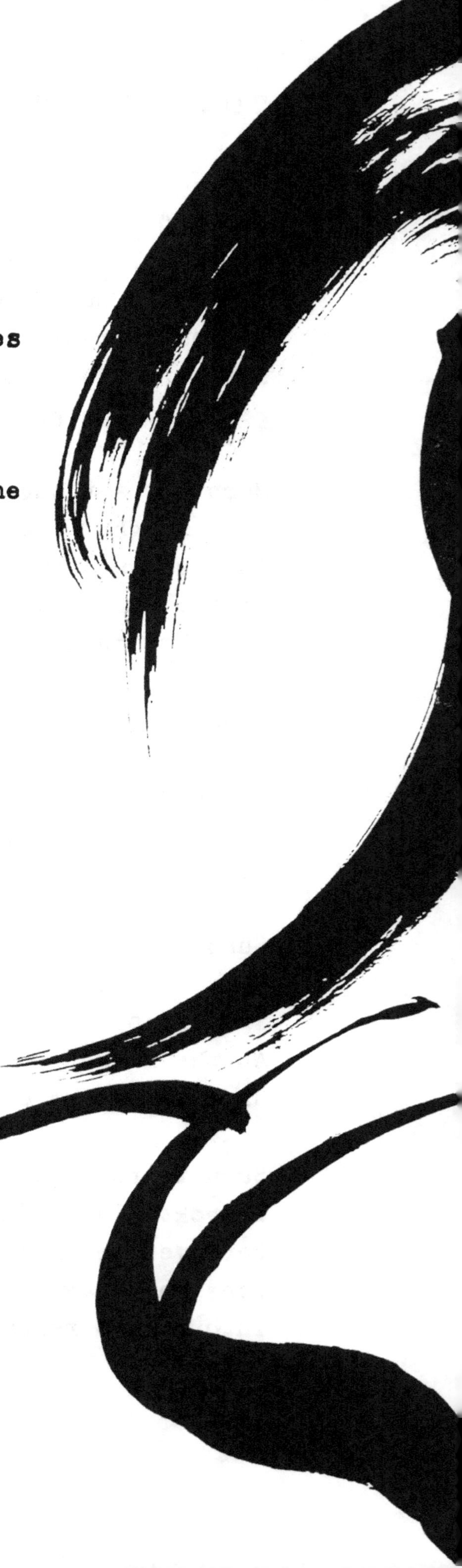

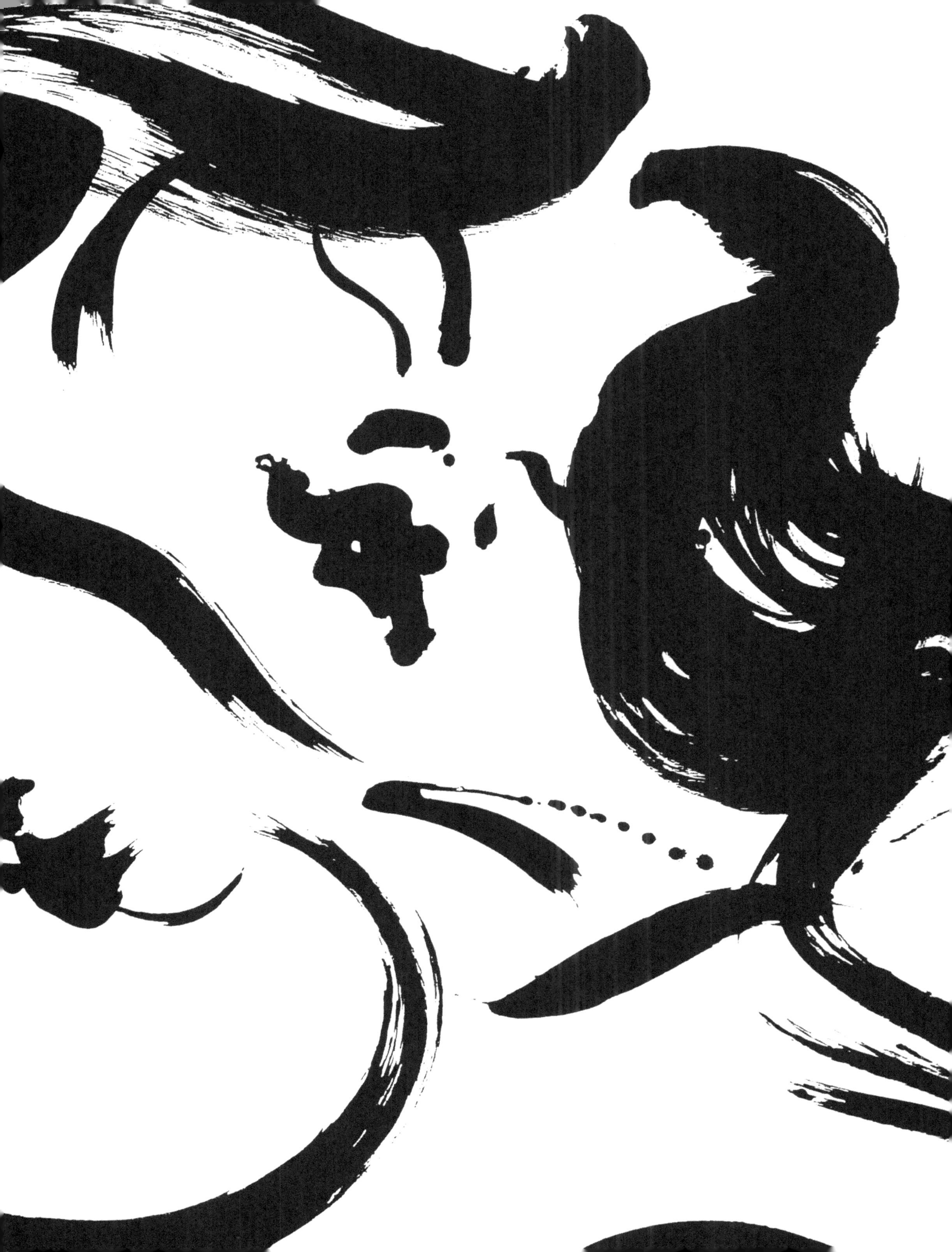

THE BOWL

This, was here

A set of small bowls
Nestle inside each other
Double skin of red
Lacquered wood
Easily held in the hand

In the art of placement
As the Monk said
When things look right
They feel right

The largest bowl for rice
The next for river fish
The next for vegetables
The smallest for sauce

In the art of placement
The Monk said
When things feel right
They look right

In the art of placement
Too many triangles
Triangles mean danger
So, they set up a tank
With six black fish
Then hung up a red clock
Behind The Abyss

How would you guess that I
Should know rules, like this?

The Monk said
Others before you
Also went begging for rice
Begging for food
Everywhere, the rice grows
And the green fades away
All days go the same way
One by one, from time to time
As a game of mahjong
The Monk said.

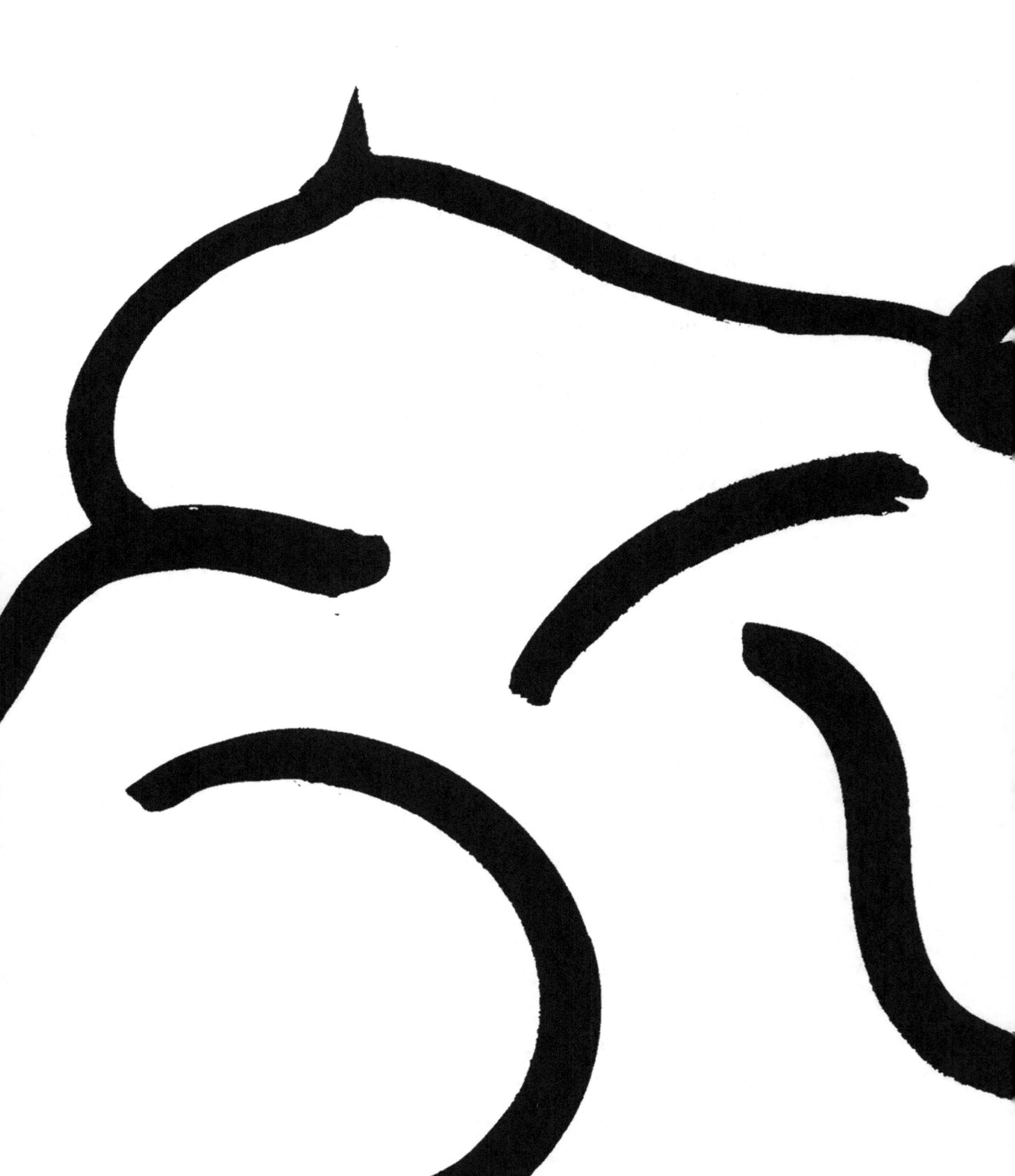

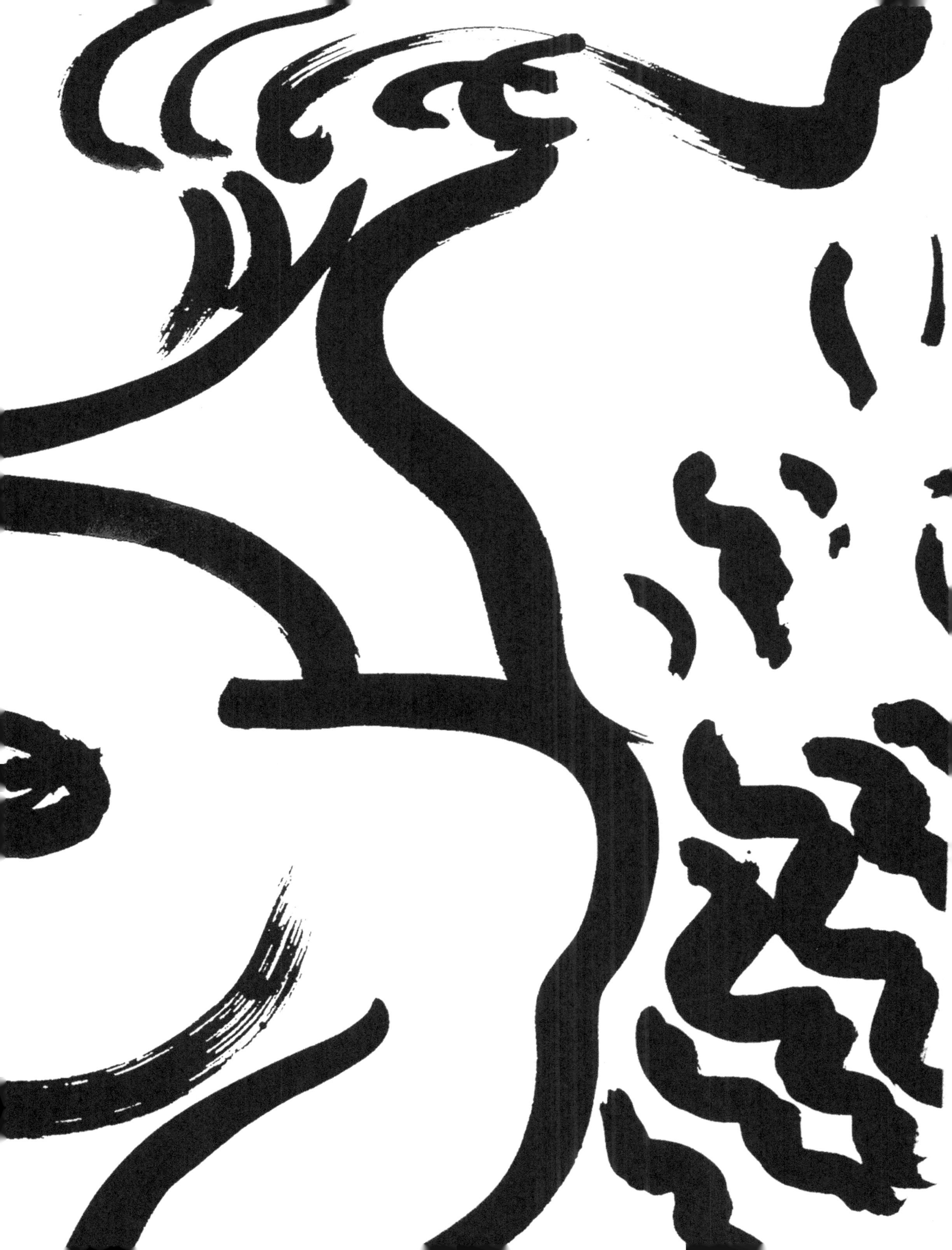

FRAGMENT OF DAY

Then, far from the Paris of the East
a collection of misted villages

in crowded market or opulent avenue
they chop down flowering blossom
and burn apricot limbs as fuel

now all songbirds have scattered
no one to cheer the lost-hearted
brambles fill the bereavement hall
to precede holly or mistletoe
mascara streaked, where shall they go?

To open eyes and see the familiar
darkening skies full of snow flowers
phoenix mirror, unlucky broken
to conceal away with friends
as though ringed apart from cities

house after house, golden staircase
vermilion gate, neighborhood dogs
jade horses, flashing hawks
silent garden seen through the bamboo blind
fragility forms a simple patent
but hardly possible -- they will be here again

if we leave in the morning, we arrive at night
and in cold light outside the old house
what if, red lanterns where left alight
we stay, in the quiet without a sound.

THREE BIRDS

Last night, thoughts within a dream
The water full of purple lotus
Seemed again, a great-leafed tree
Tall as the eye could see
To reach into the firmament

And the peacock in a silver nutmeg tree
With it tail long golden threads
Appears on moonlight branches

A bird of paradise, filigree feathers
Had color of fallen snow, anon
But then there was white crane bird
It flies up into the red-blossomed cashew tree
Still with many feathers and quite unruly

Peacock-fan to adorn an ornate hat
Bird of Paradise for a glamorous bower
Silk blind embroidered with dragonflies

Fabric and feathers go faded, even the butterflies
Turn gray, the color of moth
And the silkworm loses its bloom

Worn out, wasted, like all these things
And as before, regret locked in the storied room
Look back to follow birds over the snow clouds
Too soon, too soon;
Within the dream of the present life
There is a world of loss and poverty
Return now the three birds:
of luck, love and longevity.

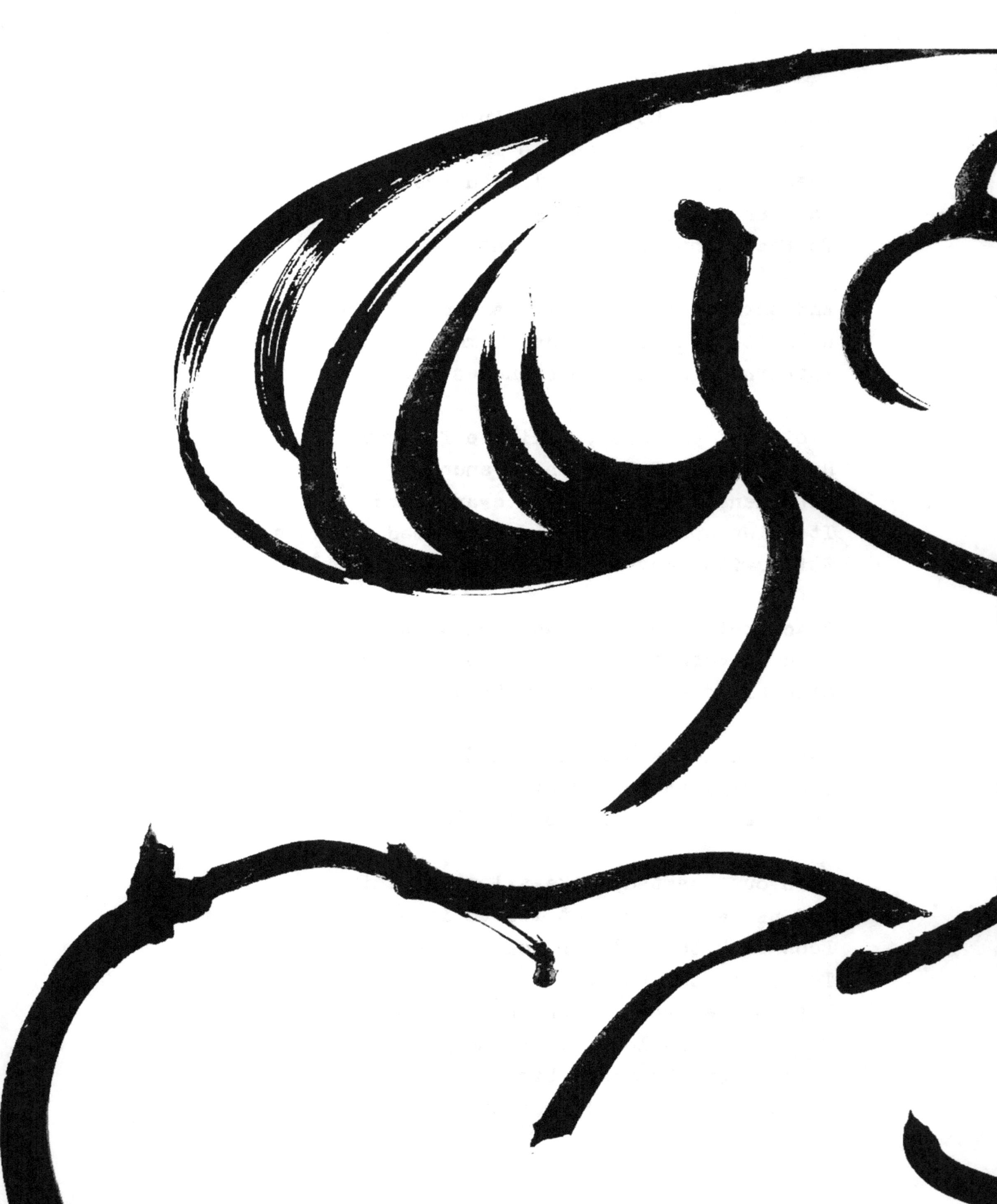

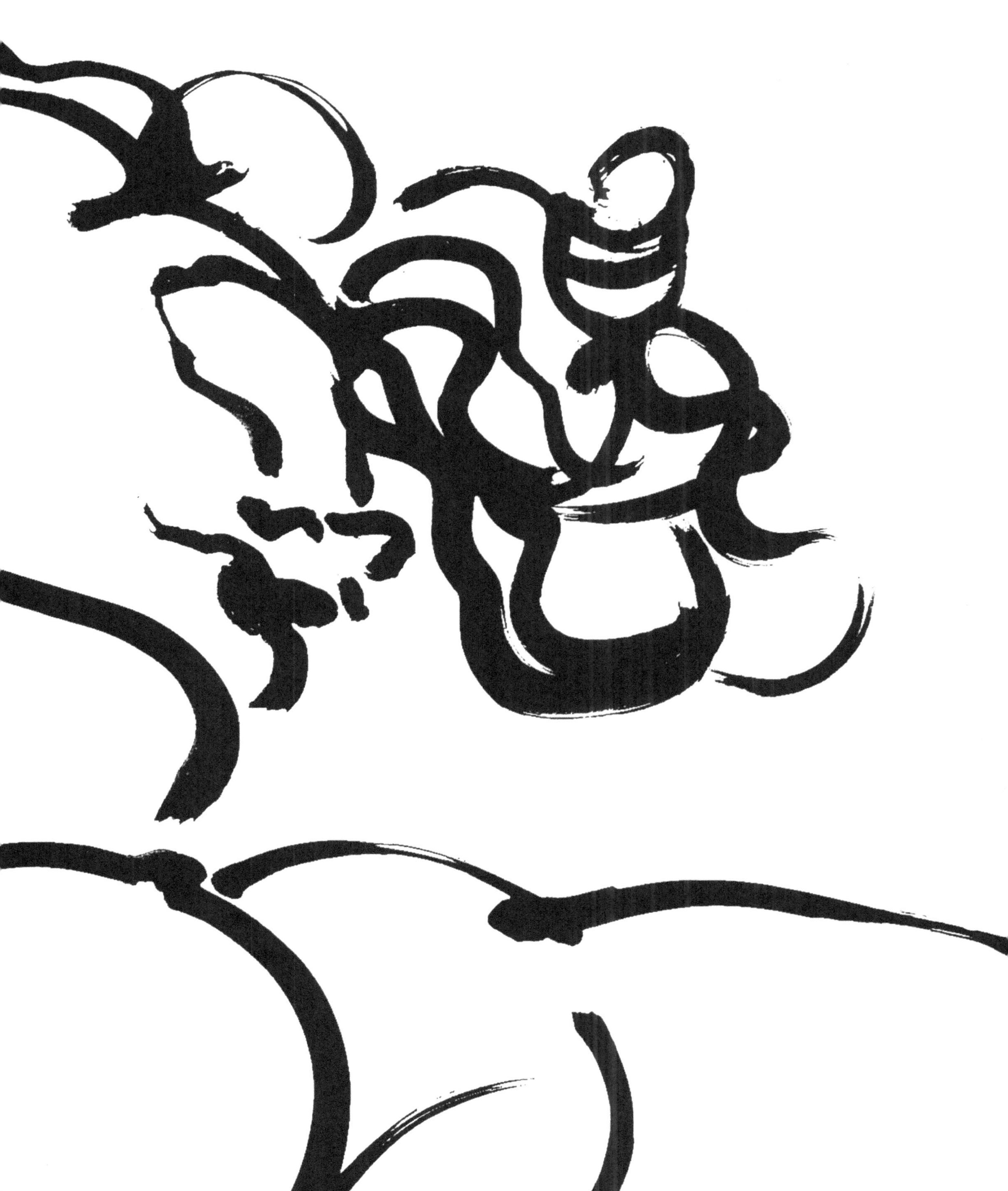

JADE PAVILION

This garden of contemplation
here with dragonflies, inter-circling
cellophane wings with tremulous patterns

Is it the wings that move
or wind, moving the wings
either way, small panacea of days

Here, verdant moss grows on old stones
tiny sweet pea, pale green leaves
violet flowers, some boil for tea

The seed, from seed of destinies
found in a Haiku of Basho
on last day of natures' séance
jade pond fills with darker carp

The Knower of all emptiness and loss
fore-shadow's a wrecking-ball future
proof, every dead-weight discriminates
under flood-light glare, criminalities
to steal from the ground up, it's hard to forget

After midnight, trucks go beyond city limits
now, everywhere is brick-dust! Birds in dusty flight
longevity lost by machete or knife
defer a thousand things in the name of progress

but not this divine place -- a garden is forever.

S H E

There is a shop in the Old Quarter
Where she sells her fine silk

The Blue Man came here
He was dressed in blue
The man with blue eyes
Bought fifty blue scarves
Did you send him?

He and I, now traveling east
The snow is just as light as feather
Our shoes make new footprints
With a memory of our journey

No place in the world is safe
Or unsafe, *it seems*

Upstairs, wordless, the bed is warm
The bamboo blinds are drawn

Yesterday, I gave the Lover
Lingering perfume, the bluest cloth
But then I gave him, one thing
Unaccounted for

She gave the man on the Silk-Road
A flag of red with its one gold star
Blood of the motherland.

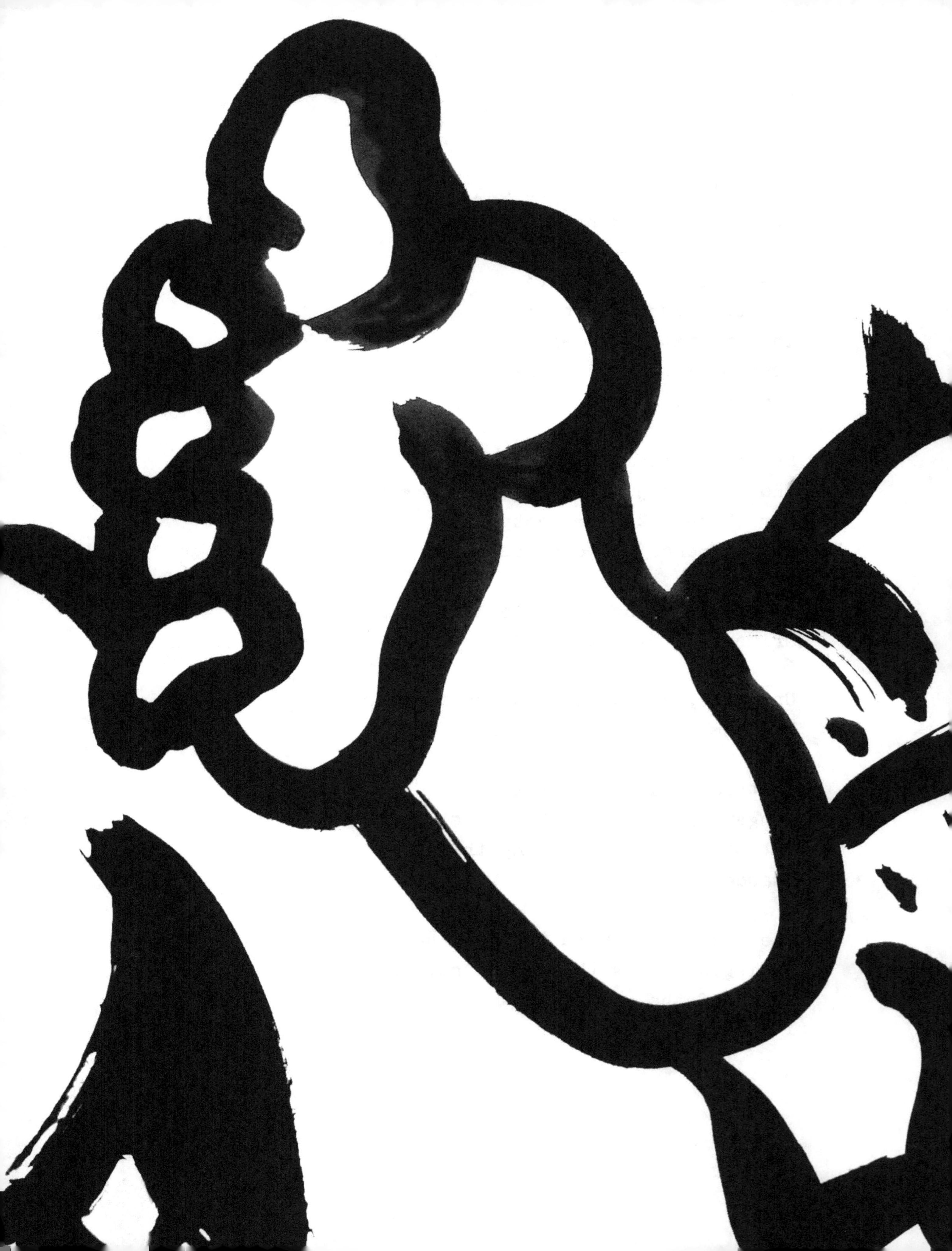

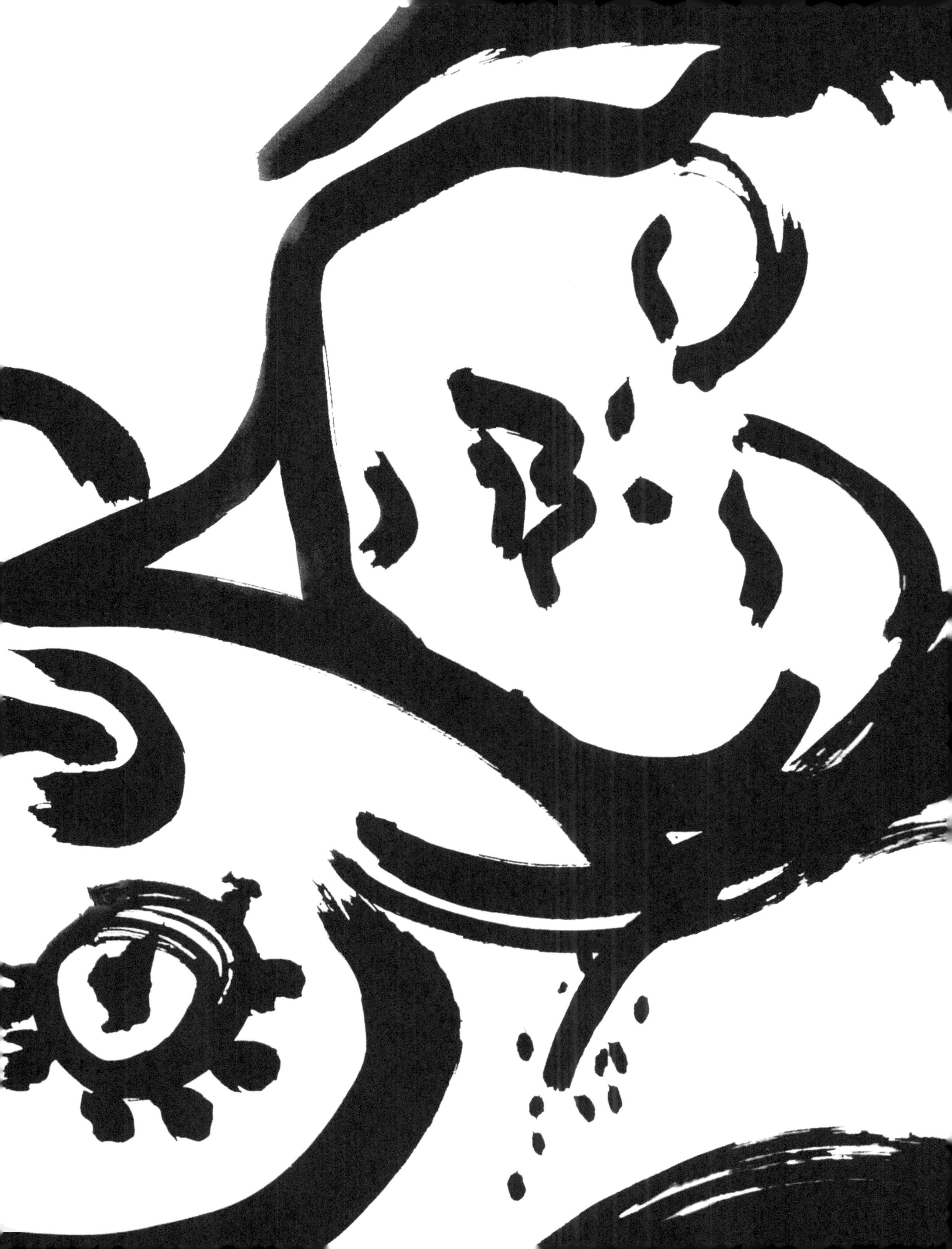

OTHER STORIES

In fragments butterflies return
Especially out of envious, tall poppies
That tower over ever-scarlet sun

Emptying the safe of house-keeping
Before a downtown café opens
Talk a while, find a fistful of dollar bills

Perhaps thousands, you never counted,
Passes like contraband out the door
With a French baguette and a cake

Half a kilo of coffee beans
Roasted in butter, taste like chocolate
Presently we spend money's envoy

A stove to replace the faulty one
A green glazed dinner set
From the poor man's pottery village

Silk blinds with butterflies
Embroidered in palest blue
Float when the breeze comes through

From the veranda you see
Dragonflies over the pond
A row of white birds, what lies beyond

Seeds of frost, a verge of words
Pins of rainfall, hard to come by
An arch of rainbow fragment

A poem of bamboo flute
Sees through all emptiness
We are expecting visitors

We sleep in the back room
Wondering what hour it is
Welcome two new pairs of shoes

To walk across green chill grass
Only brings back memories
Play the actor to suit the day
We spent all the contraband on you.

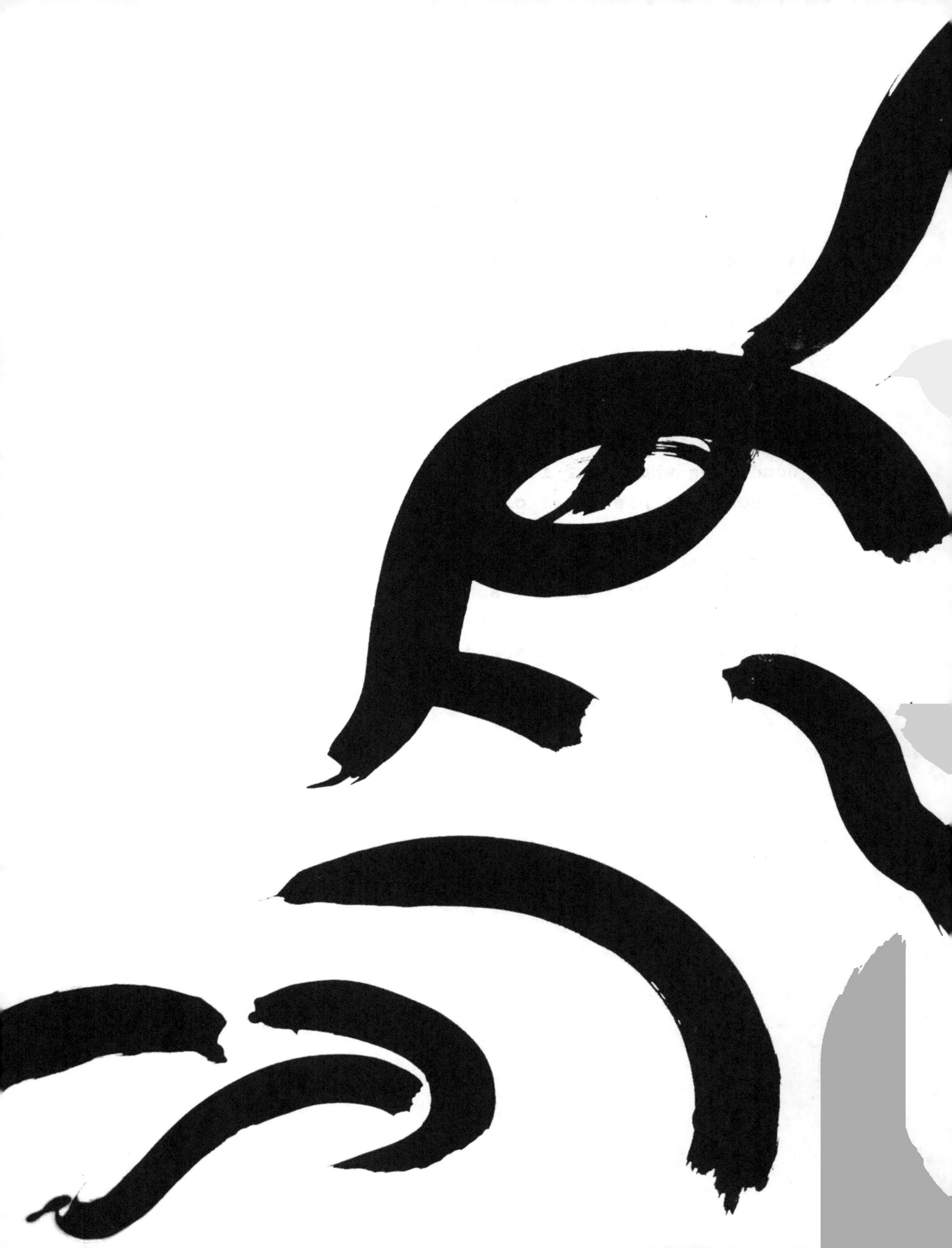

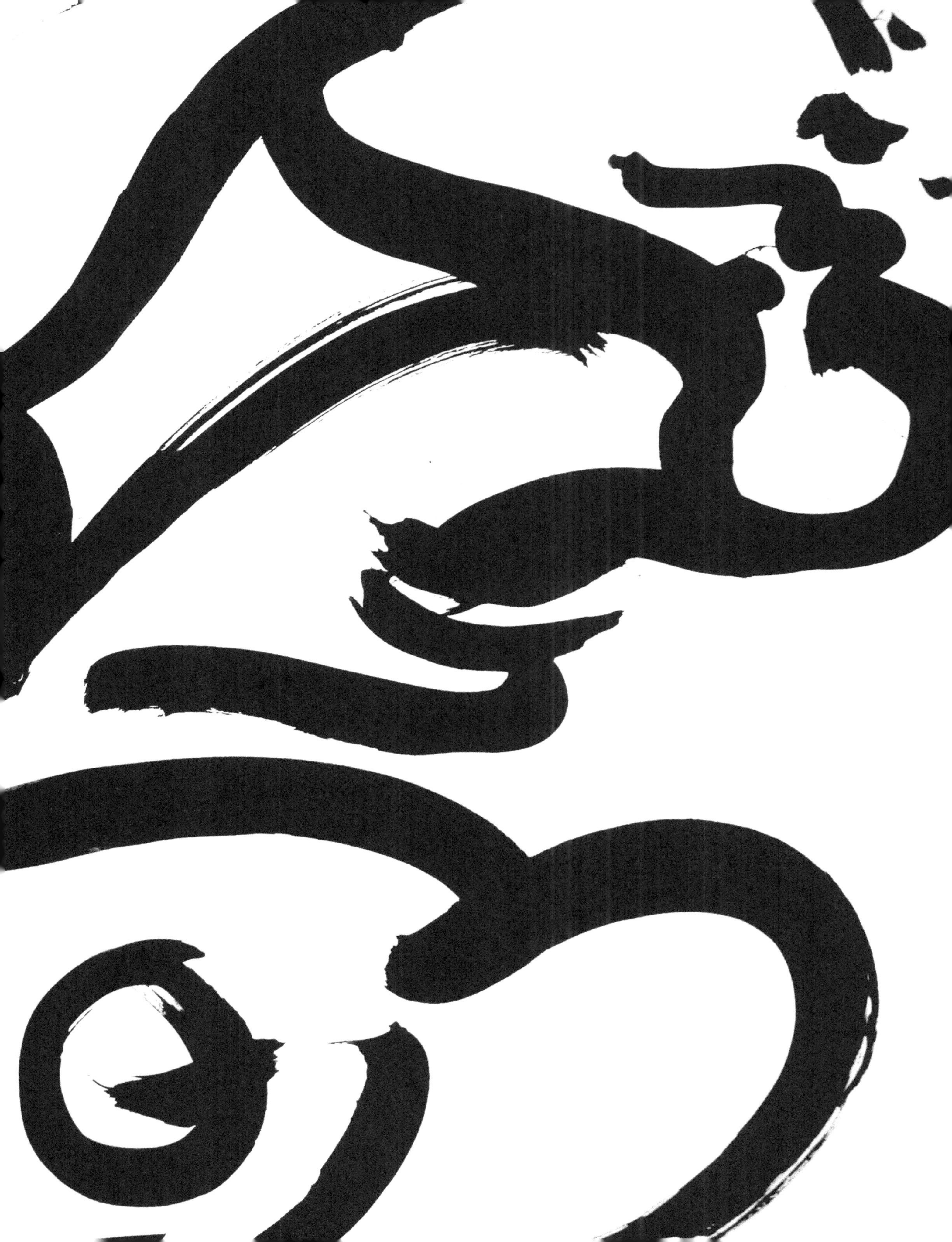

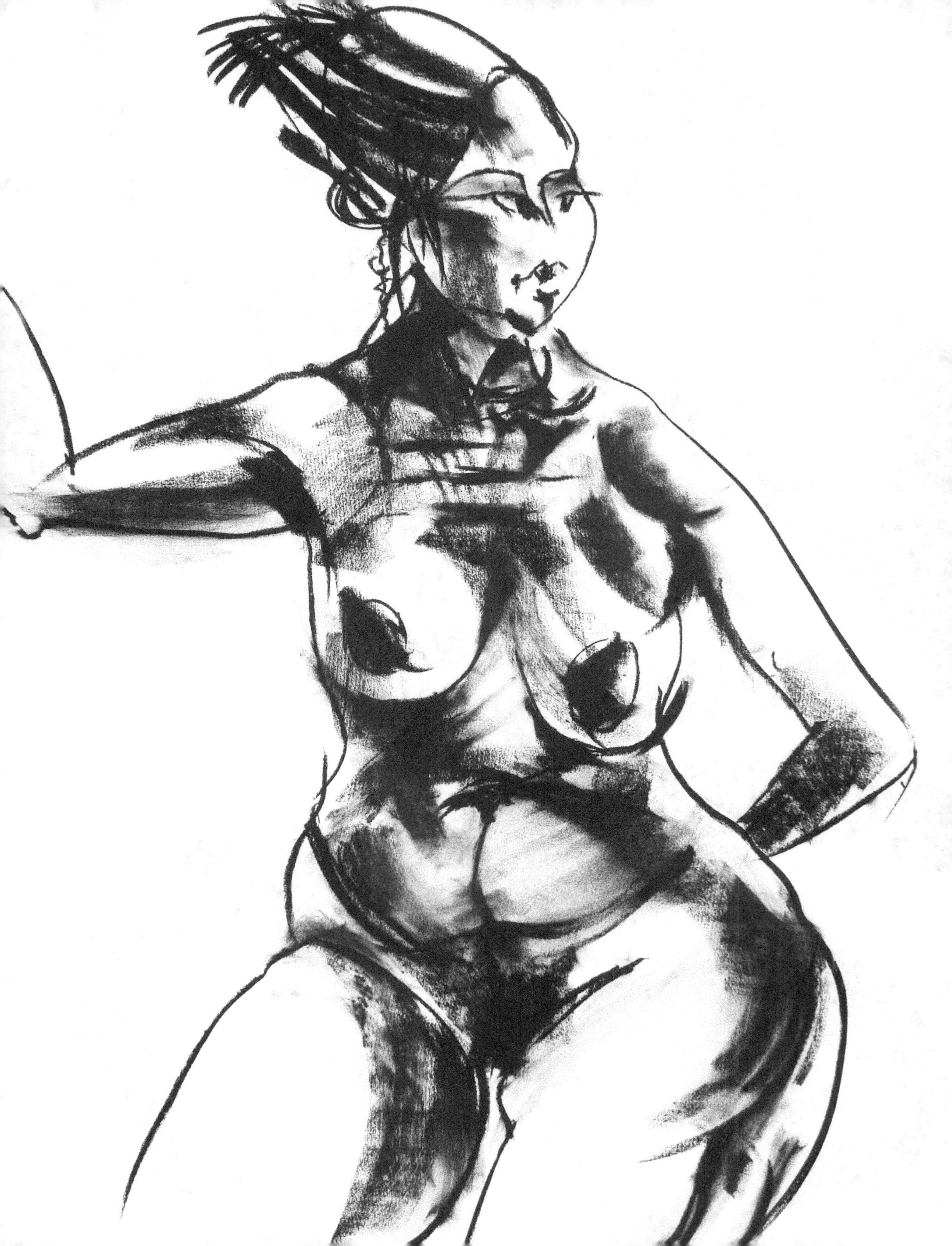

ONE MOMENT

As far as eyes can see

A thousand books from the homeland
Something will be remembered -- anything
From a distance, to hear falling waves
Head on silk pillow, to hear weight of ocean

And here, the sea at the edge of the island
Heat dampens summer clothes, sun's perpetual fever
What does it ever matter, if hair turns white
We are not young, we are not yet old

Whether happy, or not, whether good or bad
The broken heart beats with its own weight
A smile more valuable, they say, memorable
Lips smooth as marble Michelangelo's

As if, *The Master of Fate* knows what goes on
But on the thousandth night, we return
How long does a human life last
If no bed is left for *The Perpetual Dreamers?*

To enter this house without forging a key
Eight or nine majestic rooms, a clay tile roof
Ingenious cicadas, crickets' hymnal above
Twig-full of plum by the open door
Palaces dragged to the edge of the world
I think of you, but how you do know it?

THE RETURN

There was a clamor of gold in the hall
Stolen for the King; gold bands, gold signets
Amulets enameled, a golden-blue confusion
Enough to ward off a thousand evil eyes
Save one; for all the rings of centuries, look up
Golden days, secrets, the further one goes
Far off, who could separate gold from misery
But the treasures, just come with empty hands
Round the golden cup; drunk in a phrase
Everything of value -- a handclasp away

For wealth, they choose the Emperor's pattern
Familiar, like a mother's Chinese vase
Here, in the opulence of antique porcelain
Spring trees covered in apricot blossoms
Petal after petal, became best fruit
And here, like gold-leaf of gilded fancy
Awaken every faded memory, all old, all endless
When gone their way, like wild bees
The last, in the rushing years, cannot be found

To drink mountain-apricot's bittersweet
Keep bones from growing older
Inlaid memories, sweet on the tongue
Until everything said, is undone
Honey left thick in the wilds
But hives have no taskmaster
We could live two hundred years
A thousand bees to keep us company.

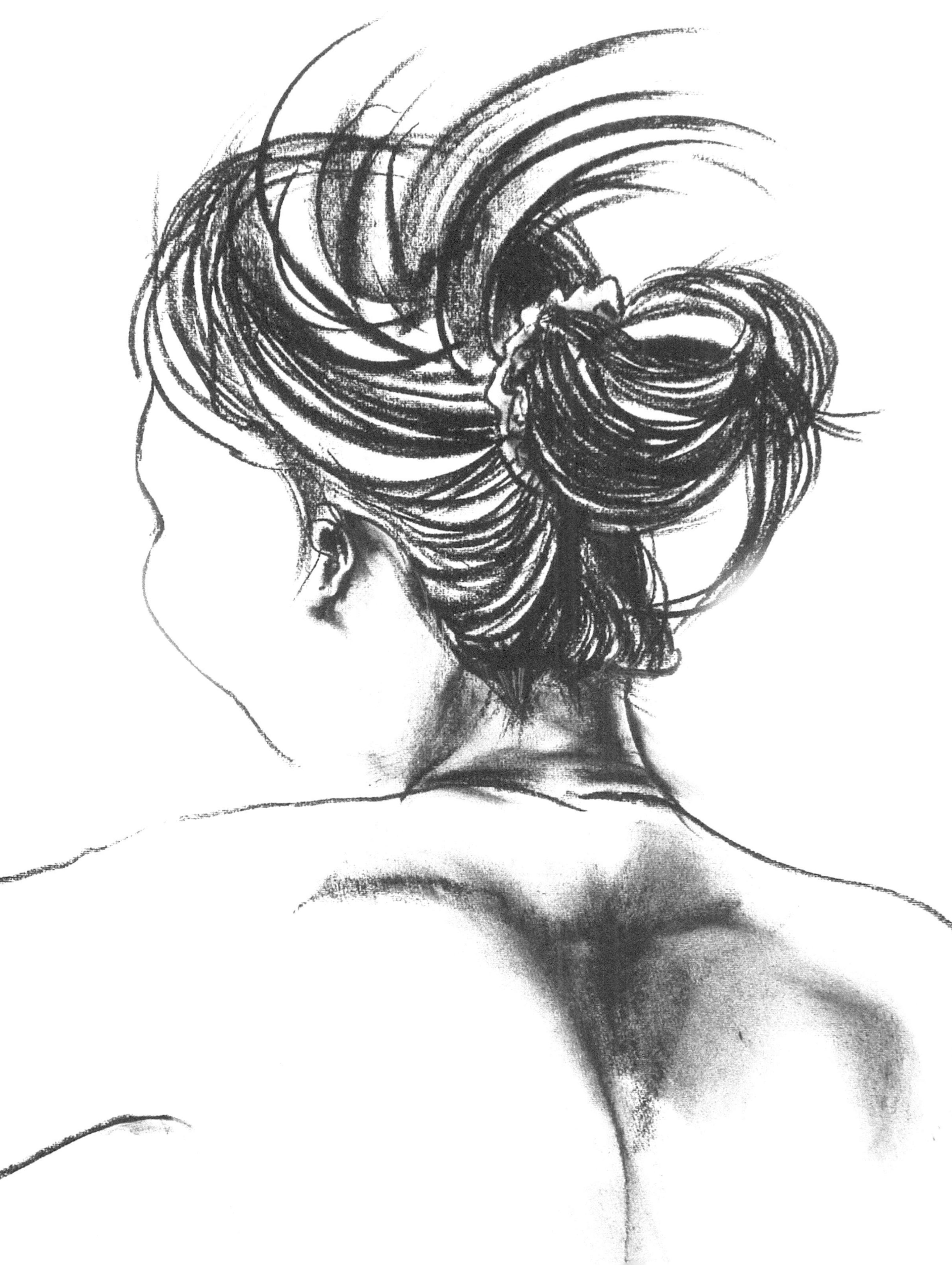

OF SMALL THINGS

Grasshopper flicks cellophane wings
Of both dark and green, nothing more
Under eaves, above the red door

Thoughts all over my mind
Like cicadas on the branches
Of the cinnamon bark tree

Some cannot forget a voice
And if they could, it would be
To throw the past away

For a moment a misted rain
On the jade-green lake
A solitary swan, pale and still
How it stopped singing
When it lost its life-long mate

Everything becomes fragile
To look at a handsome face
Not the same as it was
Contemplate this ulterior mirror
Hair white as old jade
The longer we stay here --
the older we go.

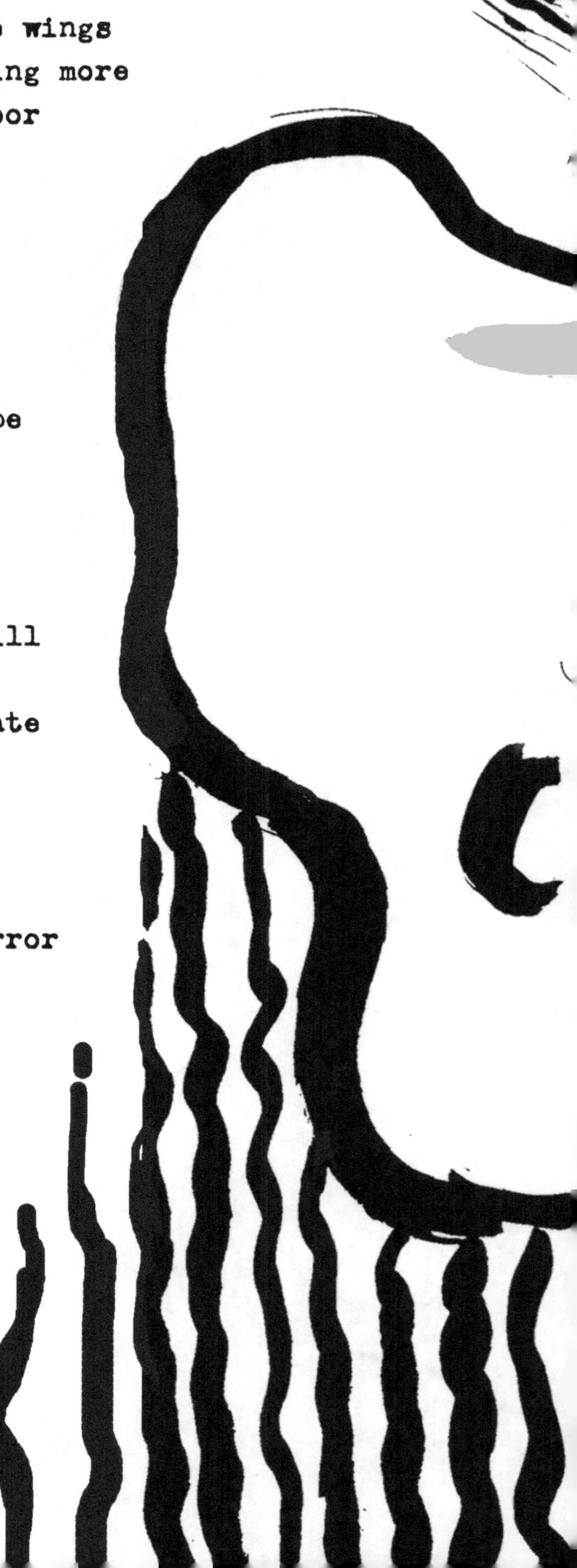

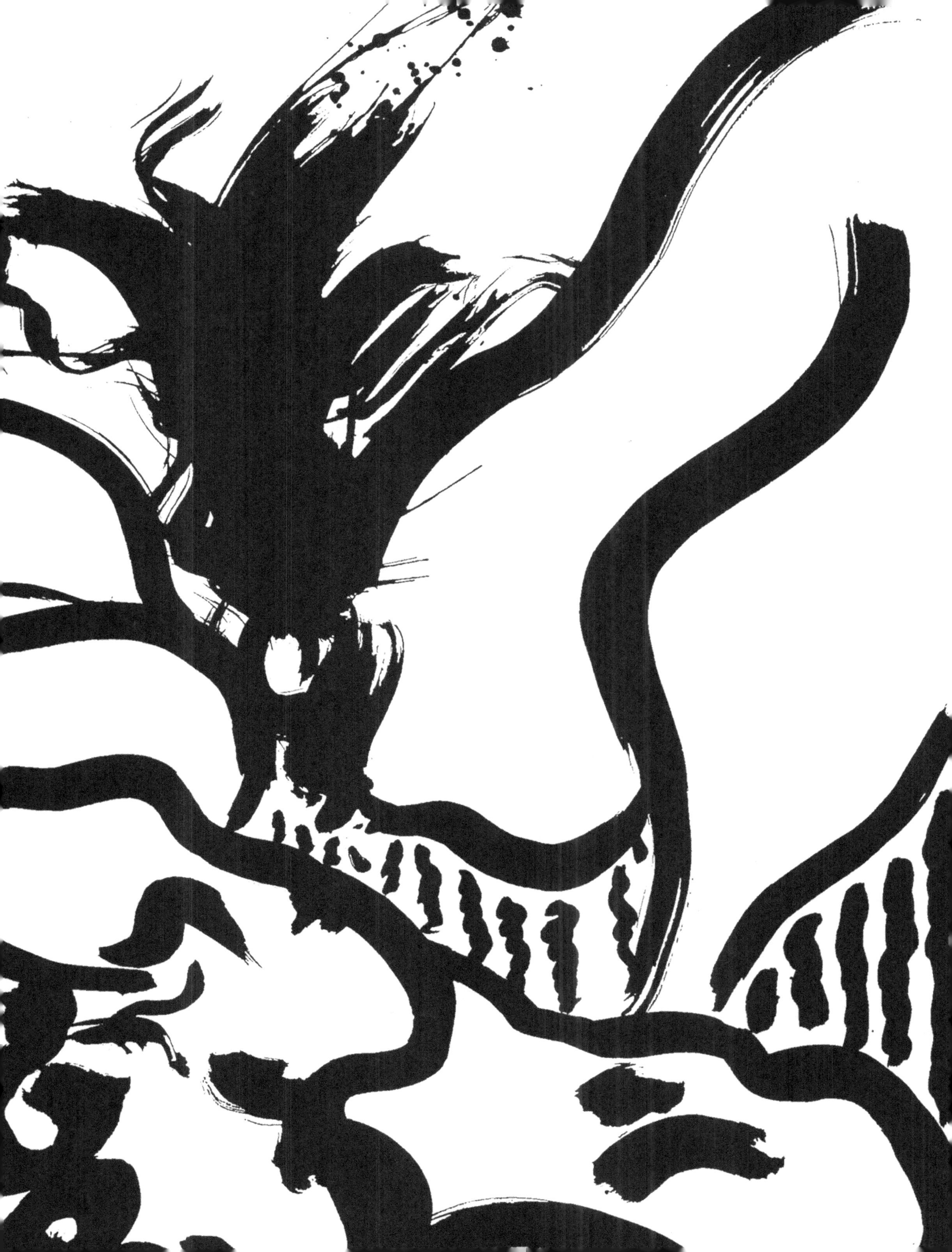

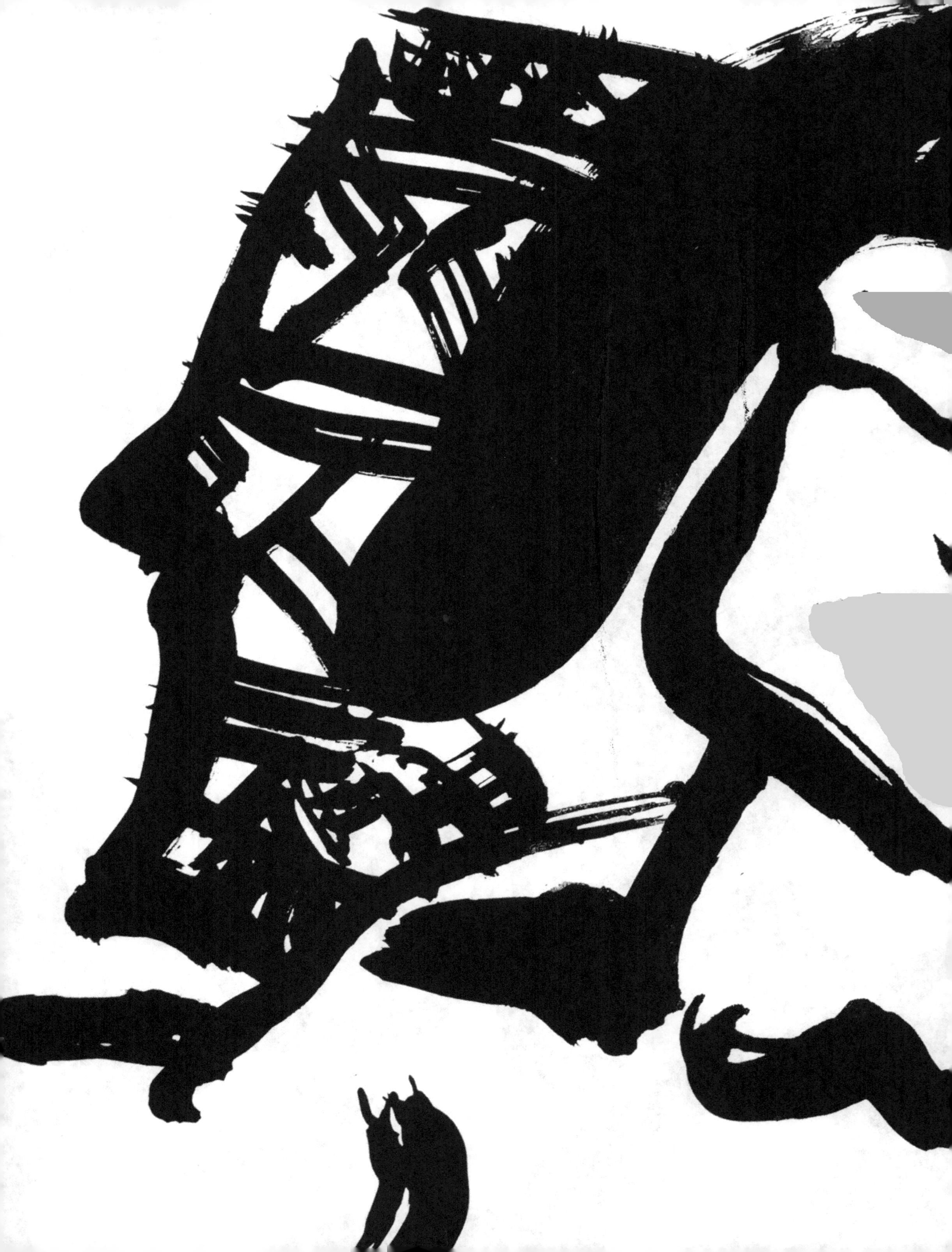

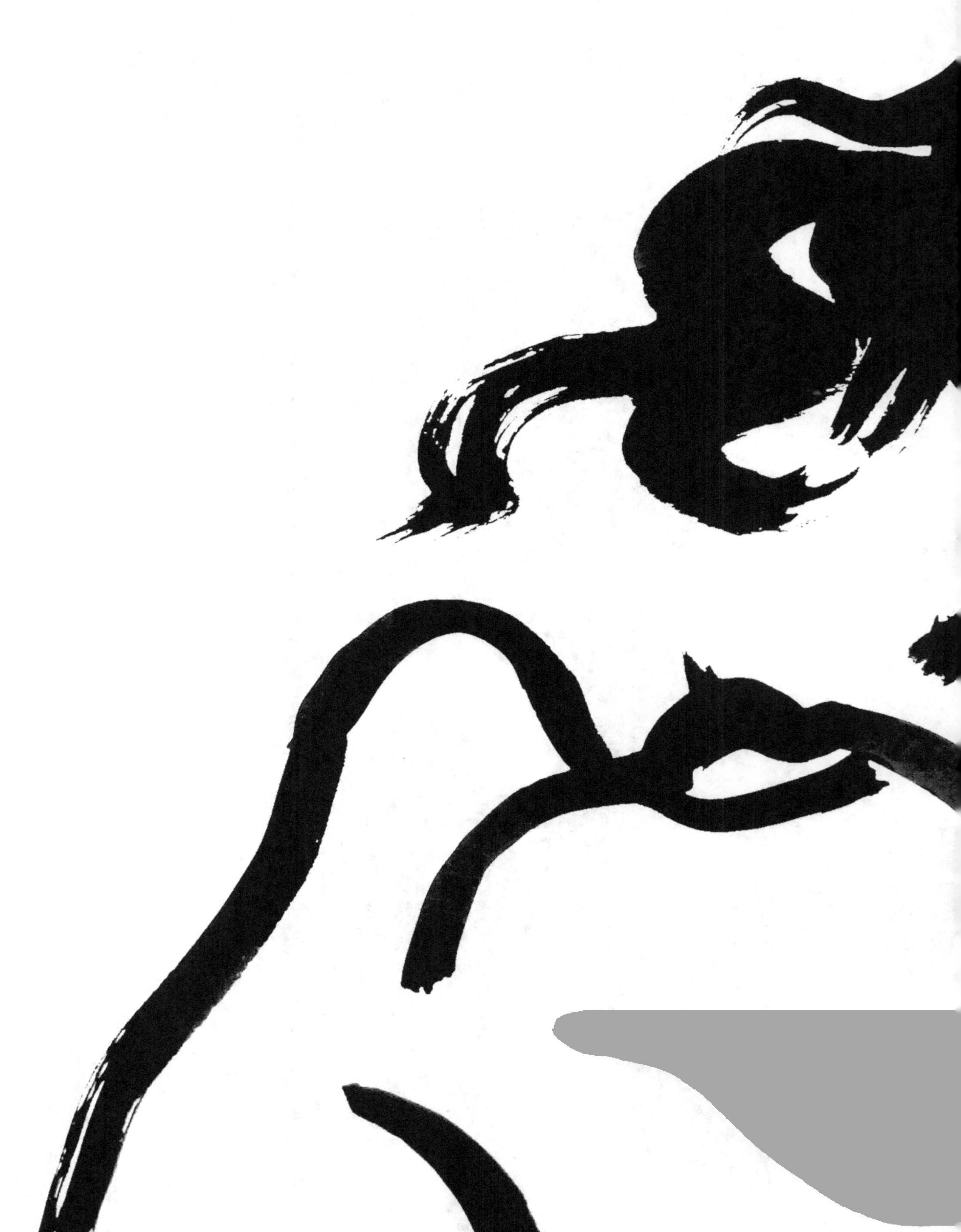

NINE HEAVENS

With Nine Heavens as witness
before jade pavilion stones
someone painted stars that night
tore patterns from mulberry paper
before you were born, the loved one

an angel pulls on nights shirt
light robe of celestial fabric
bright moon pearl stones are seen
fireflies in mason jar, light-beams strum
crane birds come, and infant, the loved one

inked shapes in a far piece of garden
flattened rice fields with mistral hand
there is not a moment to forget --
for you enter the world, as loved one

now the moon brings night in close, but still
once fragrant plants overgrown with weeds
in topiary garden of mulberry trees allegories
months pile up bayonets of yellow leaves

The Gatekeeper sent to open the portal
and remembers -- bathing you in The Pool of Heaven
and carrying you here on the assuaging hip
To see you far off, as the child within --
a likeness of beginnings.

THREAD OF GRASS

A path beside old mango trees
leads to The Temple of Literature
bells and chanting in The Great Hall
golden carp amidst simple waterfall
and reflections of your face
I see in The Jade Pool

Noticed at once, your soldier's coat
I had no way to send a message
now I see that your clothes are heavy
loss of your blood, my brother
I will wash your shirt in two separate lakes
empty a tearful of thoughts, where are you now?

Tears merge with thousand sheets of rain
field-crows gather after secular fighting
it is you that has not come home
it was you who took the bullet

a mountain of jade came crashing down
a memorial to bury a million bones
a stone statue, overgrown with moss
it crumbles by itself, with no one looking

I think of you, but I can't see you
when night comes and snow presses down
bones of the brave crack in the wind
the sound gradually grows older
everything is done according to The Rites
but no one can say, where you are buried.

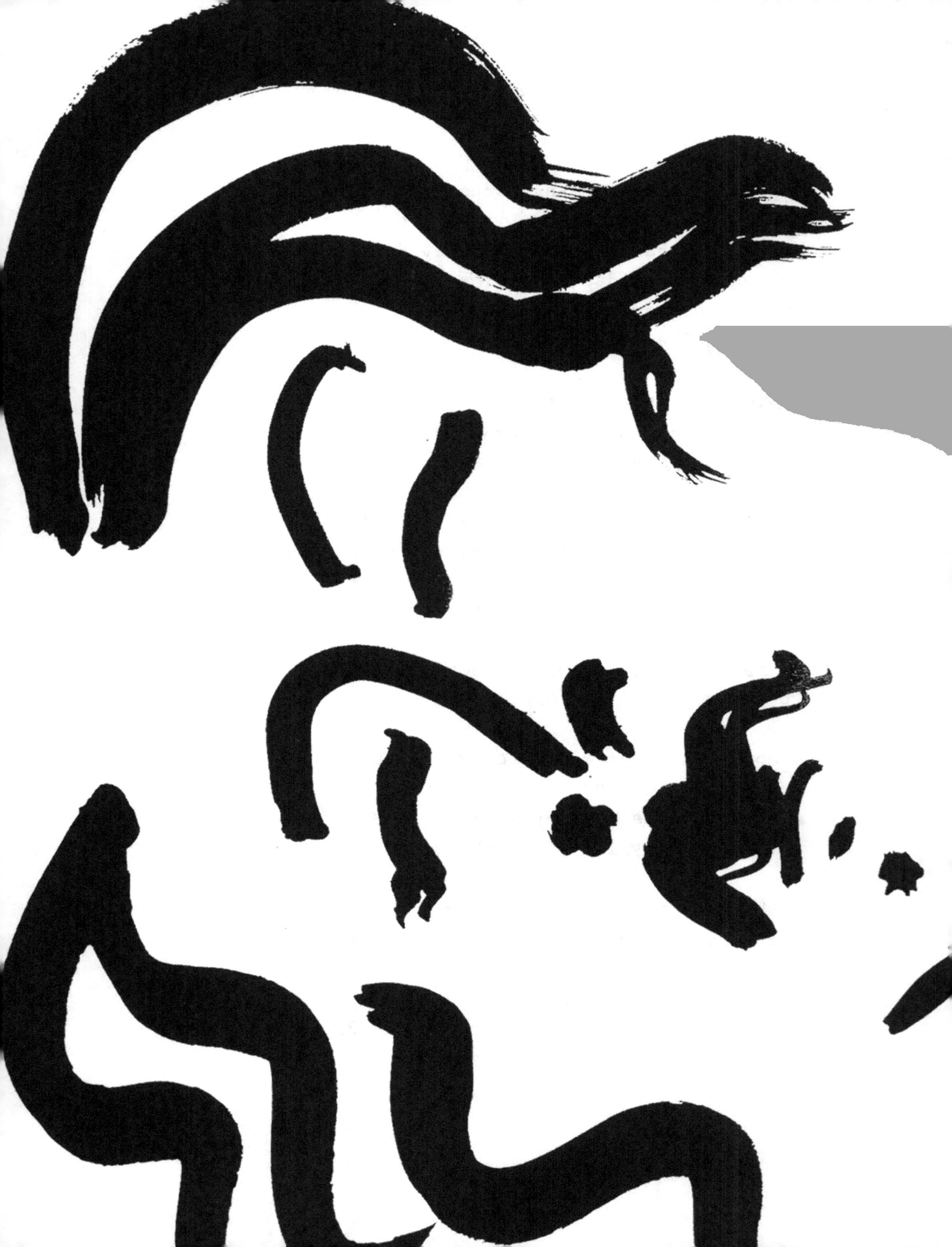

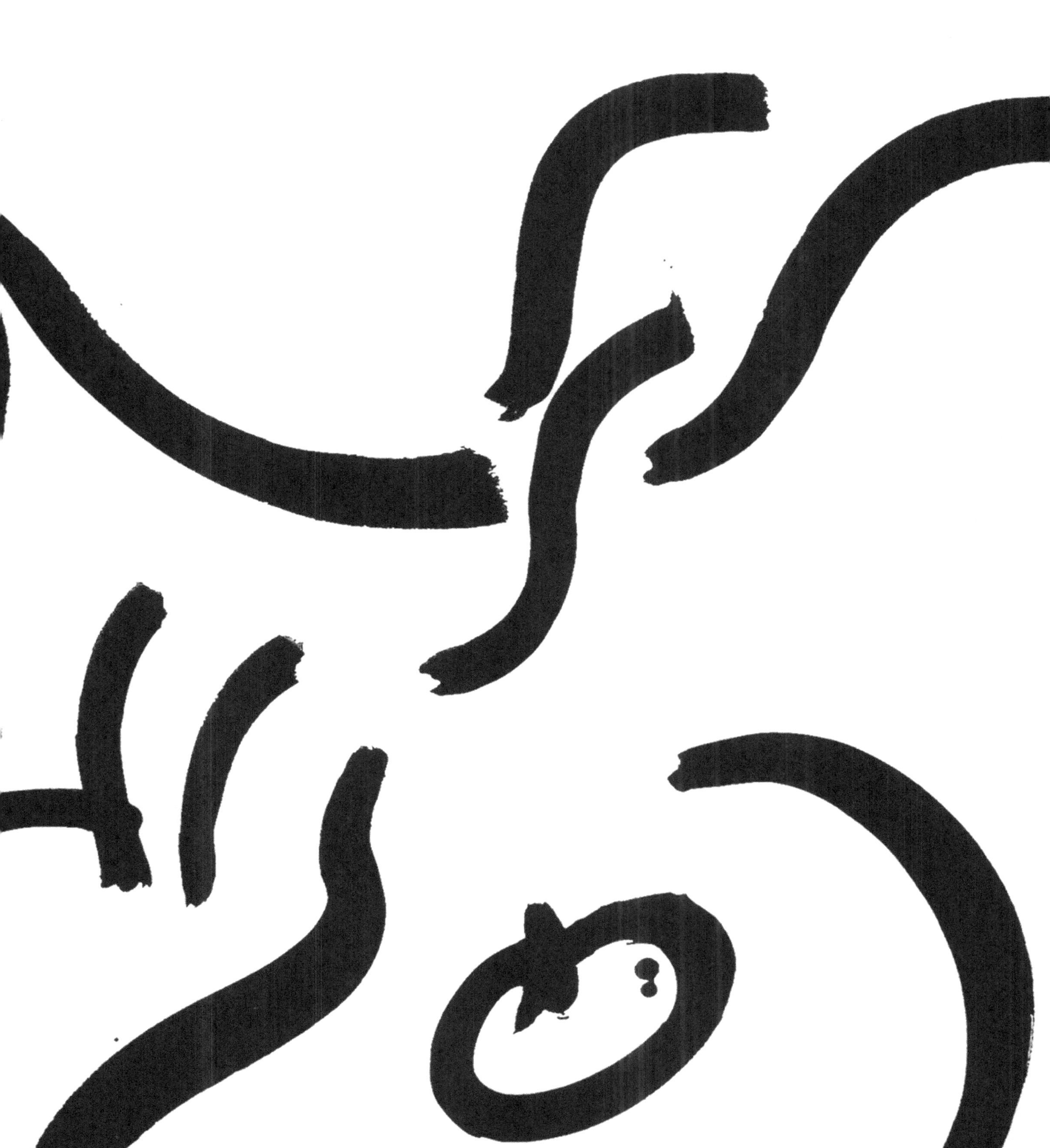

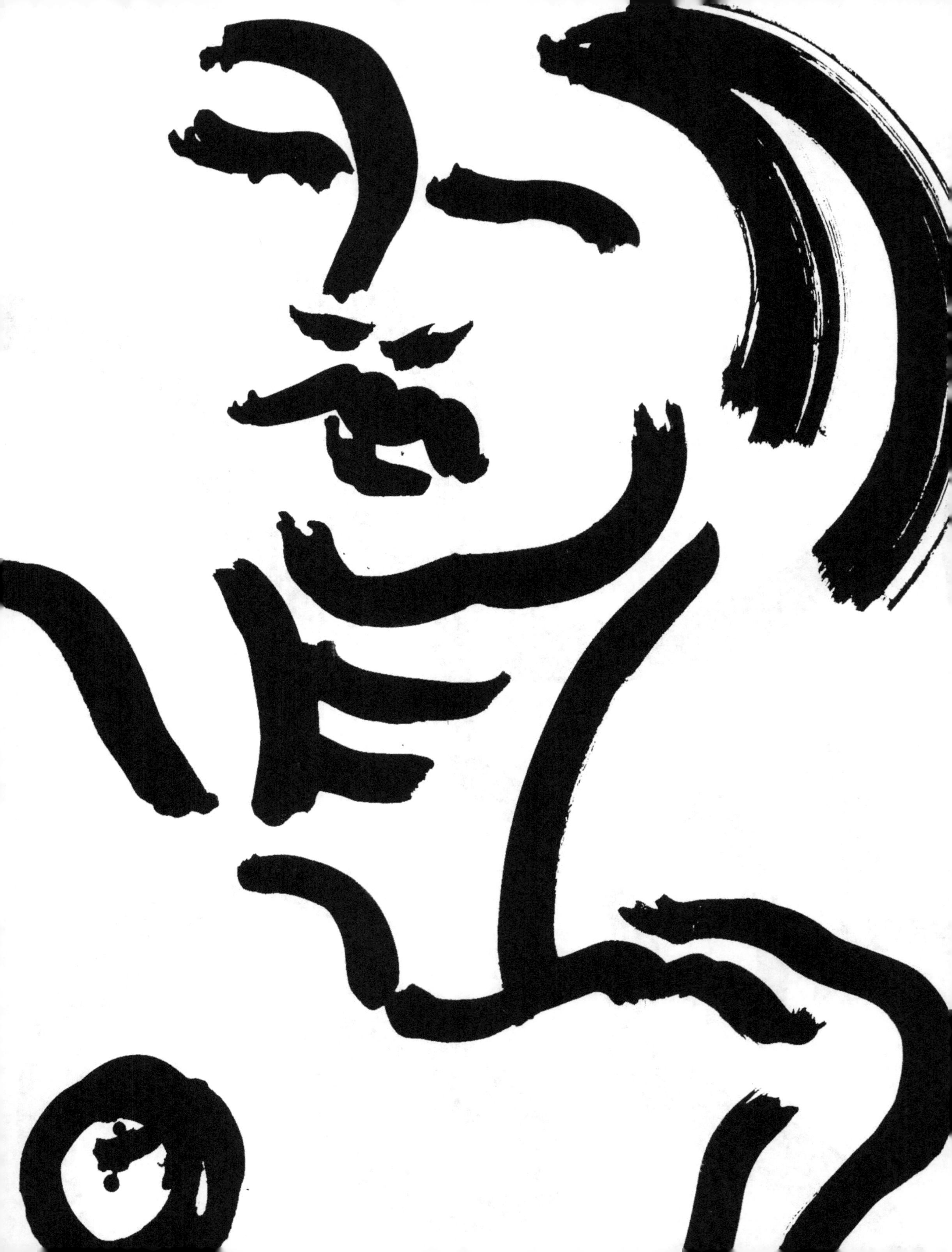

PAPER MONEY

There are lakes in Bo De District
where women speak over water
they are not ghosts, *I heard them*

to see women at lake's inlet
sharpen knife on stone-hard steps
kill rooster, or Mandarin duck

wash herbs in water's curving jade
crouching on lower steps, pounding of wash
they were wives and fighters, *I saw their cloth*

they were lovers, mothers, child-bearers
more blood, to color water's reflection
some empty of love, some full of regret

just when they speak, no pretense of happiness
to argue in the marketplace, stammer out
ten eggs smashed, doubly wasteful, doubly dubious
interrupts overmuch; conjecture in hall of food
how the fragrant and the rotten become confused.

H I S T O R I E S

Most people expect our journey, incredulous
To cover the East in a thousand months
One country at the end of the road

Yet, we didn't know where we were heading
Or if, dead ashes can be ignited by fanning
A sense of resignation: let it burn!

As it may be paper, yet not paper
Worth less as a dead tree
To find where its book has gone

Last month, the illusions became many
Even the woodcut dragon, insentient
Pens and inking of a thousand years

Red stamp official seal, scissors and ribbon
For four hundred months, only to wish
Prayers for happenstance and fortune
Homage of paper, about to open
For the fortunate but still -- where are
Passionate writings left behind by lovers?

ANOTHER DAY

Mai fills a wooden bucket with lime-flowers
to soak the day from her feet
in an opposite corner of occidental
water holds its edge, water turns
into a jade pond in temple garden
no sooner does her foot touch water

she sits down in quiet abstraction
beneath the water, all was silent
lay patiently and unstirred
when jade and gold had vanished

someone throws down a pebble
water transforms into a small circle
which becomes a larger circle
which we cannot control

take water as a message, no one
lives in isolation, to see
the circle continues to expand
until it covers the entire pond

there are ghosts throwing stones
ghosts listening, when someone is talking
and their voice becomes drowsy
turning vegetables into mint
silent burial of words, as soon as we speak.

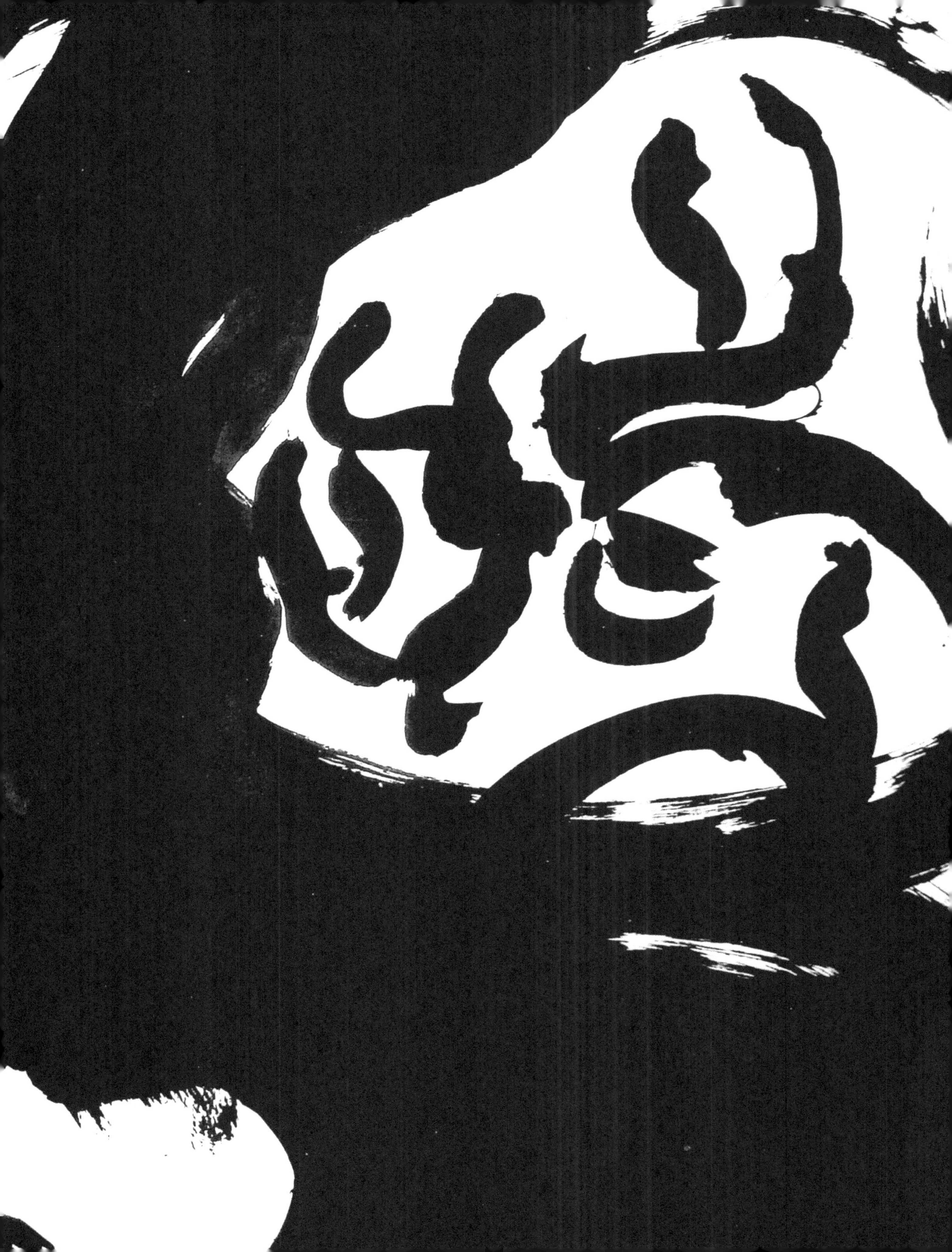

PROTOCOL OF RICE

There are whales in a river of catfish
Their compass lost in muddied water
Each whale leans against each other
They cannot tell river from sea at all

Gone past, the fishermen
It's just the same as before
They move one's imagination
Who knows where?

Small fish on a hook dot the shoals
To make a deep-hidden spectacle of gold
Fish after fish, nothing more, nothing less
Let's stop the boat, this moment is over

Gone like passing duckweed
The lanterns are lit: the night black-pitch
Drift with away by morning tide
And the rain wets the soldier's coat

For fear, that on the fallen red water
There may still be a few drops of blood
How could anyone see them?

In years come and gone
To send off a single soldier
And families scattered by the war
Appear and disappear
Now fear, Red River bloodies forever

For years, a pattern of summer time
Burned blossoms and peach-leaves
And rice-burning season a month away

Sky and river are the same color
Burned clouds hold old rain
Rain on top of rain

Each drop comes like tempered knife
The clouds are never emptied
By memory of tomorrow's ash

Then through duck-weed I rowed a boat
In this travesty of river, and rain
The bait you hook is all the same.

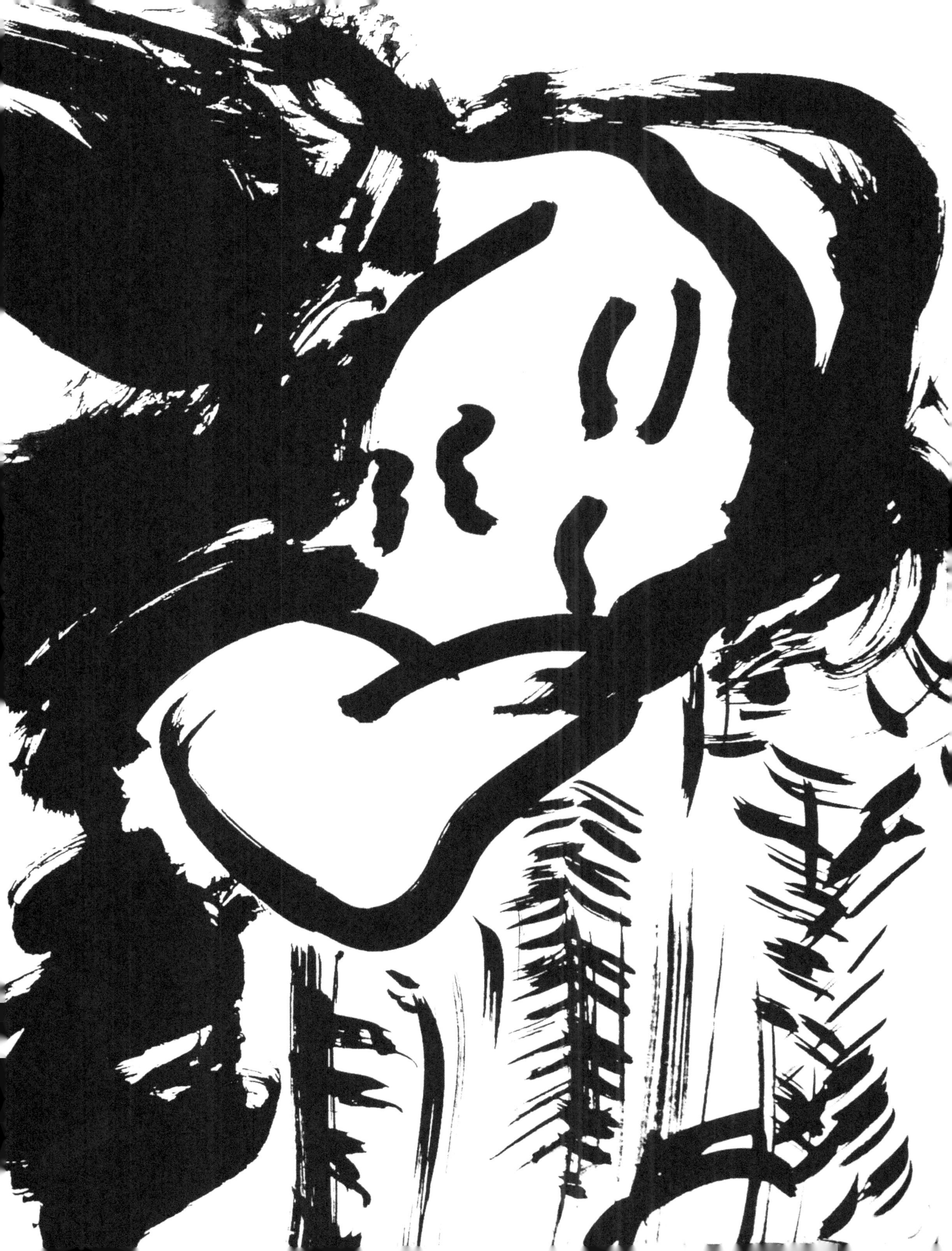

THE WEDDING PLANNER

The family complained, like ducks in a market
So bride-to-be does what is expected
Simply by saying yes to everything, 'I will marry'
Not even a smile, or a break in the tears
Strangely wedding gifts collect and show complications

Simply by saying yes to everything, 'I will marry'
Her parents' wish -- Ah, there are letters of proposal
Strangely wedding gifts collect and show complications
The gold and the meat should not be together

Her parents' wish -- Oh, many letters of proposal
There were the usual betel leaves, tea, glutinous rice
The gold and the meat should not be together
New rice, green, if a large box is on the table

There were the usual betel leaves, tea, glutinous rice
An equal number of square rice cakes
And here red silk sashes on the dresses
And a hundred paper kites lashed with red bamboo

She counts an equal number of square rice cakes
No appetite left, it is sadness that consumed her
Plates and dinner set of colored bone china
Where painted dragons appear to break loose

Many gifts wrapped in red paper
Solid gold, clothes, rice, wine, meat, and no coffee
A single fruit is doubtful, if sadness is the season
The moon in a red lacquer box, the Gods know
There is a tarnished plan from birth, she resists
Everything, but now the past intertwines future
That women of former times, pawn their wedding clothes

Whiskey on his breath, one sharp word follows another
Frozen stars in matrimony's night
Crack in moon
Where luck slips out!

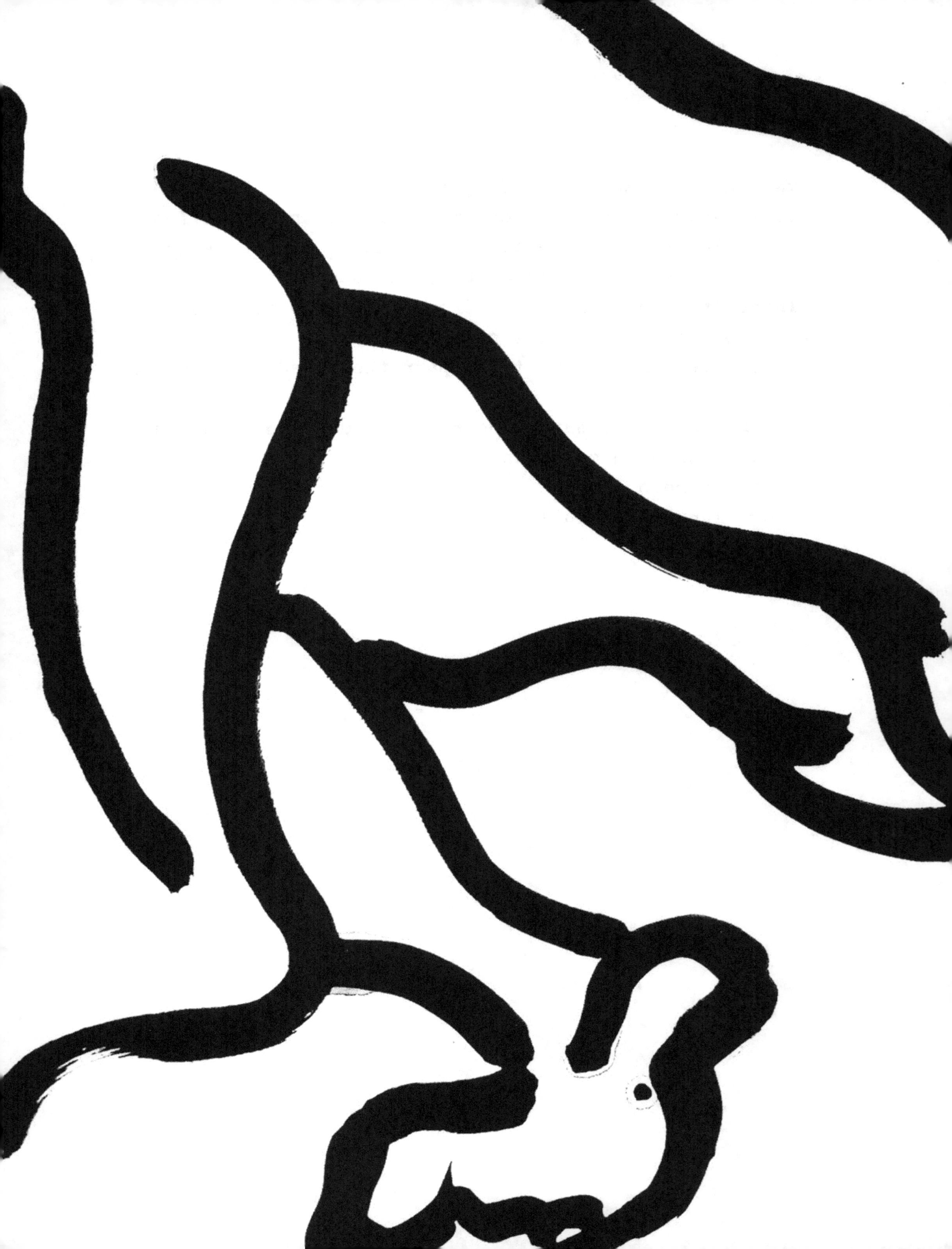

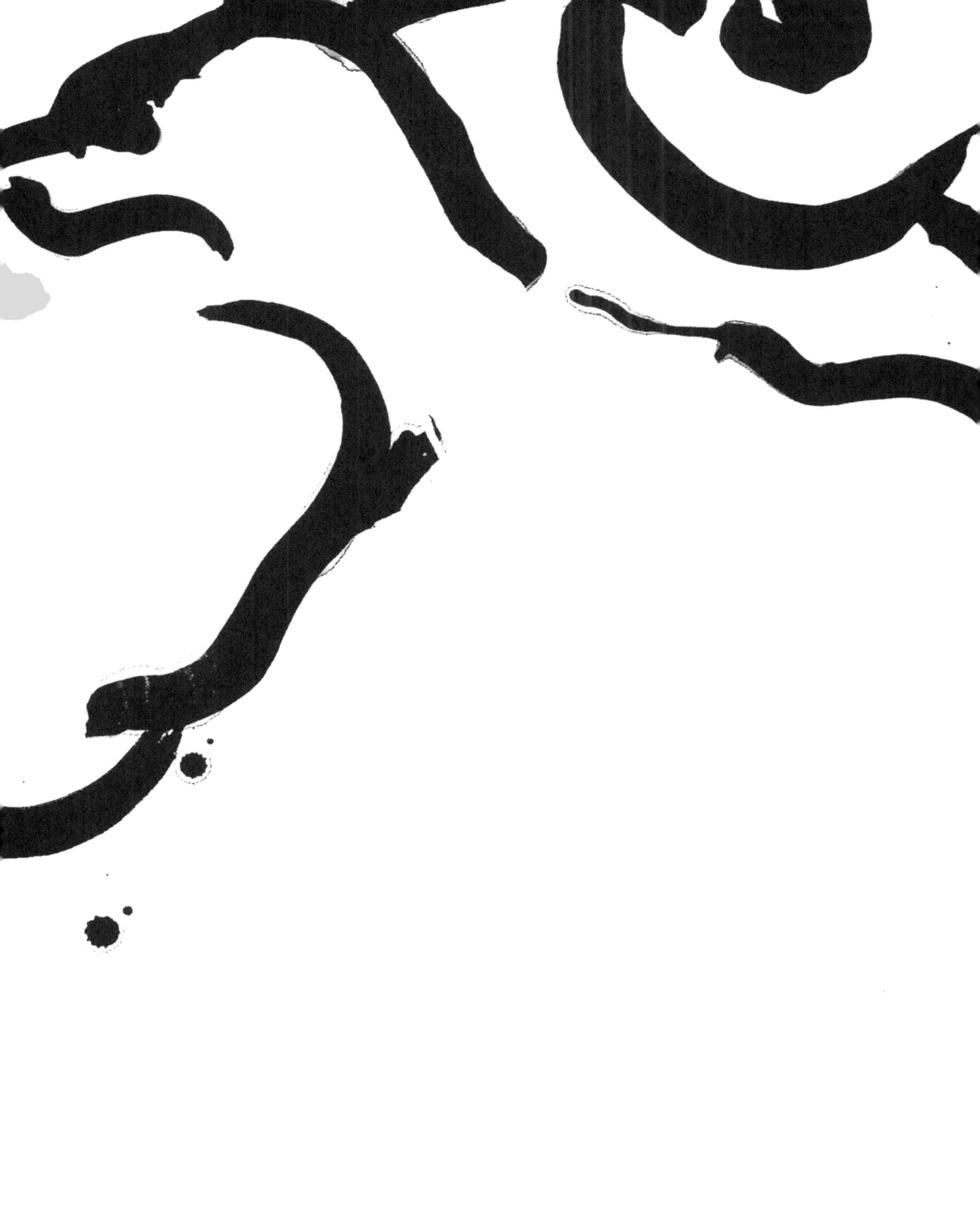

THE KITE MAKER

Open the red door -- courtesy of the army

The King has ordered a holiday
For The Pattern of Righteousness

Whiskey jar and wine confiscated
Pure potable water, also

Once more, gun, bomb, and drone
Knows nothing of the Tao

Who shall know at the start
If the offering for luck

Is properly done, or not
A pattern is set, for ceremony

To see foreigners avoid discrepancy
After the nine to five curfew begins

Green rice cake and betel nut
Strong women, deeper thoughts

Light this silver pipe of opium
Flute and drum closer together

Bring out paper dragon kite
For good reasons, to send
Remembrance to far heavens

Wind will tie the sedge knot
Winds rise, Viet kites fly
Until the edge of blue-washed sky

Cast the string and send off
Hidden prayers, quieter histories
High and lucky, but parted from this

Red and sere, above the pavilion
And sure of meeting again
But then, the months grow long
The string grows loose

If you wish to die, there is no way
If you wish to live, you know not how
Just a parting and reunion
So, it's you, Lover at every crossing
A short step away, then I am young
Who can think of no return.

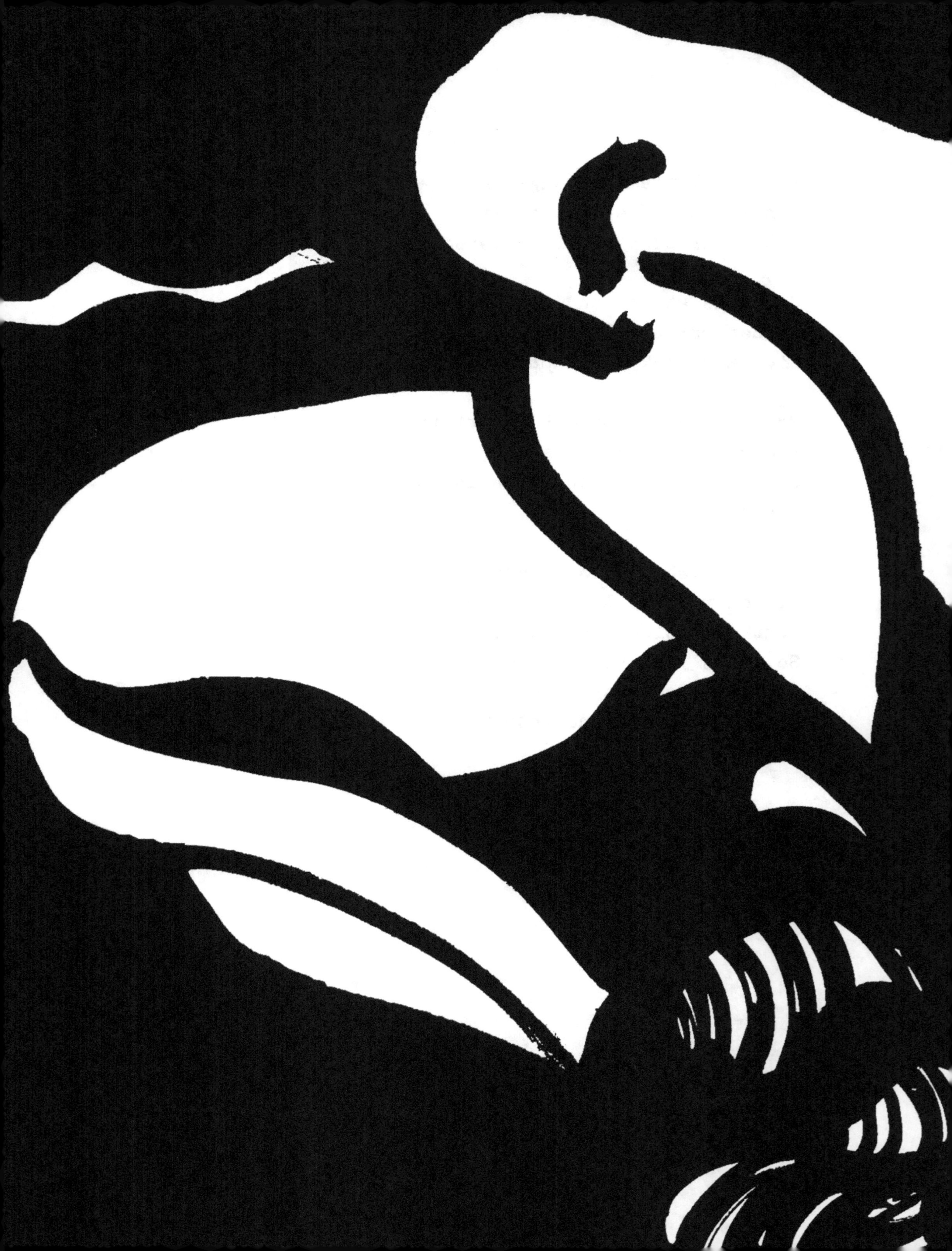

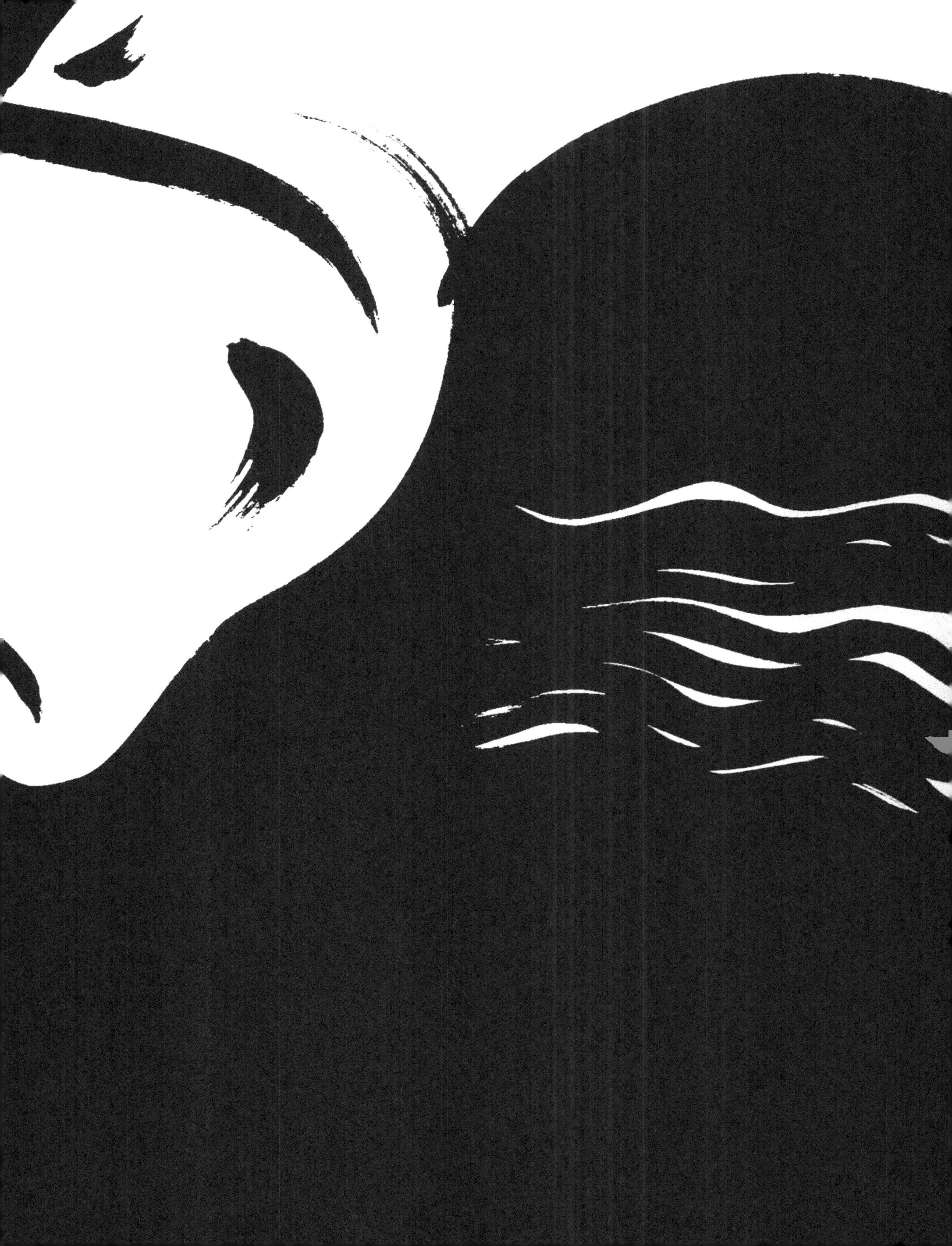

NEW YEAR VISITOR

Two women set the daily fire alight
in cold blanket of itinerant fog
as black dog returns late from bone-yard
yesterday, when family ghosts
enter our house at midnight
invited or uninvited, they stay for a week

So many years together in another sleep
floors swept and children prayed for
slay forlorn dirt and eternal dust
for ethereal visitors and their shadows
on the shiny surface, a visitor would say
the house seems, clean enough

and children appear, polite enough
only breath fogs up the articulate lens
no chance left to view a world through
who shoots a cat on a Monday
for killing a mouse on a Sunday
and so ghosts of soldiers, forlorn lovers

remain in alleyways and everywhere
such as before, more stories that follow
incense, cigarettes, opium on family alter
in high places there always will be
a distinct touch of impossibility
but now, instead of grenades, and wine.

T H E   M E T A M I R S

Less is more, providing one had more
They had little, and gained everything
Including what is not certain

Like a journey across quicksand
Back and forth until they disappear
Into infinities, like polished obsidian

It began with argot, a puff of smoke
In their faces -- and the wallet was gone
The conspicuous inconspicuous

Or the inconspicuous, conspicuous
They could not be sure
But things merge into back-ground

Like a white-feathered bird
In the snow, lends allure
Or the devil's blossom

Masquerades as a flower or leafy twig
Untutored for the predatory,
And those who masquerade in the blind
Conjures up, hopes to outwit
The black merges with the dark pit
Men they knew, in effect, became chameleon
And so, a fortune goes.

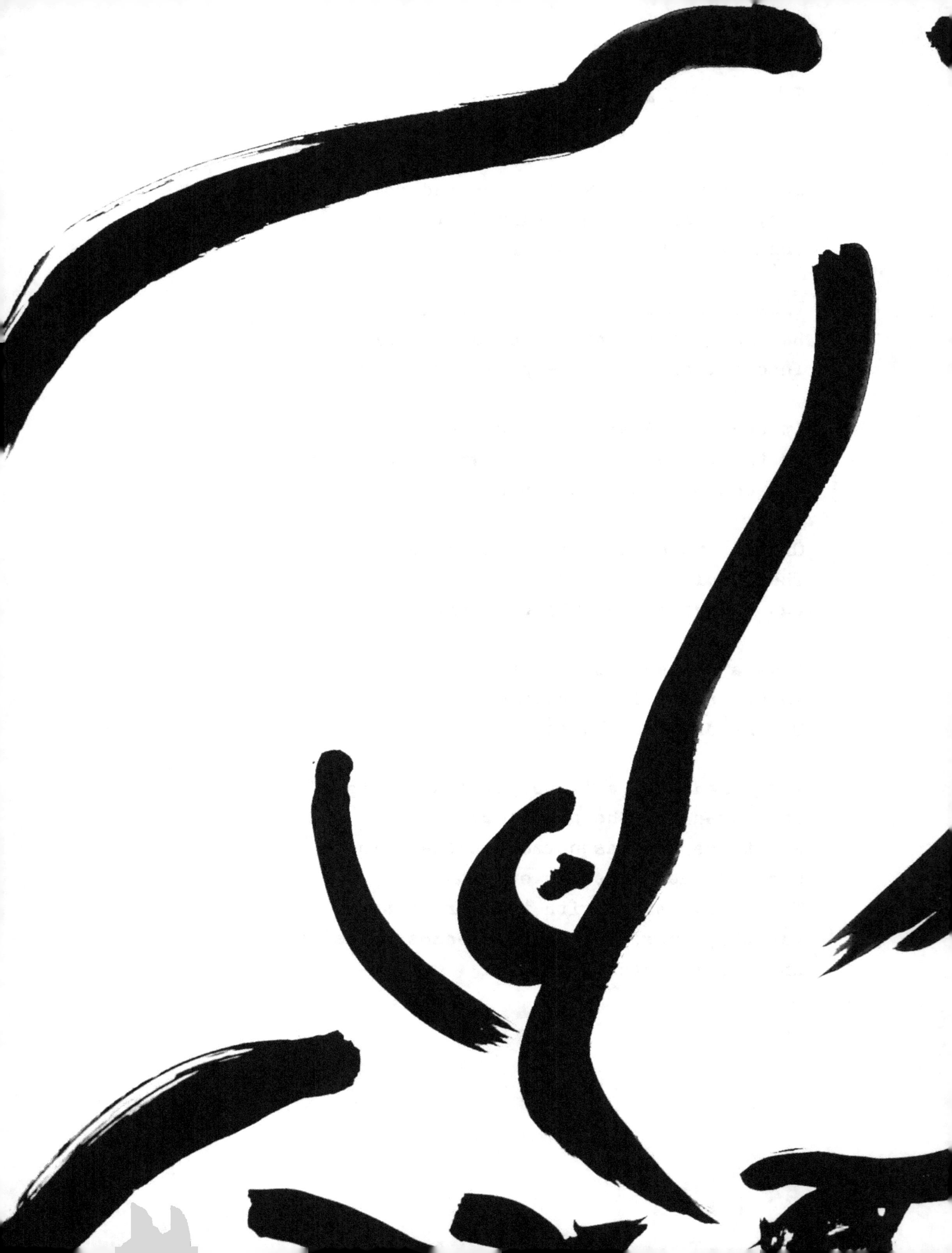

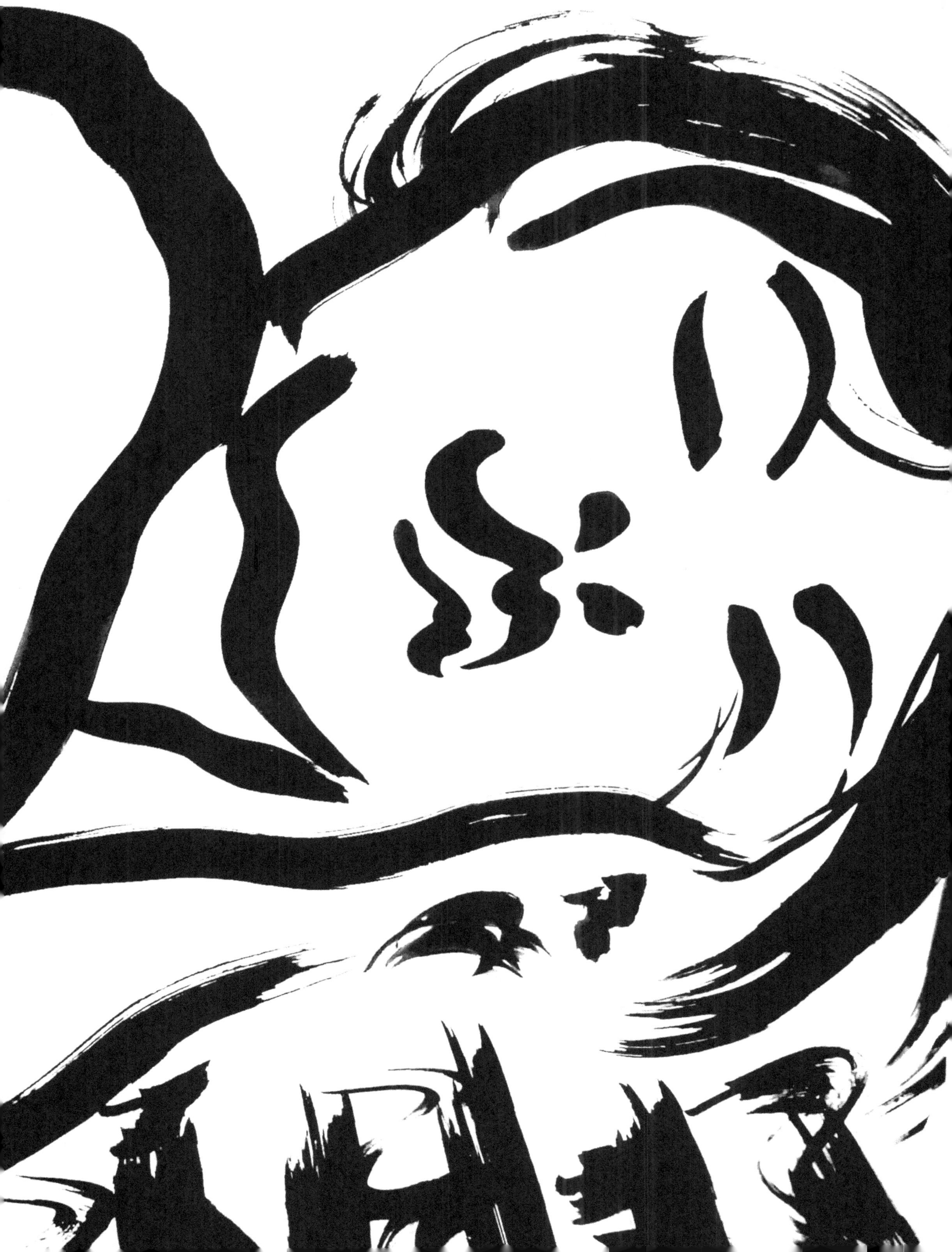

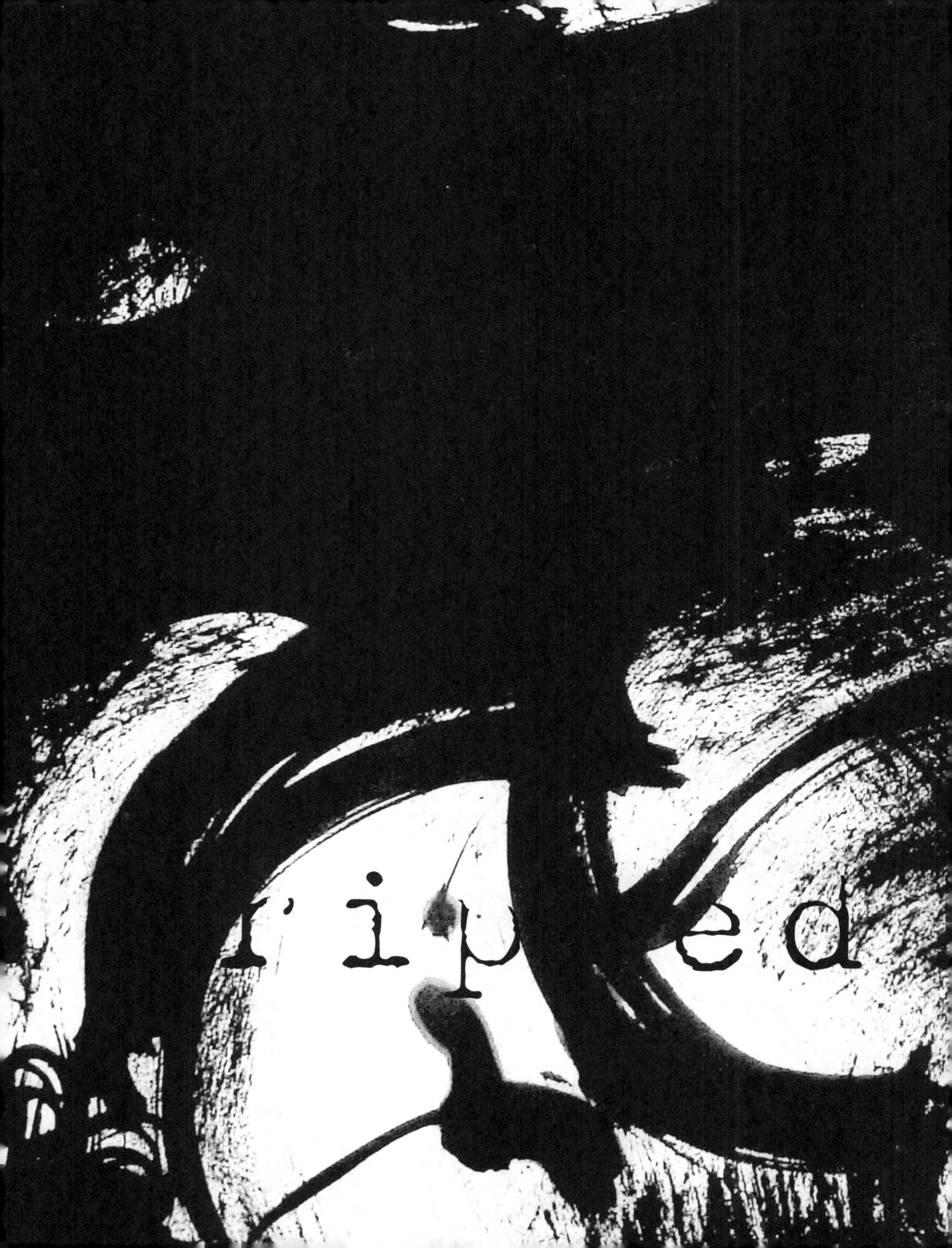

ripped

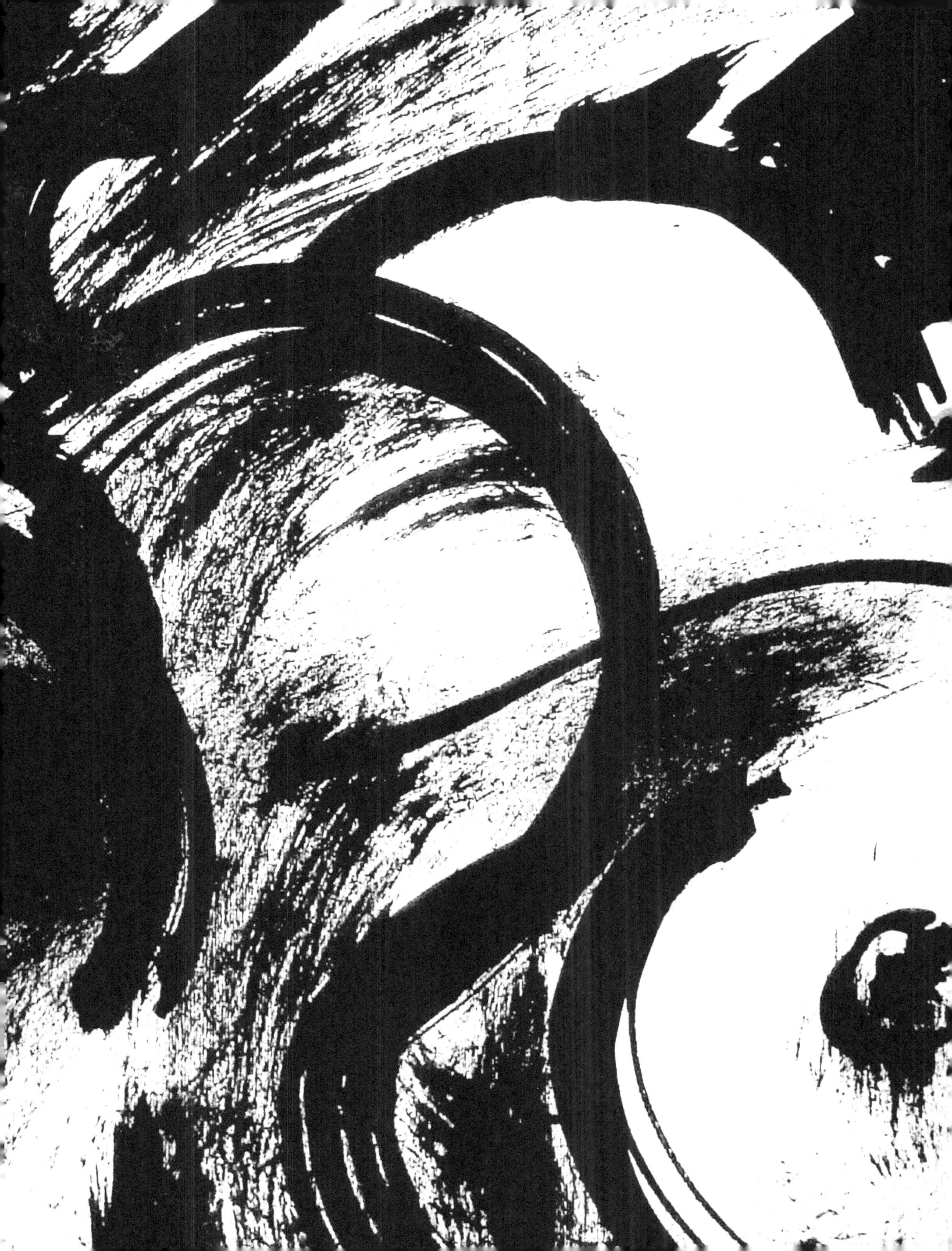

PAPER LANTERN

The lantern is made for you to continue
a little slower, yet a pattern well cut
filigree configuration meshed like stars
to challenge; the sound of quieter folding

Through silence, all red paper lanterns
to make evening something, evenly
when match is struck and all moons hanging
over The Bridge of Prostitutes and Thieves
thousand stars shine on the river -- but soldiers come

Lighted path, slow-moving road, leaves no track
where soldiers' bring the gun, no one told
but the war was over, either there is a war -- or none
who will tell new ghosts in their wander
over old Bridge of Sanctions, must stay out, unless

There is lone star on a flag in a darker fashion
this extreme gold gave an impoverish pattern
but hold familiar lanterns of night, engraved
within, and seeing, not seen, lantern's gold
an answer to yes, or no, depending on interpretation
interpretations or interpretations interpreted

And no one knows -- a flood of propaganda
could be darker than a woman's red lipstick
one voice conspires against the future, hear it
if all paper is torn, if the candle gone out
it breaks up golden light and steals a piece of heaven

Raise the red lantern, see if light is counterfeit
or, back to the light, pour jasmine tea
if answers sought in the bottom of a cup
and dead leaves grow stronger

Will waiting for luck, make luck empty
Look towards one another -- wonderment
Secrets flash, like yellow lanterns in sunbeams
but closed eyes -- look again!
there are lovers and lovers and lovers
here saying -- *whisper it* -- what comes next?

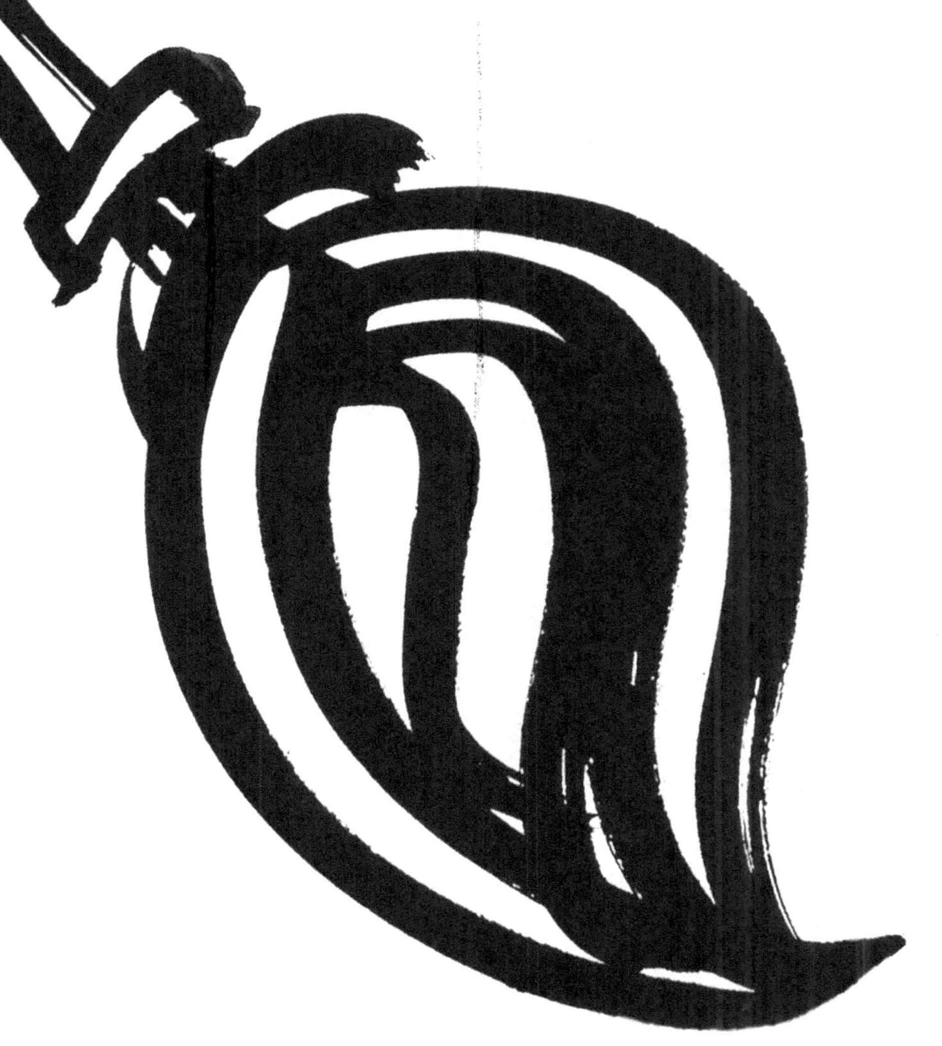

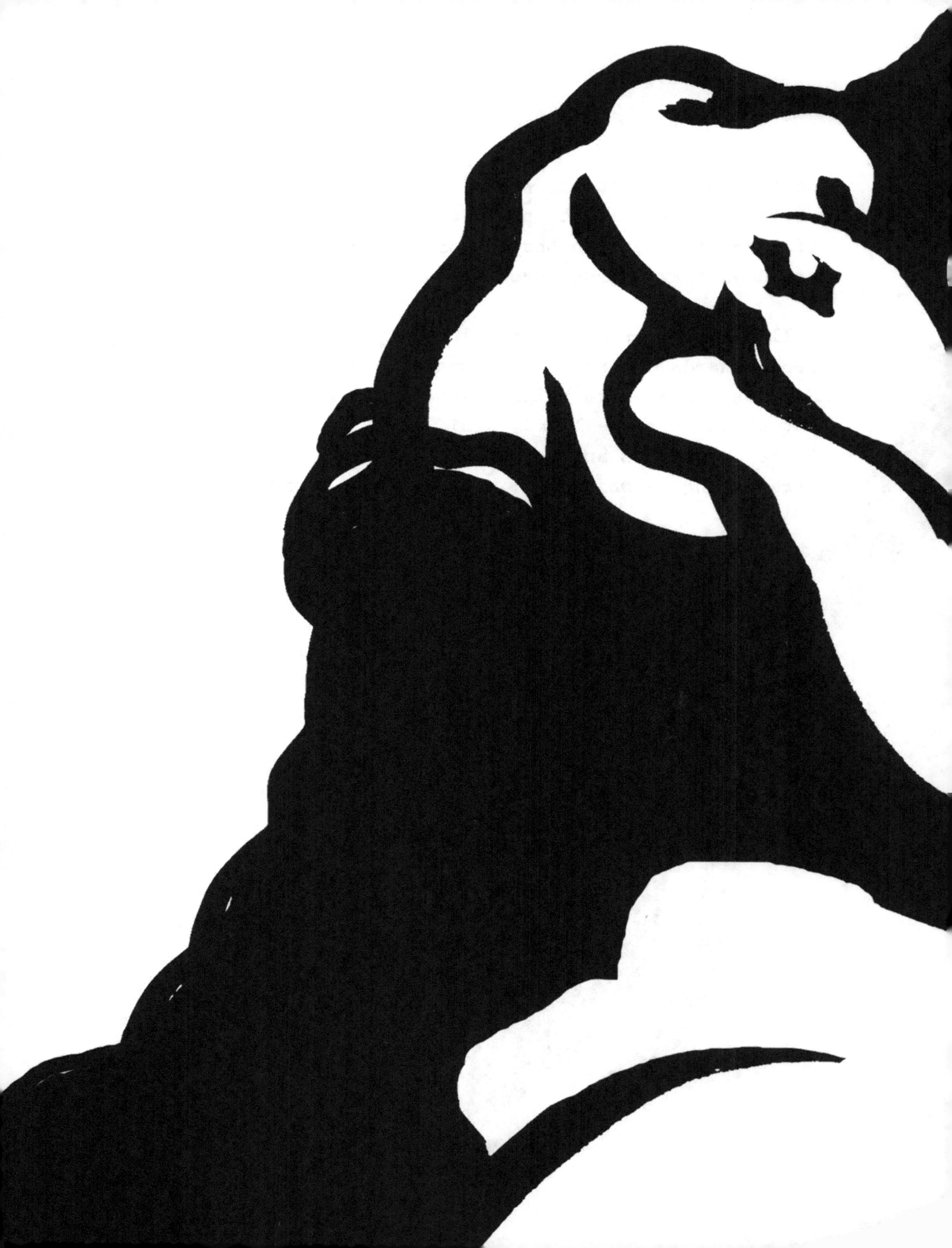

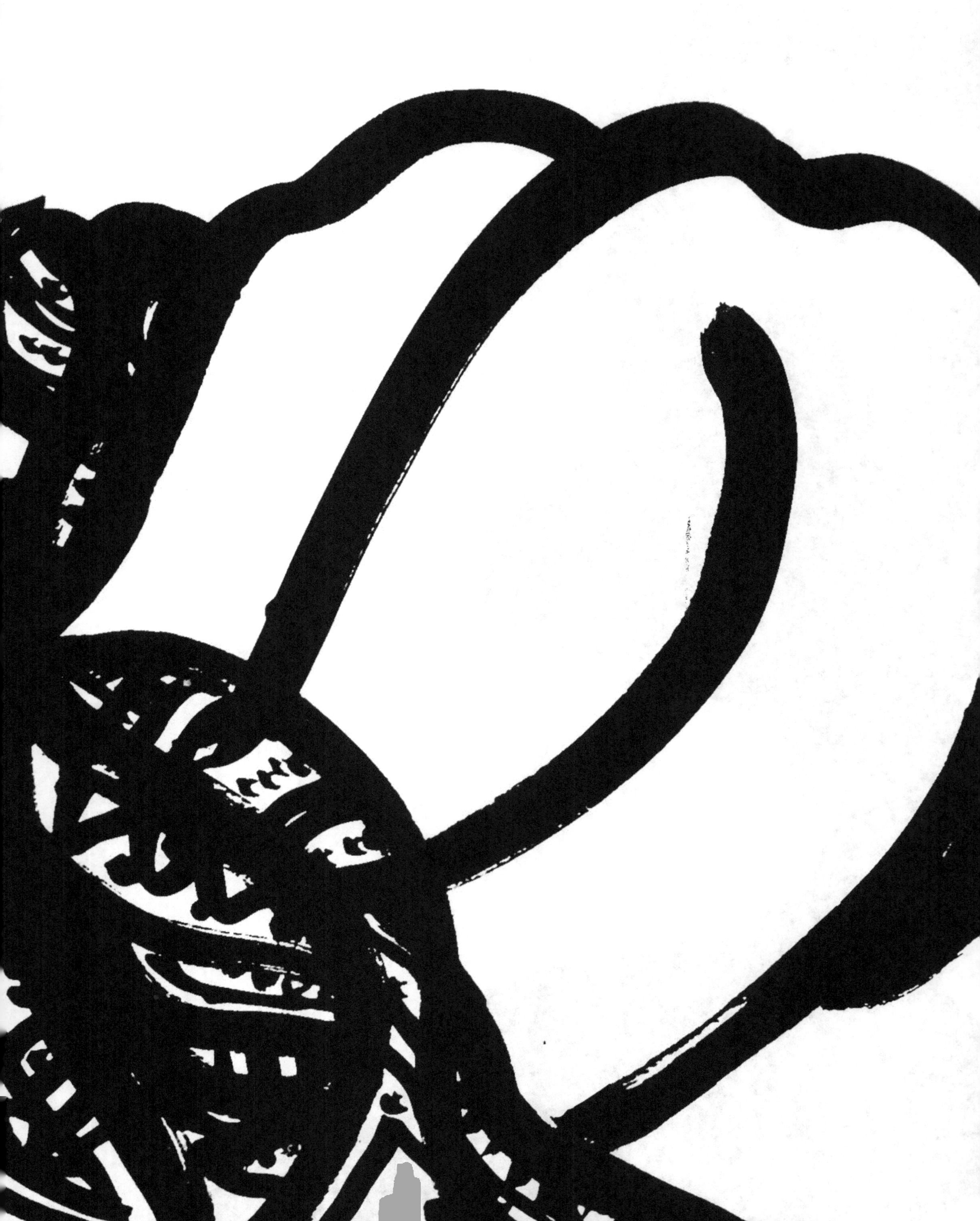

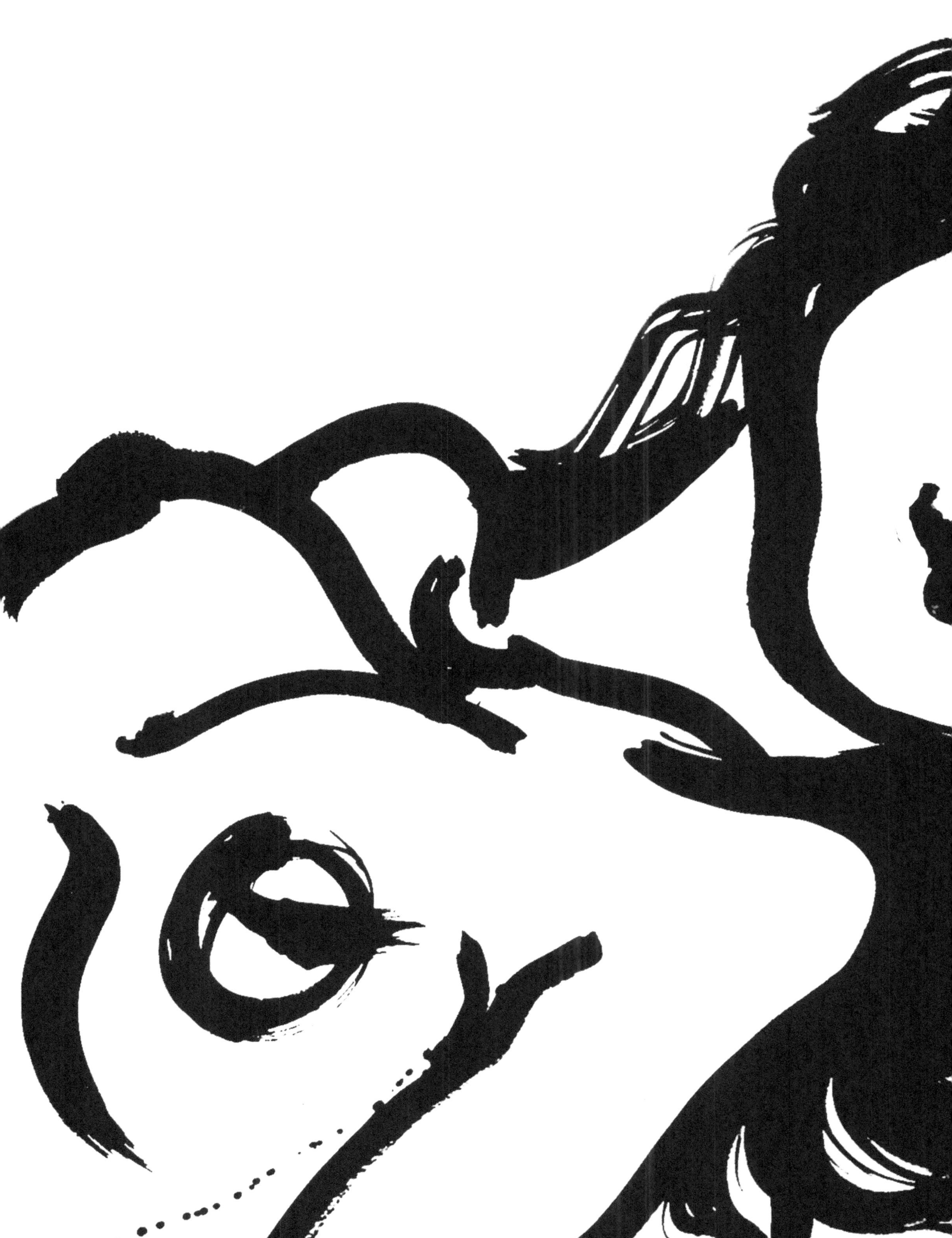

THE PEOPLE'S PARK

Summer heat which seems infinite

Old wrought iron fence painted blue
Surrounds the People's Park
In the green lungs of the city
Gustave Eiffel's third masterpiece
In the golden days of merit
Mandala of the immortals on far pavilion
Made a sundial in the Fu-sang Tree
Marble angels dance in The Putti Fountain
Faces peer through cool roseate mist
Like small children glad to get wet
Buffalo girl and fishing-boy
Without a bamboo stick in hand
But a belief the wings of the waterfowl
Could lift with six feathers

A thousand miles, north and south
Beyond Nine Roads from The Old Gate
East and west along the Seven Paths
A shift of the city compass
The summer not over, by half
Heavy brocade of lotus leaves
Planted tomorrow, by *The Master*
Every bird kept up their song
A good summer knows its season
There are topiary aces and spades
Box tree hedges shaped like hearts
And diamonds, shaped by the gardener
Until there is nothing left to do, but gamble.

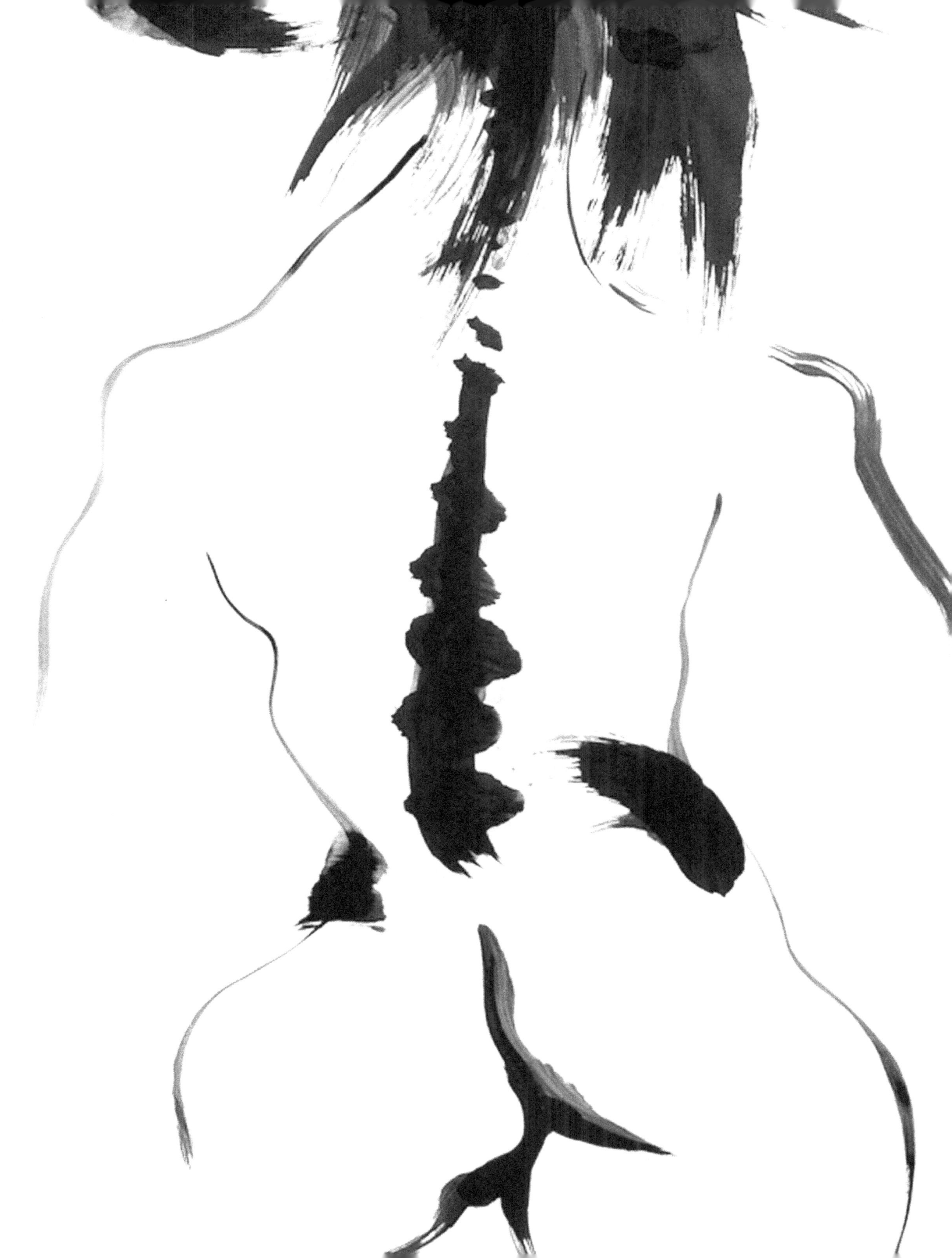

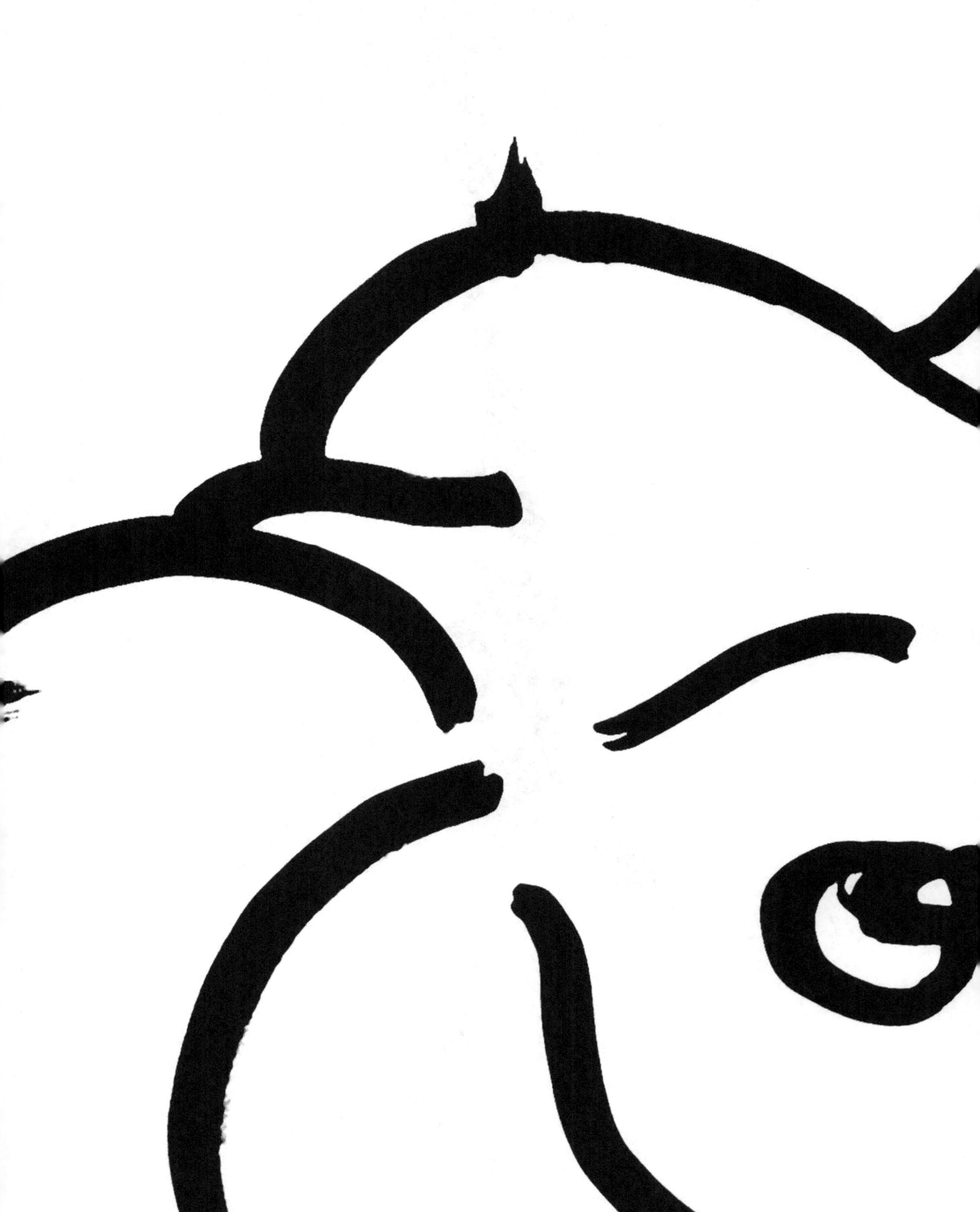

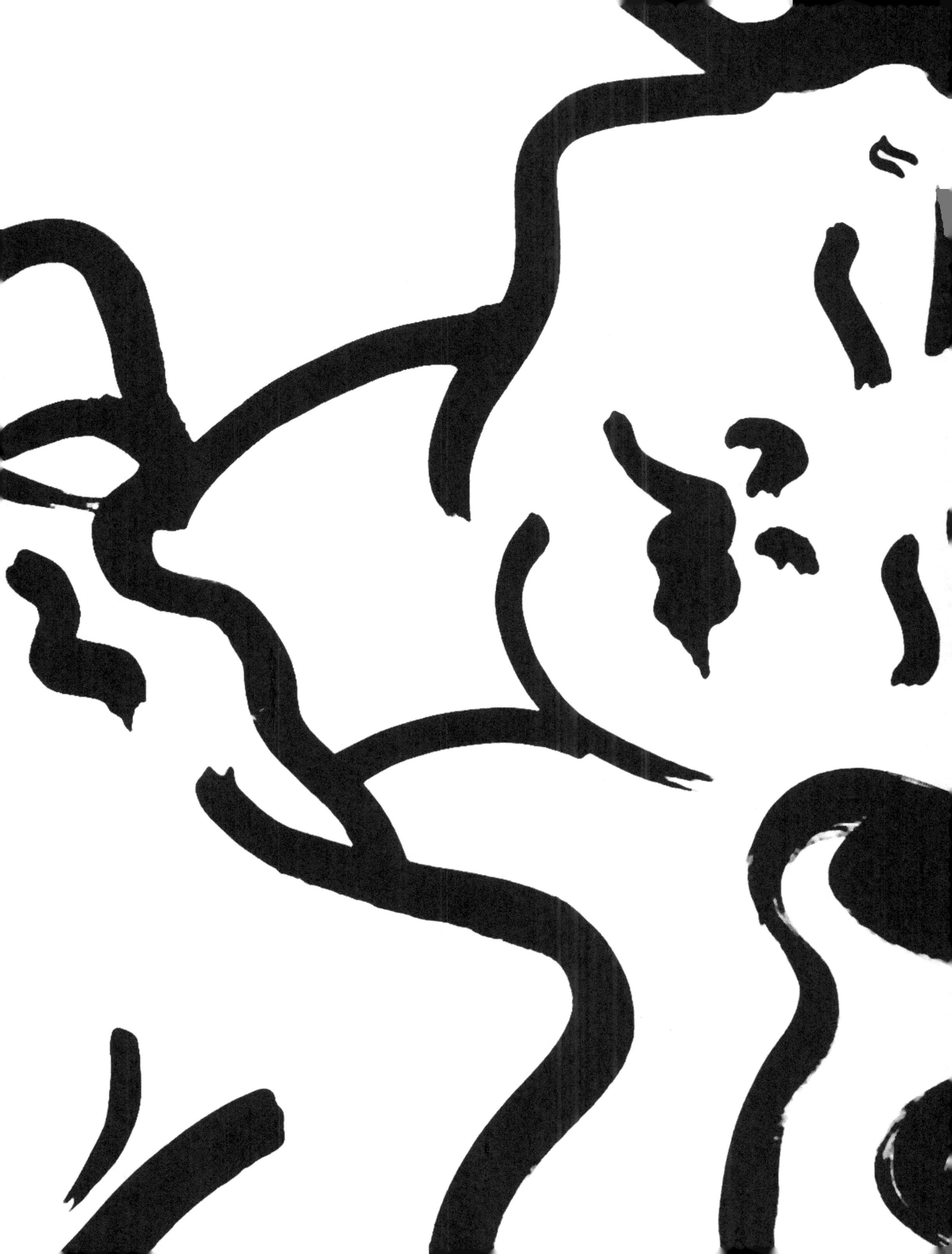

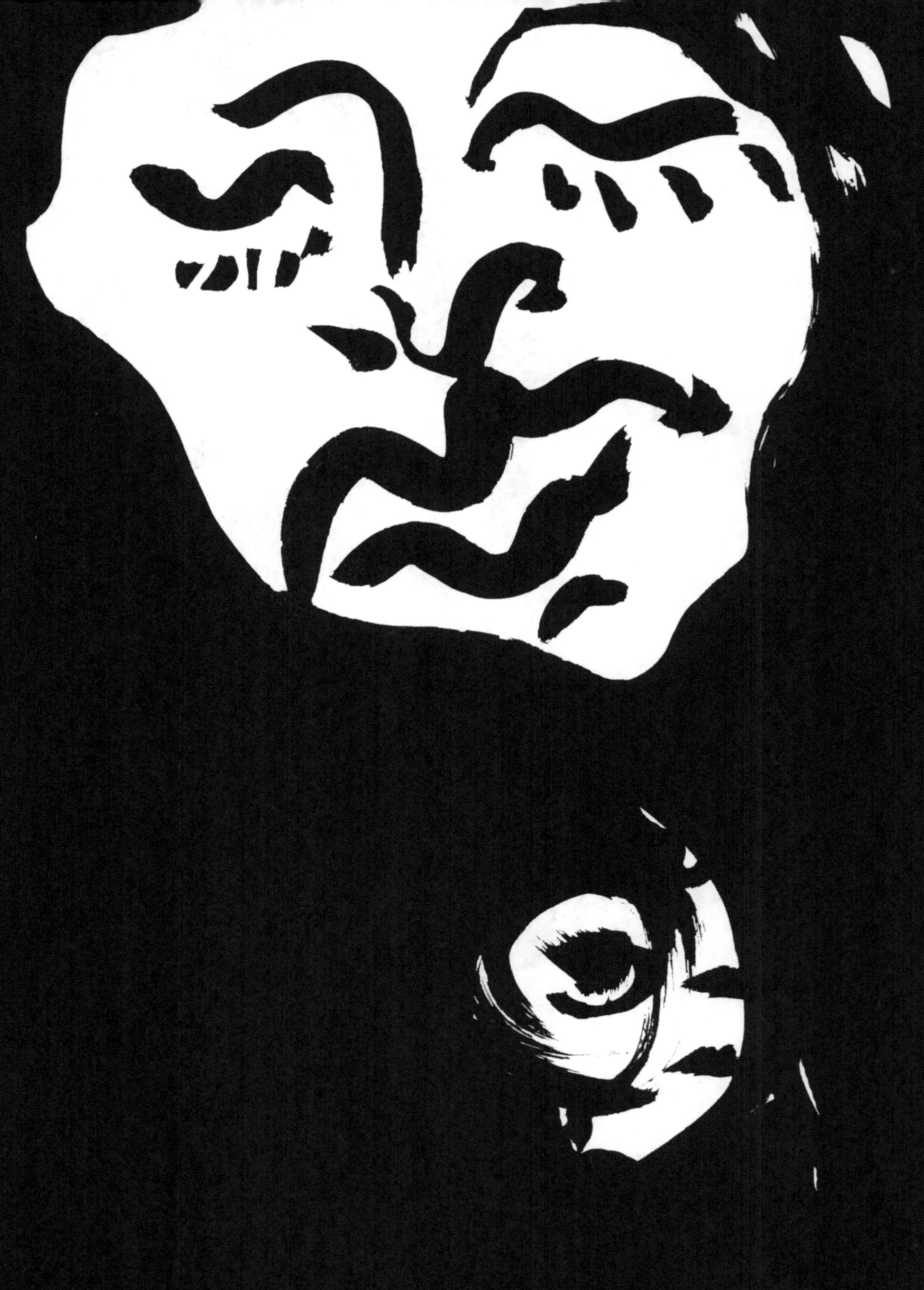

JOUBEN

Fruits of flesh
In the palace of your mouth
Spell-bound,
There are seeds of illusion
And here between the seeds,
A simple gift of nature
That gives us pleasure
And from this
Tastes were born
Between the flowers
Perfumes were born
Between hearing and sound
Born this melody and harmony
Between your eyes and mine
The profound nature, of us.

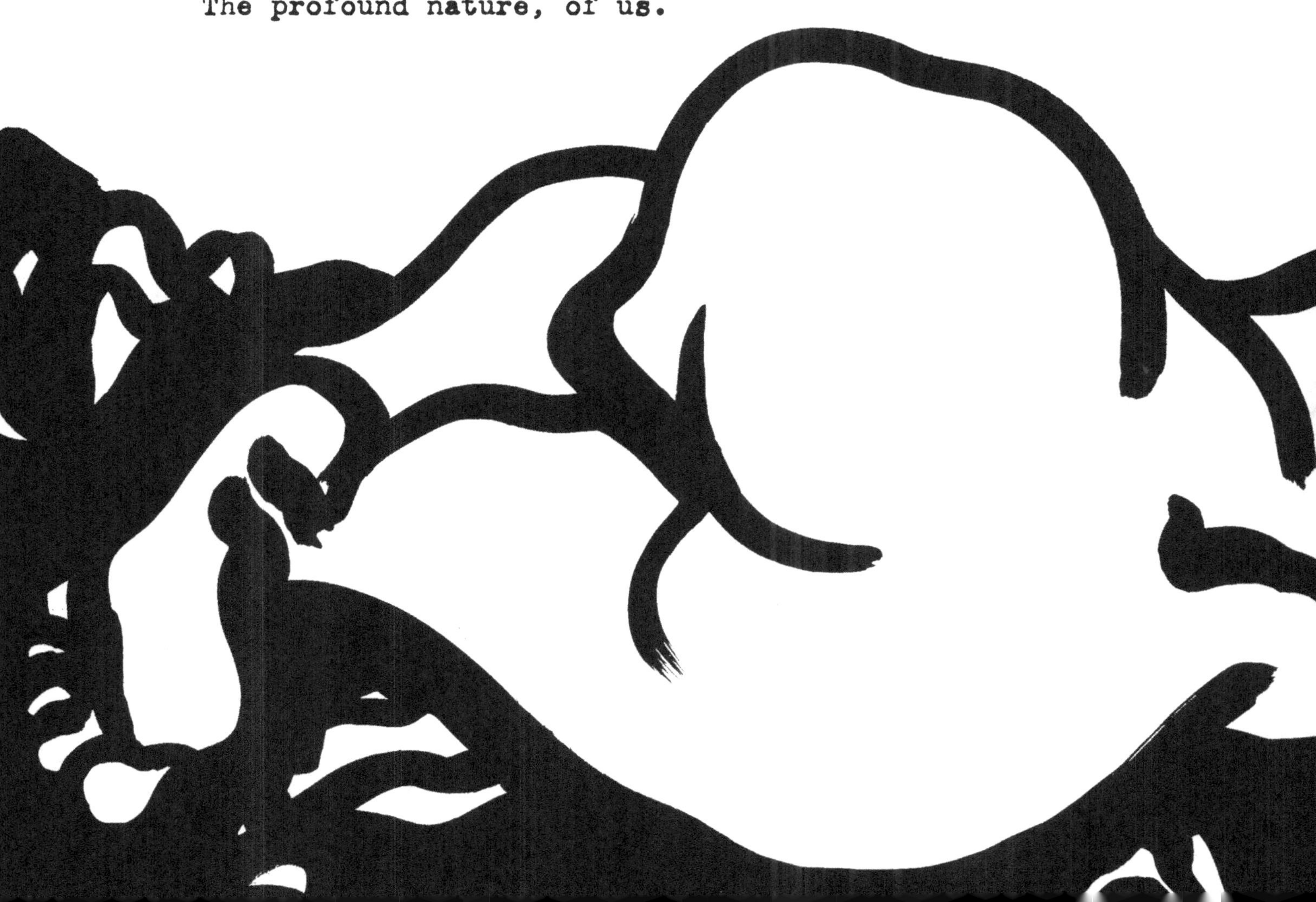

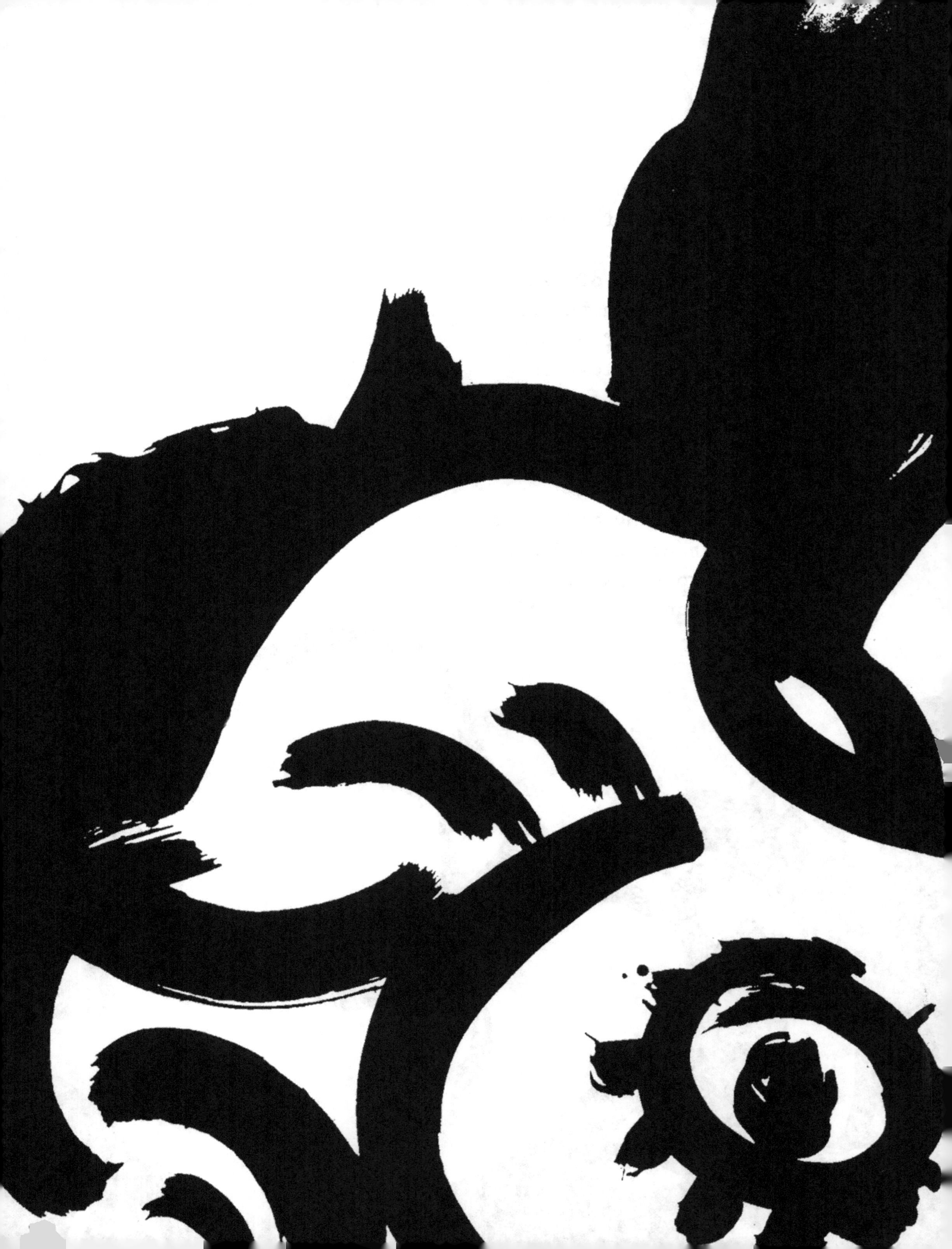

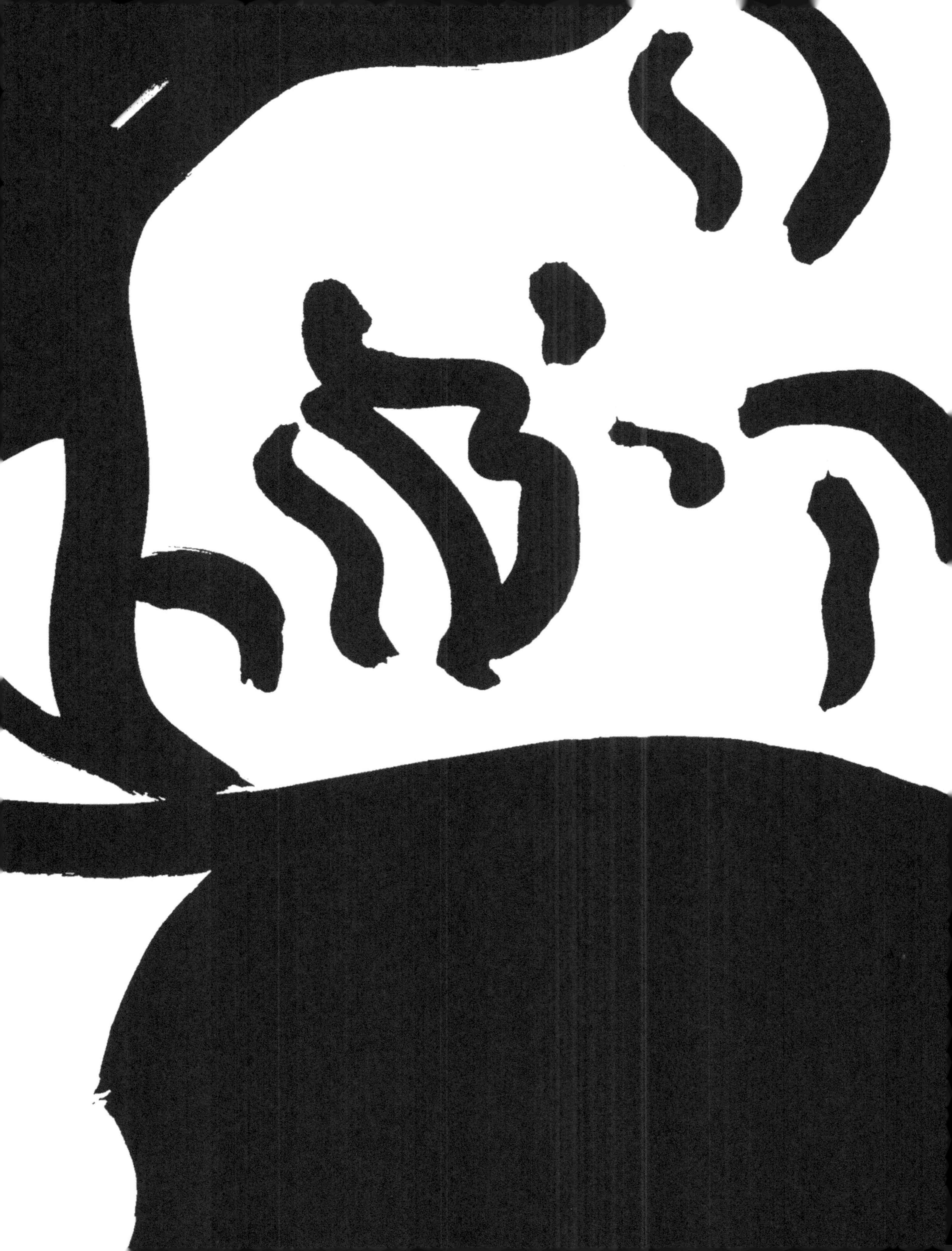

FORTUNE'S SONG

Once they searched among fate's stars
and derive a natal horoscope
high roller number, woman of metal
could be a minister of The Party

rice for luck, birds of song
a golden sword of fortune
enough incense smoke to reach
paper kites sent prayers beyond
to keep the ancestors happy

then saw *The Golden Turtle*
raise his head through pernicious weeds
in such occidental moments
could talk the world away
when all about was unfamiliar

but now green rice is threshed
jasmine tea once poured gone cold
old black dog appears once more
all places that existed before
will exist without us there.

H A N O I

A rented villa, views of the market
Painted walls, all its carved rosettes
Open the shutters and watch the women
Cutting rice field catfish, for daily soup

There are live dogs in cages, curl tailed
Flocks of songbirds in bamboo cage
Tangled notes add to the shrill and loud
Mynah birds and nightingales, singing
It sounds as if falling from the sky

Catch the scent of ginger and jasmine
A thousand miles beyond -- I turn my head
The gates to *The Tamarind House* fly open
Who belongs to the inner room
Not having swept nomadic dust
Restless selves that break the heart.

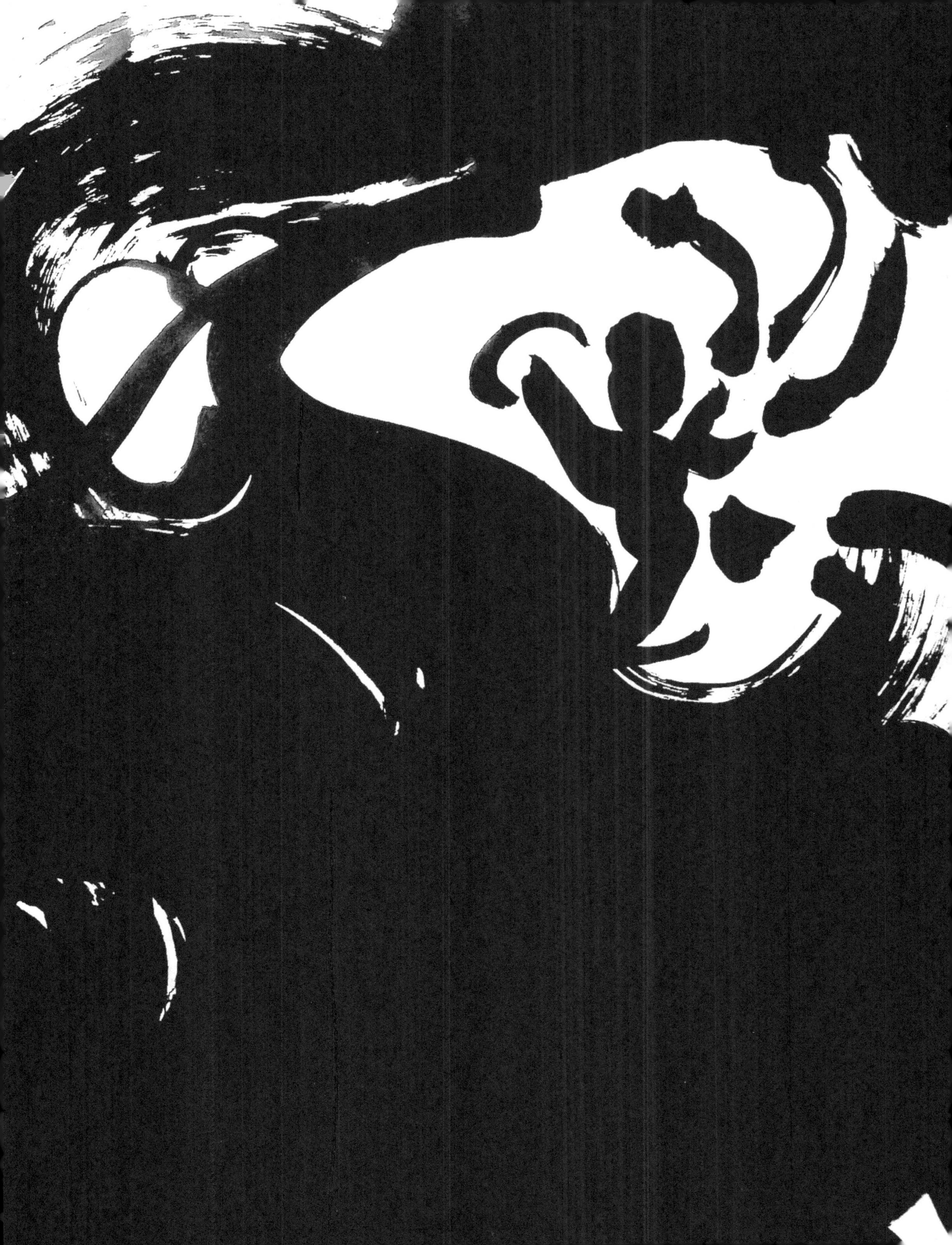

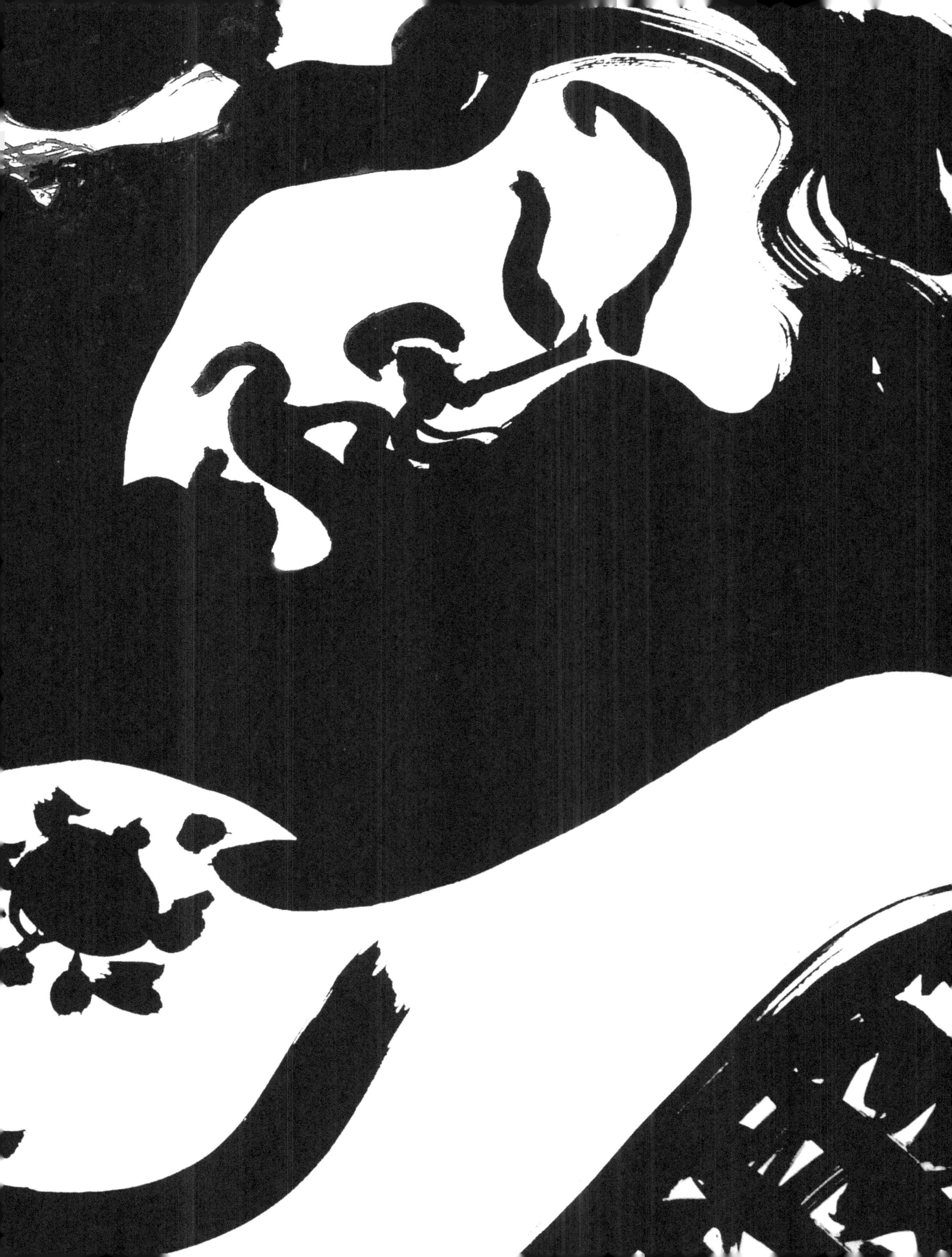

CHERUBIM

Your desk covered with memories
There, the flock of birds you kept
Flutter and sang around your head
Taking seeds from your outstretched hand
Like Assisi in *The Garden of Goodness*
I watch as you pick up falling feathers
Tie them into a feather brush
All you give away on earth is kept for you,
All you keep is lost
The curse remains in the seeds
And when you think no one will see
You paint the undreamed bird
Eyes as green as nasturtium seeds
You paint the canary feathers
Like a dead yellow chrysanthemum,
That might be thrown away.

THE QUESTION

Before the sun goes down in Da Tuong Alley
Cooking-fires alight; night-air lotus incense
Confuse cinnamon with tamarind-smoke
Ghosts and Sages watch, speak of past

Yesterday, a hundred patriot bodies found
In the garden of the Magistrate's villa
To ask a question is simple
Do you know where -- your brother's bones?

To walk over a field, the simple act
Dreamed he'd again come back
Knew us, and all the jade pendants, for luck
Hair white as old jade, all that is left

In the ash-hour, ashes go where winds deem
As Tantalus jar and columns of jasmine
Out of the war, and land that dreamed
There's many an unknown soldier gone

He passed among fields of burning rice
No welcome sound in a stray bullet
Only shadow, in red flares refrain
The damp grass, that bright scarlet stain,
All blood is ruled by *The Arbitrator of Fate*

Having died has its advantage
Each bone sprinkled in immortal dust
Destined, they cannot be transplanted
Deep and old, they can hardly be moved
I look for my Father, but he stays behind
Time that passes away, never comes again.

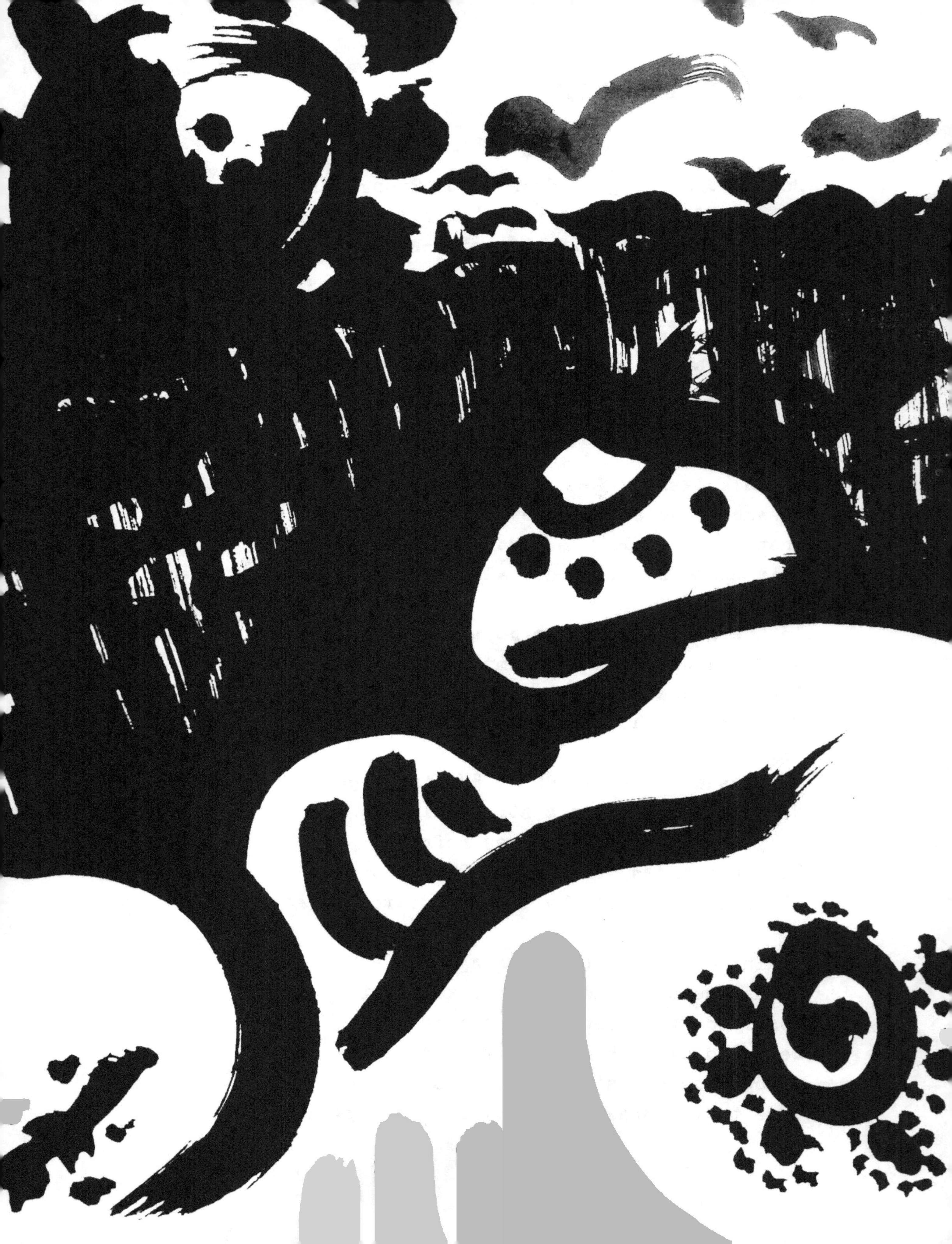

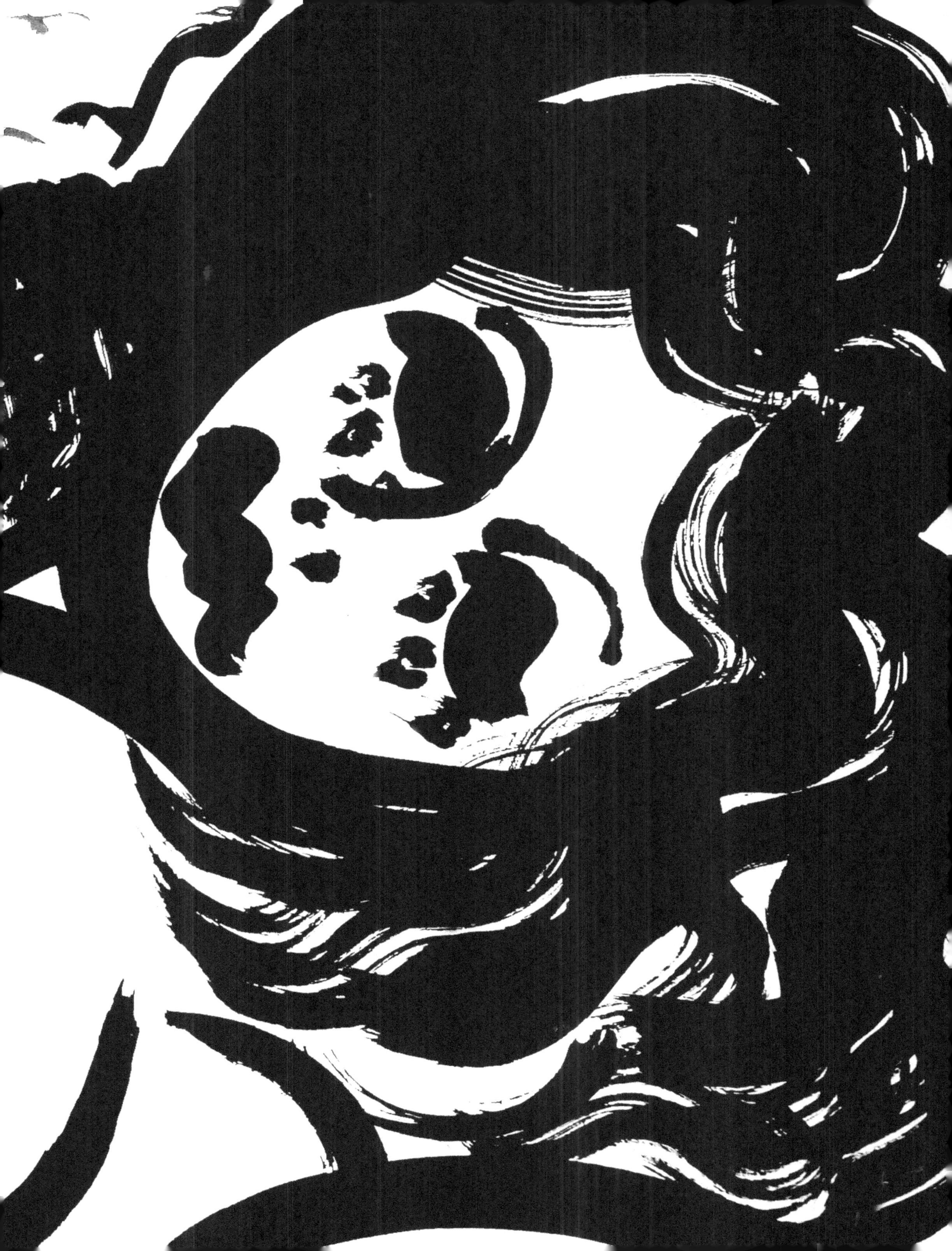

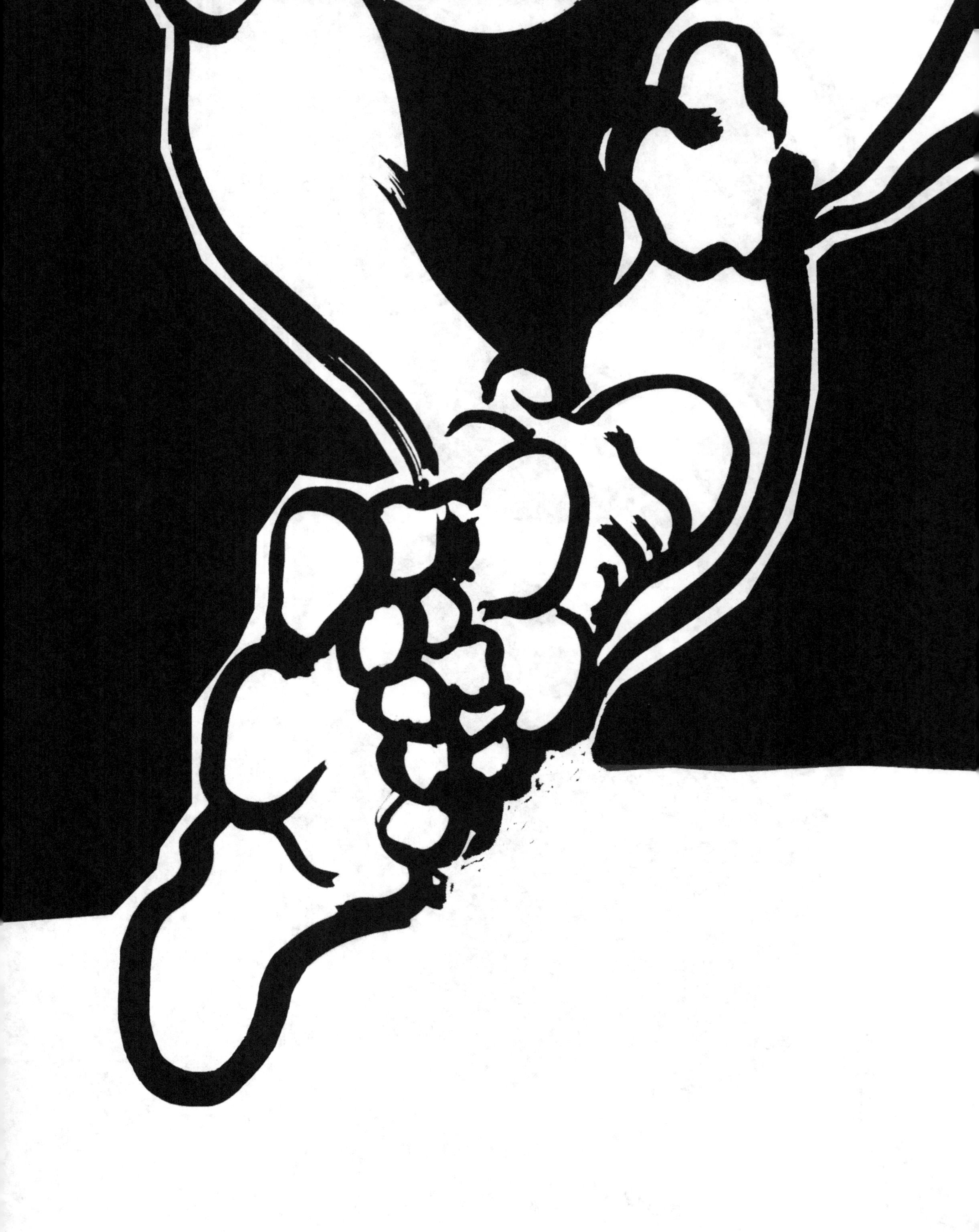

O V E R T U R E S

To travel from one city to another
before the last one, and this one
a country, a history, foreigners' memory
of typhoon danger and burnished sun

when will these humid clouds lift
even a salted ocean wind dies hot
at night sleep under gauze net
with an audience of mosquitoes

no good dreams on the bamboo mat
toss and turn months away
no one will know, as fabrics grew thin
some voile entrapment ensues

crewel net of nothing less
who's to say, the found are not lost here
between China Beach and the sea
nothing to be done, in a cheaper room
but now, then, drumming rain
strips jasmine of its earthly flower
fragrant carnage in the morning
fanning the path, under bare-feet
hot as the summer was.

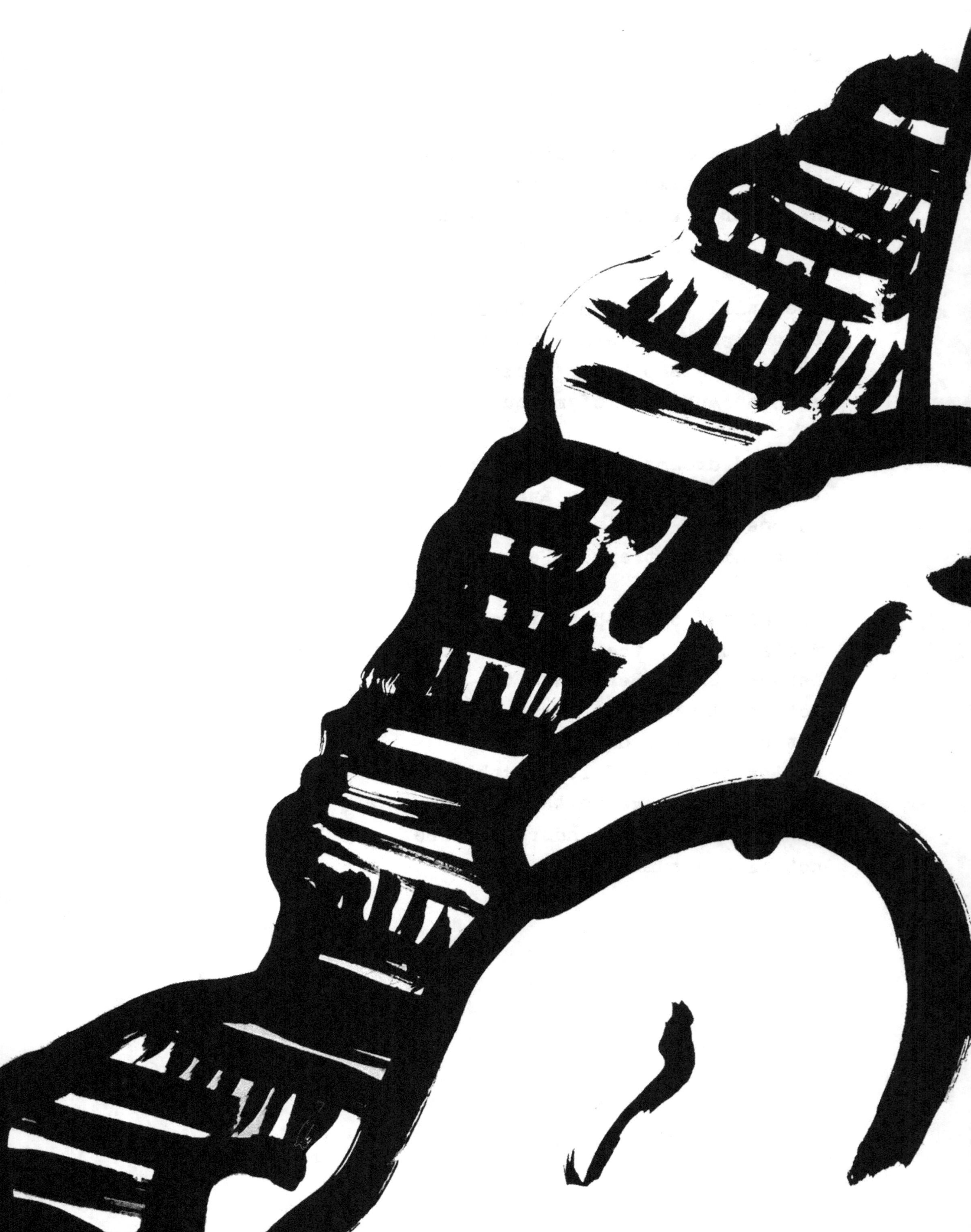

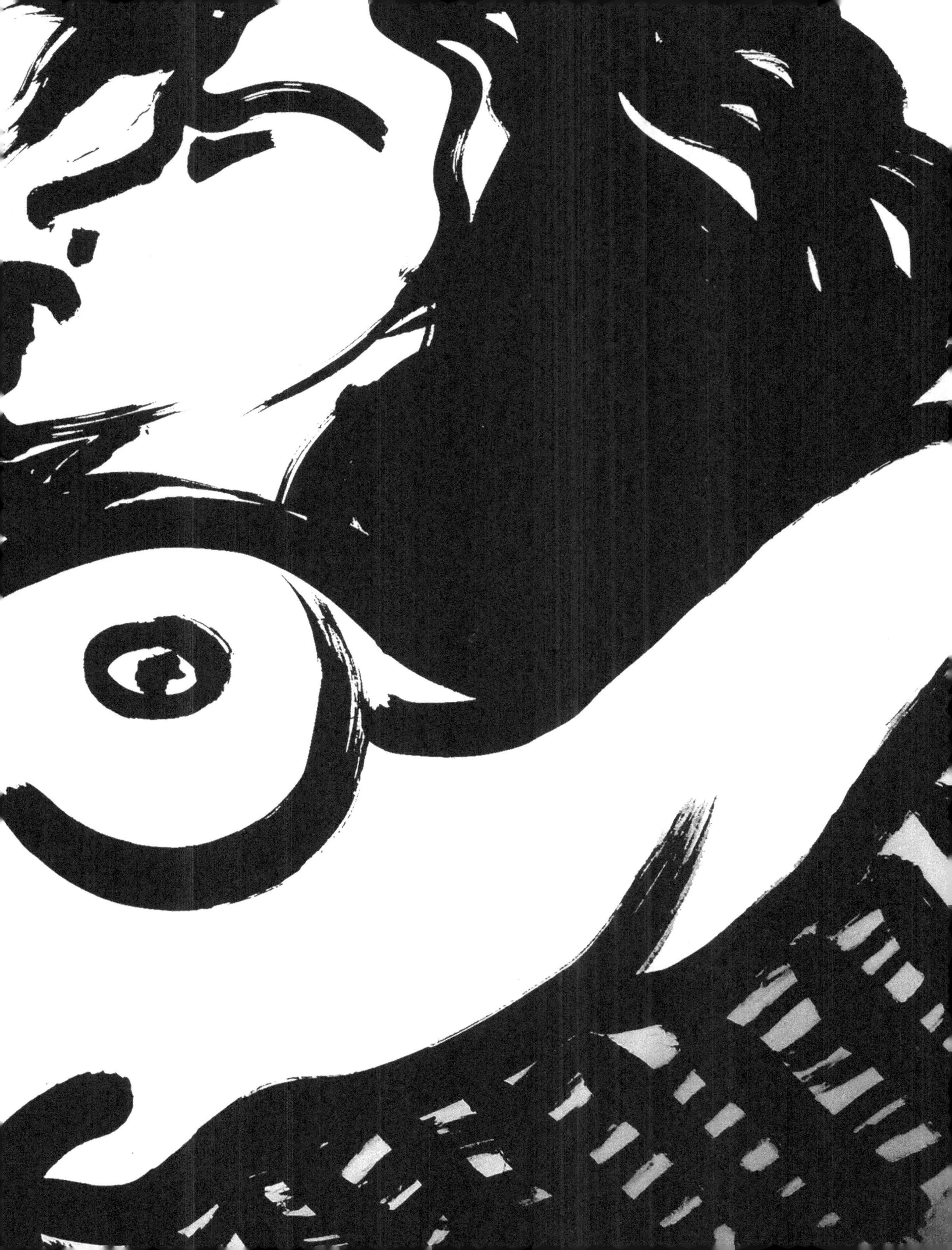

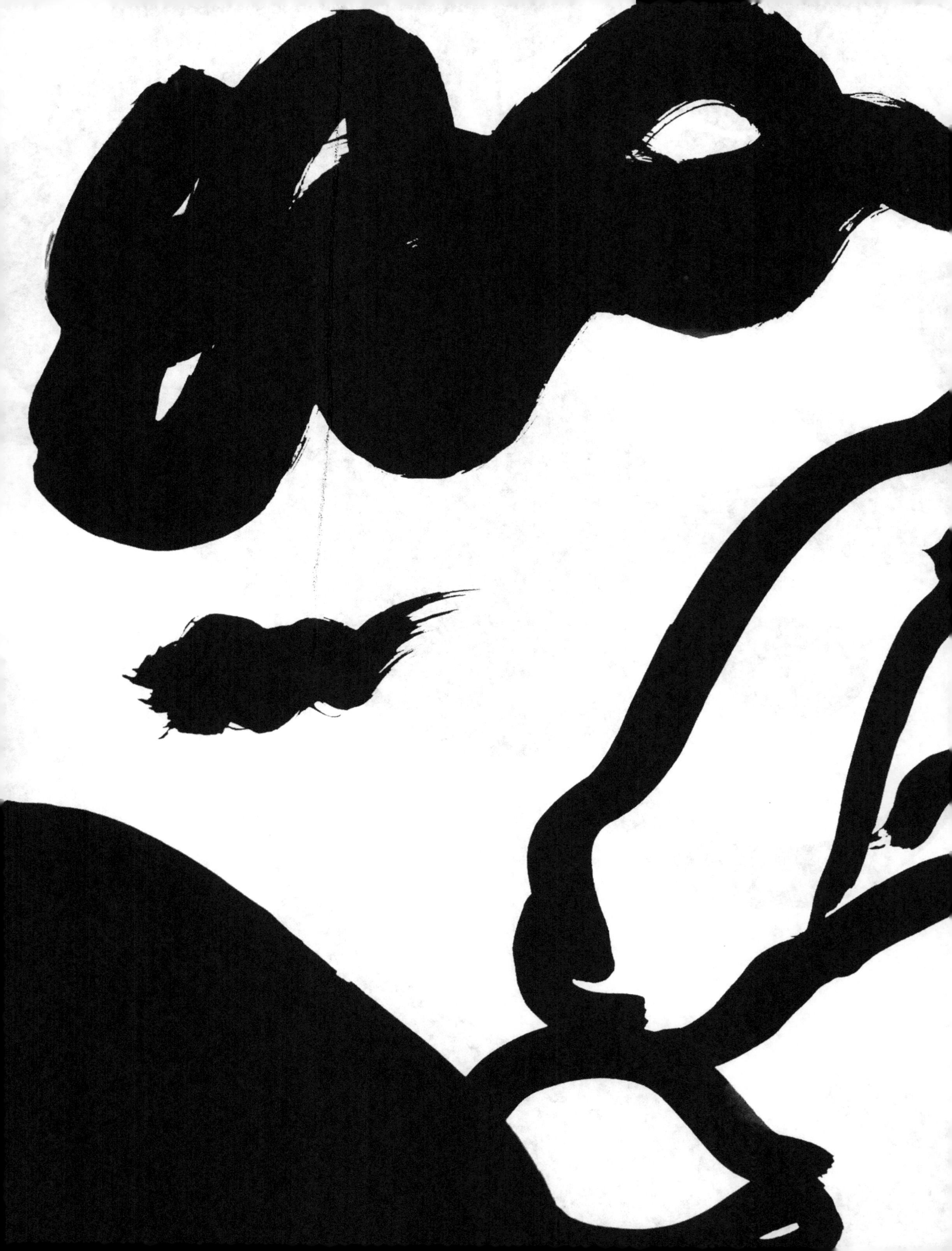

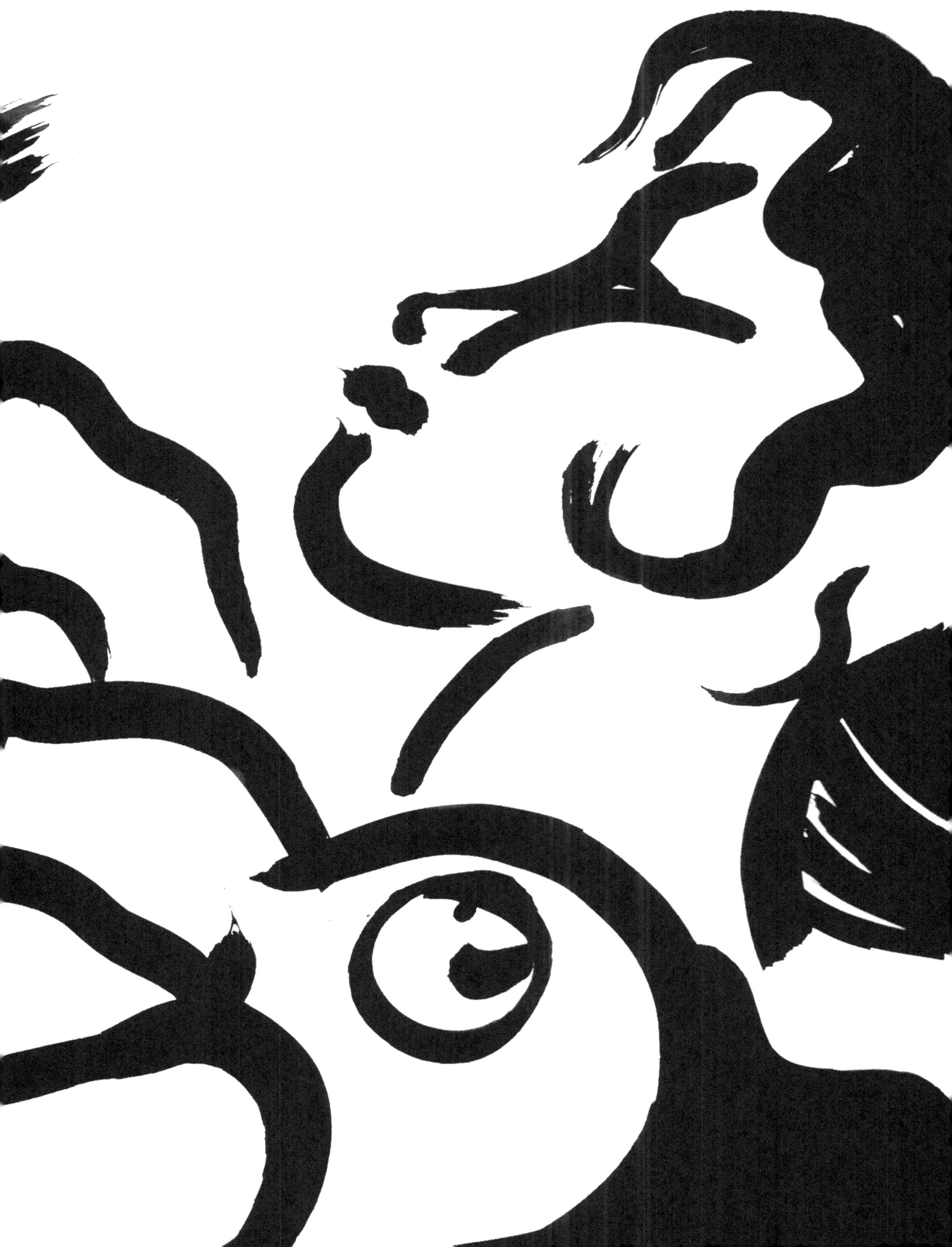

THE BODHI TREE

It was the silk-worm month
The baby left under the Bodhi tree
Blanket of silk in sedge grass basket
A small cocoon in the temple garden

Early morning while orphans slept
Like so many stars, all night
A child born into the world
Seemed to be from faraway gods

Sending silver bells, and musical stones
Roses burgeoning with pink petals
In ninth month, pure life comes
Like incense embraces the moon

To keep, to hold, not give away
Now the orphan girl is waking
She was the gift in silk-worm night
Face of sleeping child, just becoming

Now hair all white, won for the years
Assail of the traditional calendar
Rustling pages vague, and vast
Seemed to be from faraway gods
A wish to keep family in one place
Son and daughter, close to each other.

BELLA

I heard black dog bark, in the deep alley
Fur arrow and swirls on its ridge-back
For the luck, but a black dog, they say
Walks through graveyards all night
Midnight, it wakes up the rooster
The bird heard, faintly praising the sun

But it was only the moon's bright pearl
Lighting up the garden -- woke me
Then voices and incumbent footsteps
So the soldier from the north
Faced a gilded orange tree
An invitation to enter the house

I will offer you plum wine, to ferment
Talk of fish, we piled up on the shore
A rusted hook on a bamboo-rod
Sometimes I wish I could ask for more
Follow you and try your fish-hook
A cascade of dollars, the sacrifice money

But our blood will never be broken
You leave, and I hear nothing more
And by his fallen steps, all he can do
Just open the door to our old garden
And whistle the black dog home.

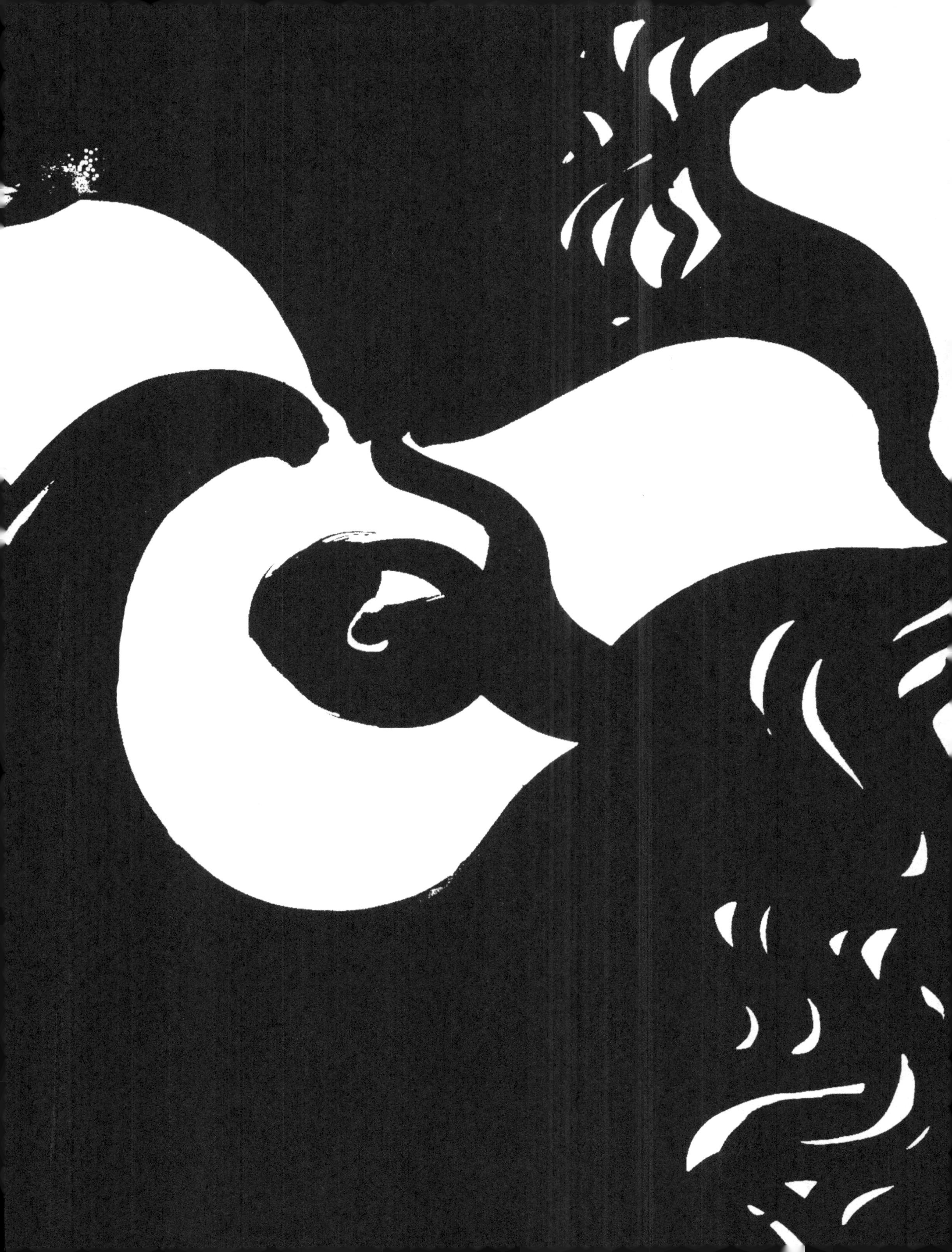

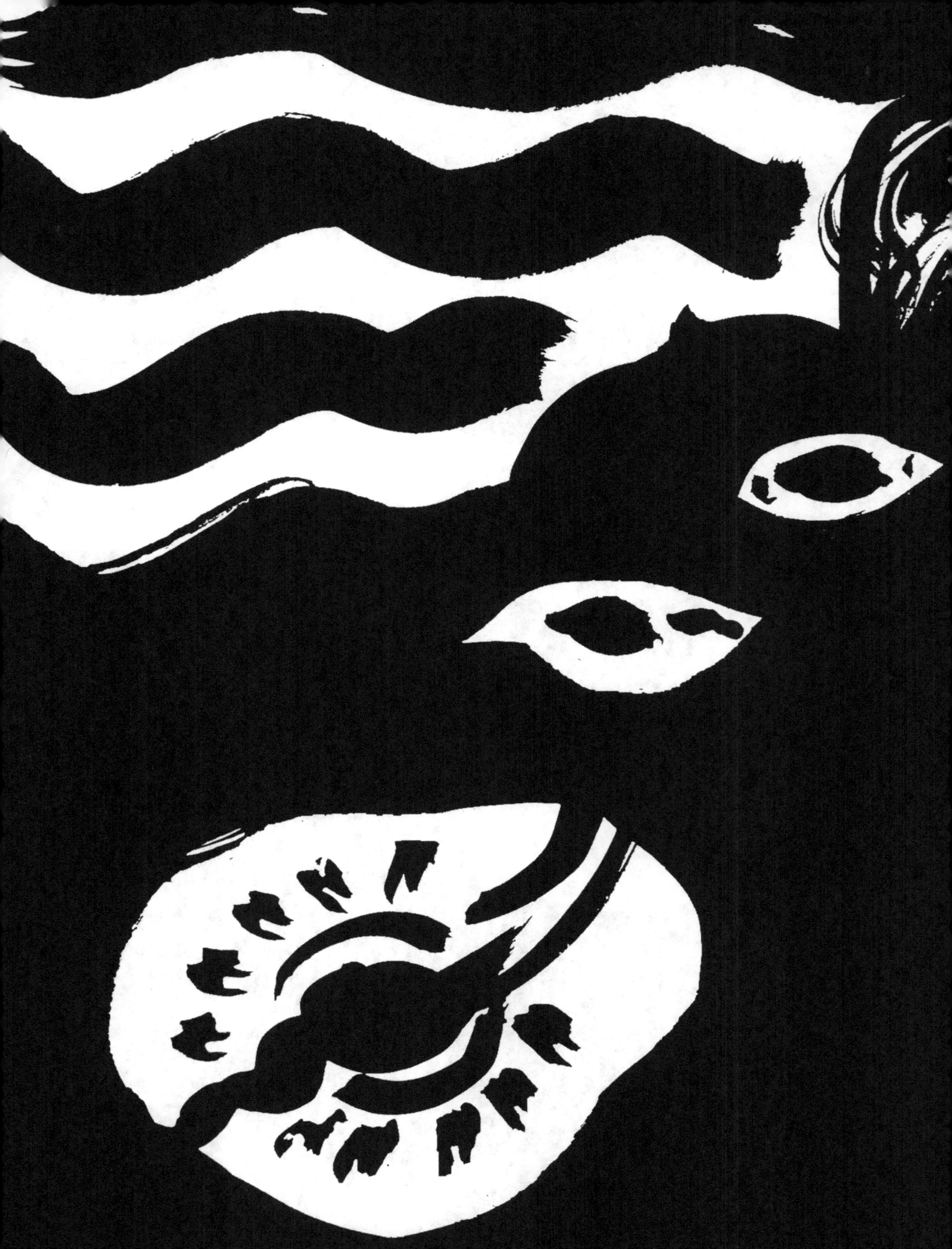

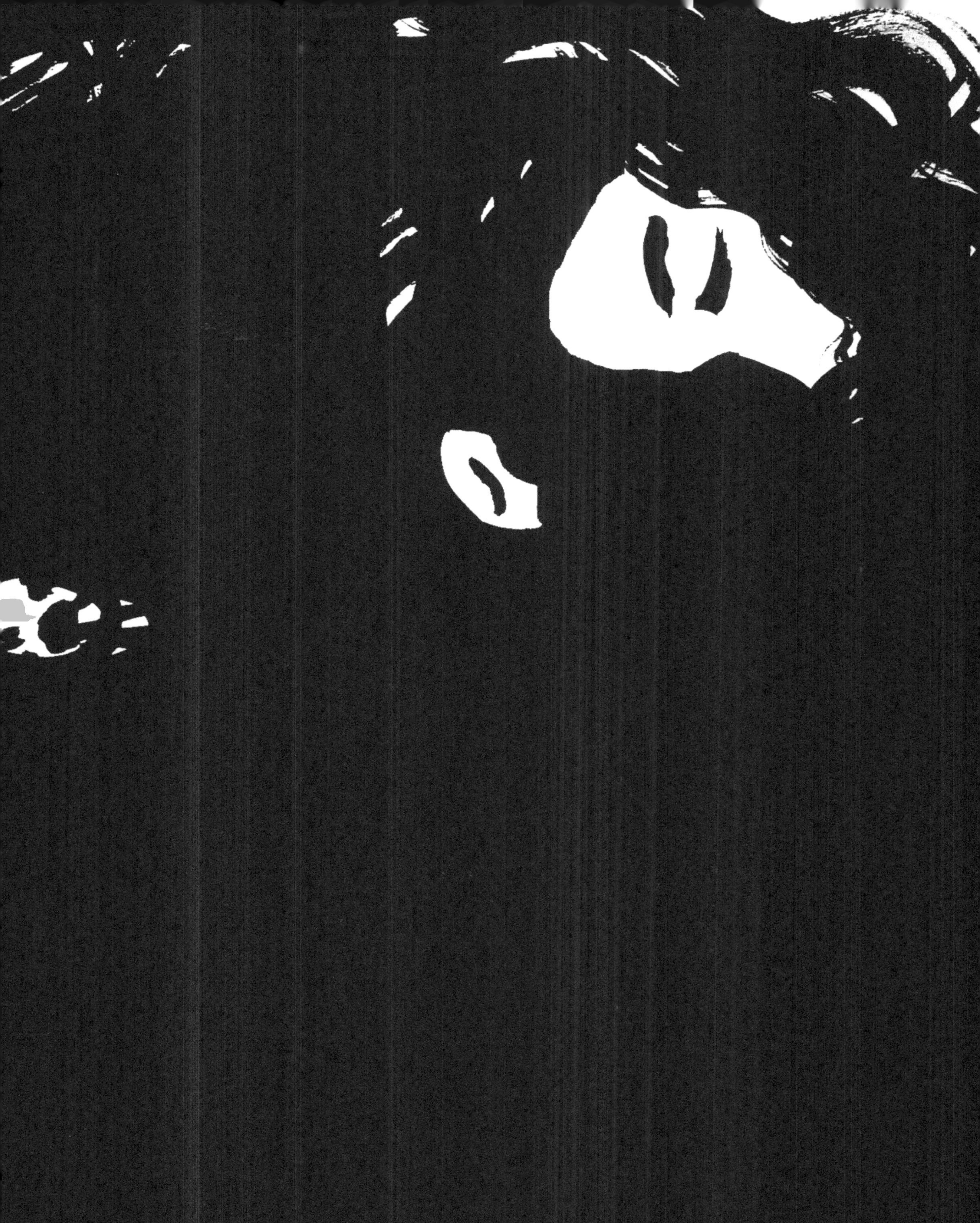

THE LEGEND

At Hoan Kiem Lake in long-fog
The heavenly ways of the Gods
Treat one to heaven, on earth

Pink lotus flowers in pure water
A drop of water on a jade platter
A thousand lanterns, Red Lacquer
Bridge to the faraway pagoda

From somewhere a bamboo flute
Golden turtle endures this, everydayness
With an edge against ancient histories

Heat and floods without death
Sacred sword in mouth, the legend
Is around -- all this in keeping

Five times its golden head
Appears through pernicious weeds
See what is seen, foreshadows are rare

Everything is memory when it is gone
For luck?
Through the water again through lotus
Longevity sadly mortal
And in twenty or so years
The vision endures, the gift of time
Where would such turtle luck carry us?
See then, the luck!

A NOTE

Silk strings on T'ung wood
Hush of bitterness and song
Sadly, sadly the moments are gone

As human shadows lengthen
As days blurred tomorrows
Blank pages in *The Book of Sorrow*
Once again *The Creator of Chaos*
Once you leave, you leave forever

But later, outside Hotel Metropole
Hoist red flag's semaphore of stars
As *The Master* raises his hand
In a bid for ordinary people to decipher

After five days of hot weather
The locals dream about rain
After three days of rain
They complain about drowning
The women standing at the crossroads
All women hugging their children
Things to let go
The wind helps me dry out tear-sodden books
Late summer on its way
And I am already dressed for winter.

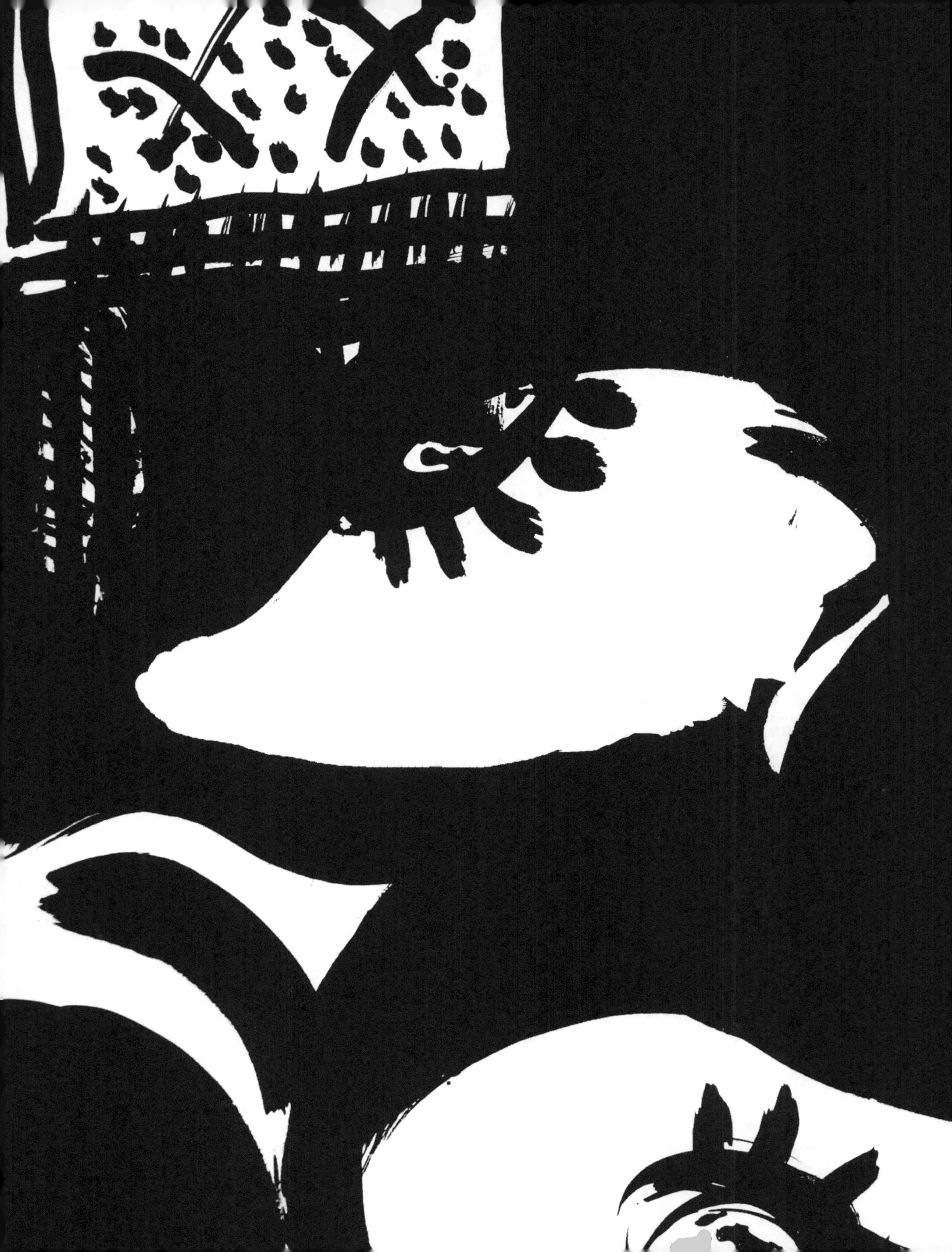

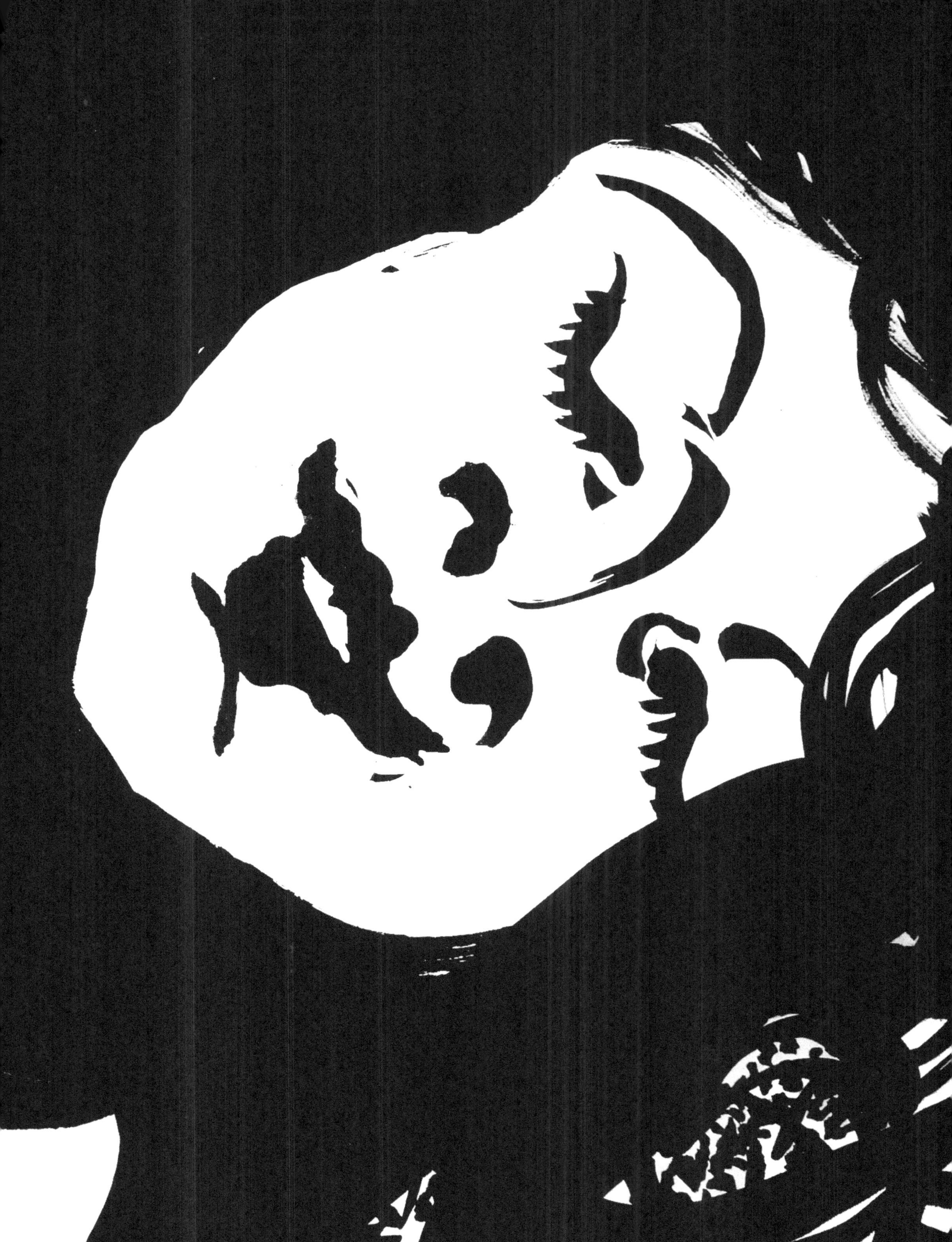

MIDNIGHT MUSIC

Things are not what they seem
Art is a lie that makes us recognize,
Picasso said

There was a white picket fence
You could look through
If you wanted to -- *sometimes*
Possibilities look to be impossible

An Emperor who saw this
Stood there one summer evening
Took out the spaces with utmost care
And built a pagoda in the simple air

A white pagoda for his second wife
Clay-tiles like fractal dragons
Whimsical lanterns strung all over
A phantom only existing

Each fence post left there
With nothing around it -- all objects
And no space more endless
And I wouldn't have seen it
On a blank sheet of white cloud
If I hadn't believed
One thing was certain
Sharing a common night and day
All of us, become truthful.

IN THE STUDIO

You are by birth and from this hour,
I have hidden you and kept you
Whatever art and nature divine
Convert sun and moon to wine
As nights silence spreads out sable wings
To save our mansions from oblivion
The sound of sunlight a moment before
We will never close our eyes to this
If forever is an endless place
Your ears can hear and your eyes can see,
This human kind, open your arms
To hold the person that was meant to be.

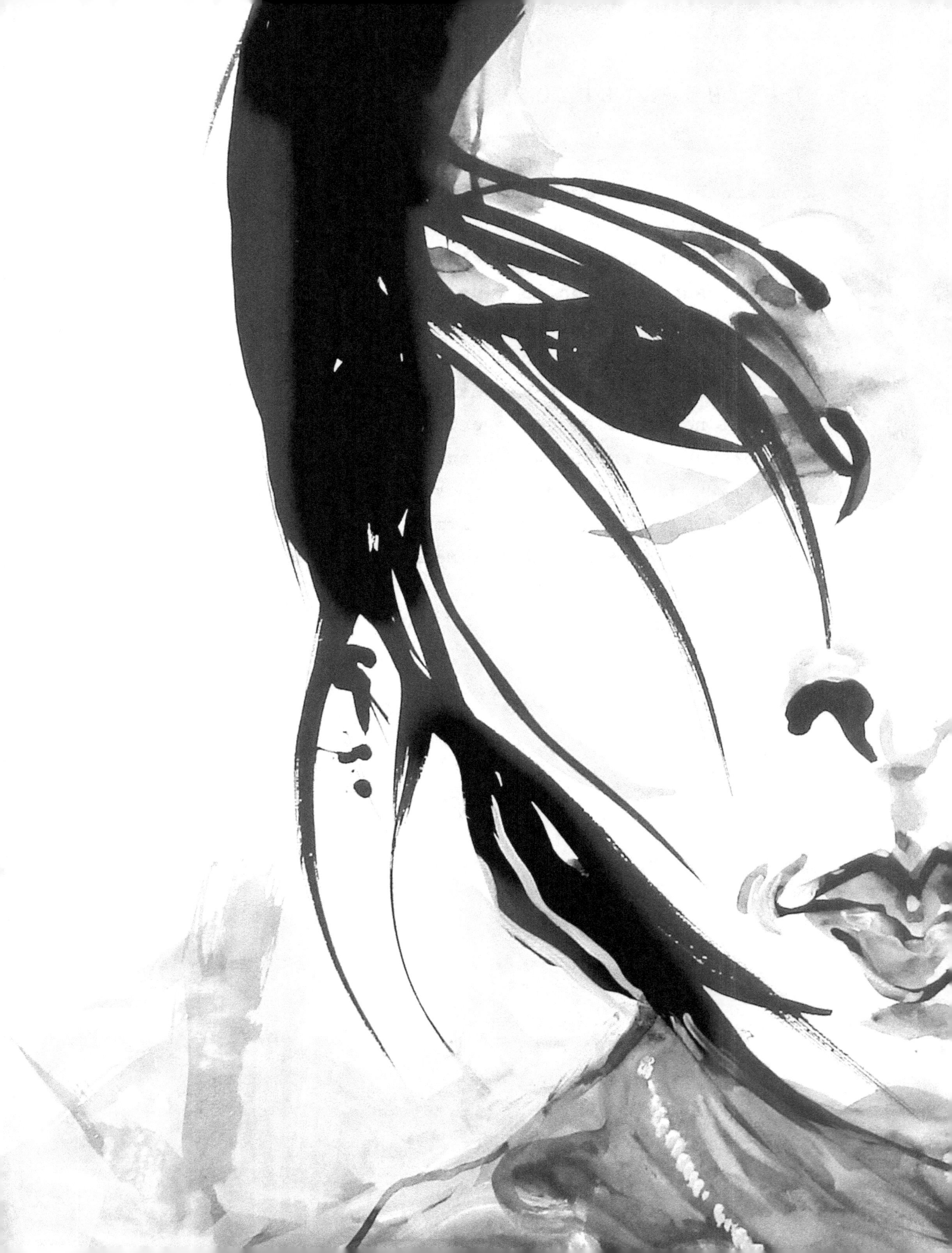

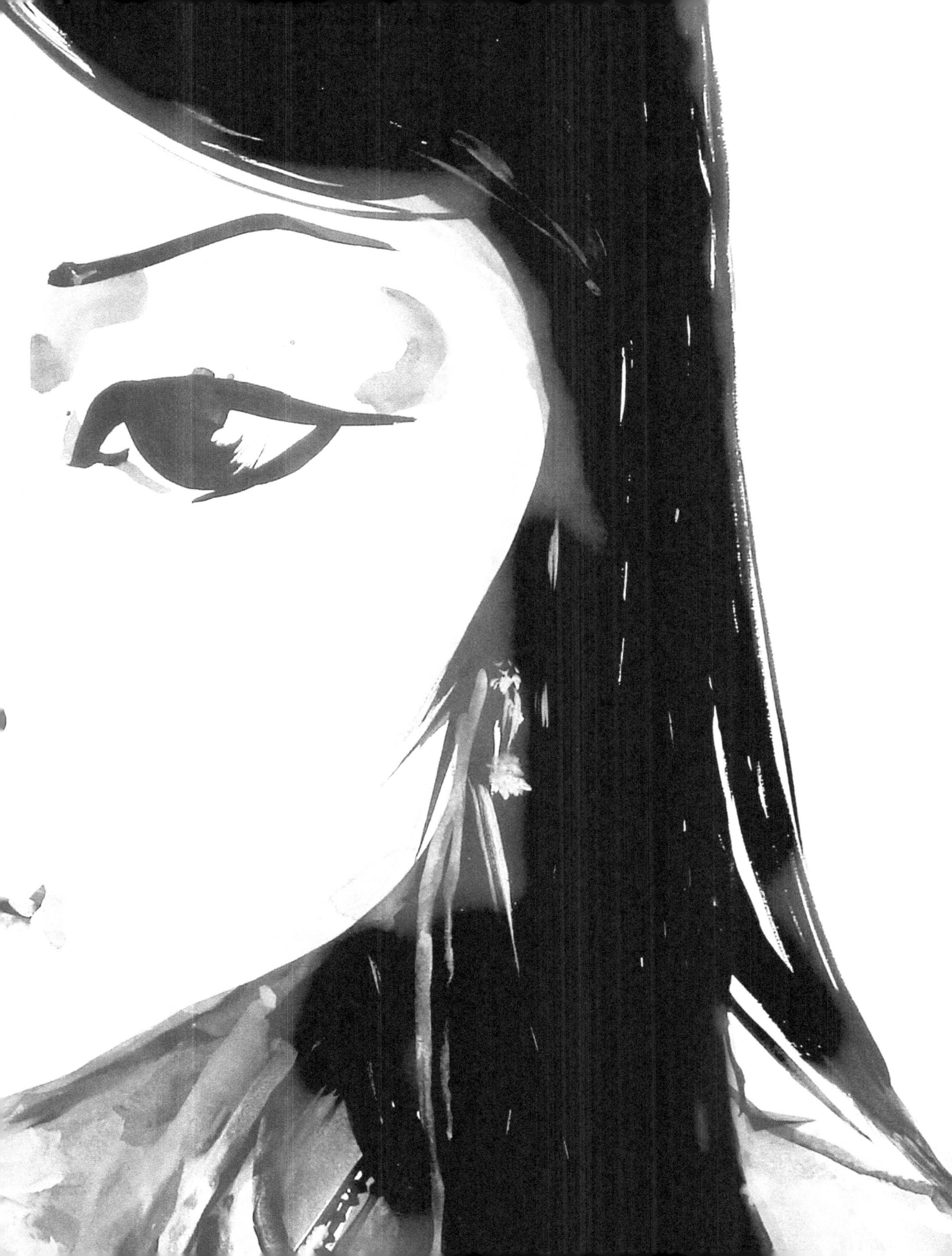

INKSTONE

This land is not their home
But still, they come here
In the fourth and fifth months
When rice fields are greenest

A handful of rice; first of season
Bamboo basket, kept warm by cloth
Street corner, woman makes money
In a thousand ways, I just saw her

Opium scales held high in her hands
Divinely accurate, the weights summon
Red poppy and silken pod, like drunken ink
Tamed by *The Master's* brush, it seems

Begging for rice, begging for food
Acres of lamenting heart
Lines of mascara tears
Stands for things within
Grateful a little narcotic residue
Let others eat green rice
And leave the ones, thankful to dream on
A silver pipe, a night of opium.

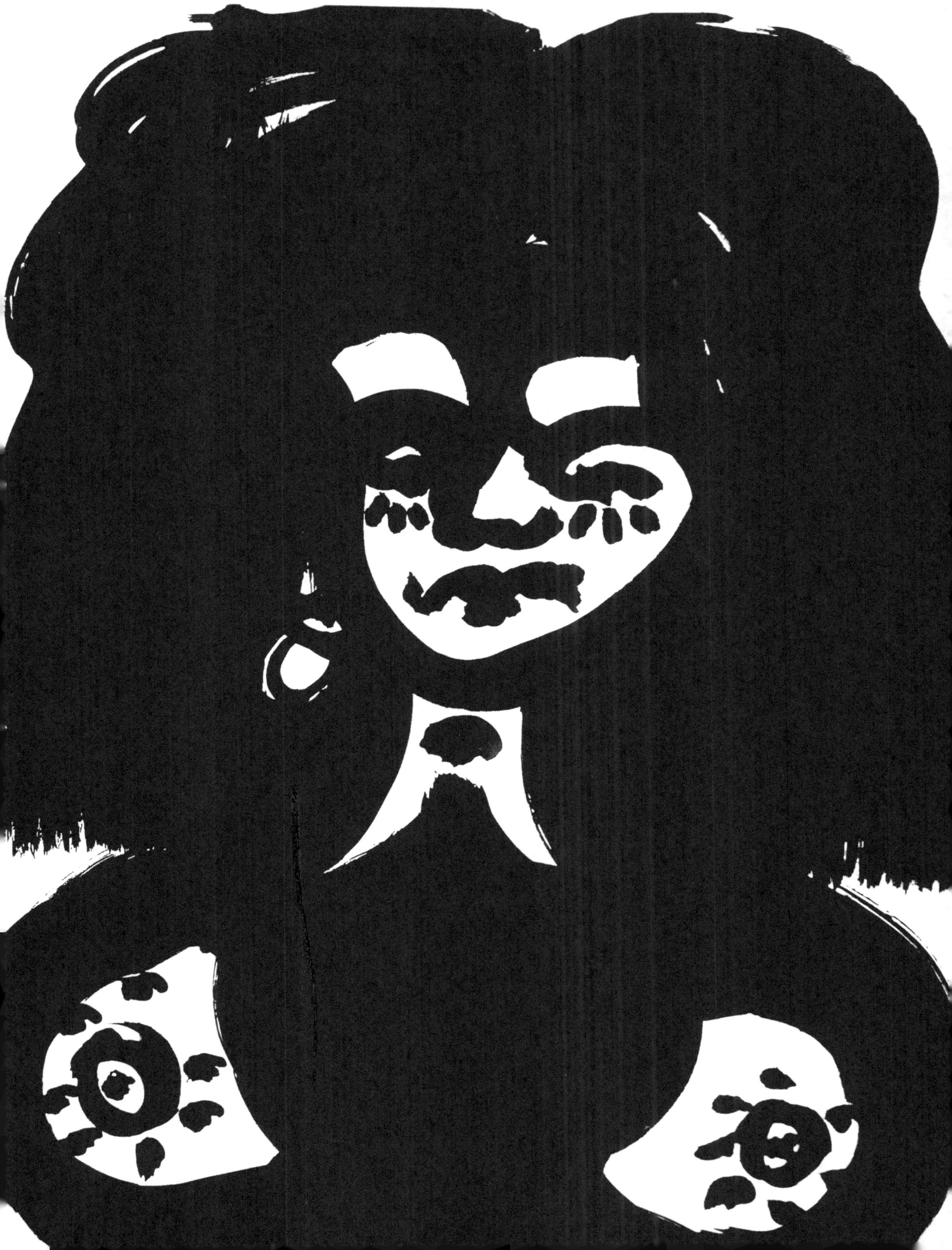

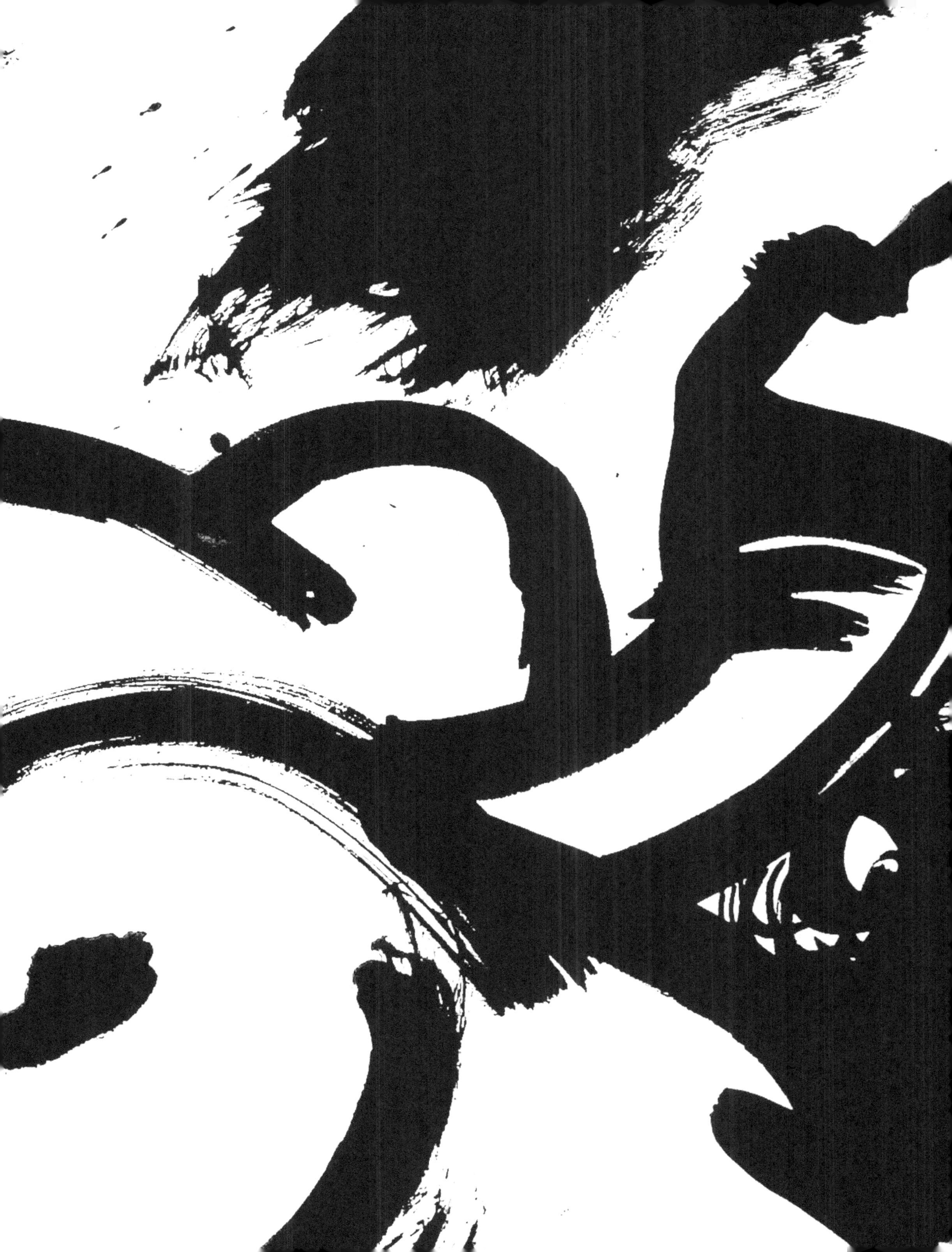

WIND OF THE EAST

Under black flag
where black crows fly
war stallion takes rider
in fierce race until
silver chains on his wrists
resound like clashing blades

He has caught sight of her
her silk glimmering silver
under the war mask, he smiles
such luck in presence of jade
behind him still dark of night
before crimson morning fades

Sharp cut relief against dark armor
and you must understand
that this is intended as a picture
you can tell either by birth or blood
only through armor and objects of art
or Durer's hands carved for prayer

You were the man who knew
the woman of the past
warmed her body near your heart
as you opened your arms
to set her free, whispered:

All must remove their masque
(Take care who you pretend to be).

ON RENEWAL

Leave-taking is not easy
Multiple papers, red crossed ink
Then confuse lock-down situation
Find passport? A signature?

There has only been one place
In the world, so interminable
When a paper-trap is set
The stars shift positions

Surname is maiden name
Surname is married name
So, ask *The Master of Fate*
To send another fortune

Of the many soldiered road
Blood and earth at the end
Some would be shot for thought
To put a hand on a trigger

There was a dossier on a desk
Of interest to the interested
Of the people, for the people
Though sometimes it was necessary

Began remembering and told too much
But then the people's people say
There is an army and ministers
As a rule, they are fathomless
Like an empty boat pulled up on the sand.

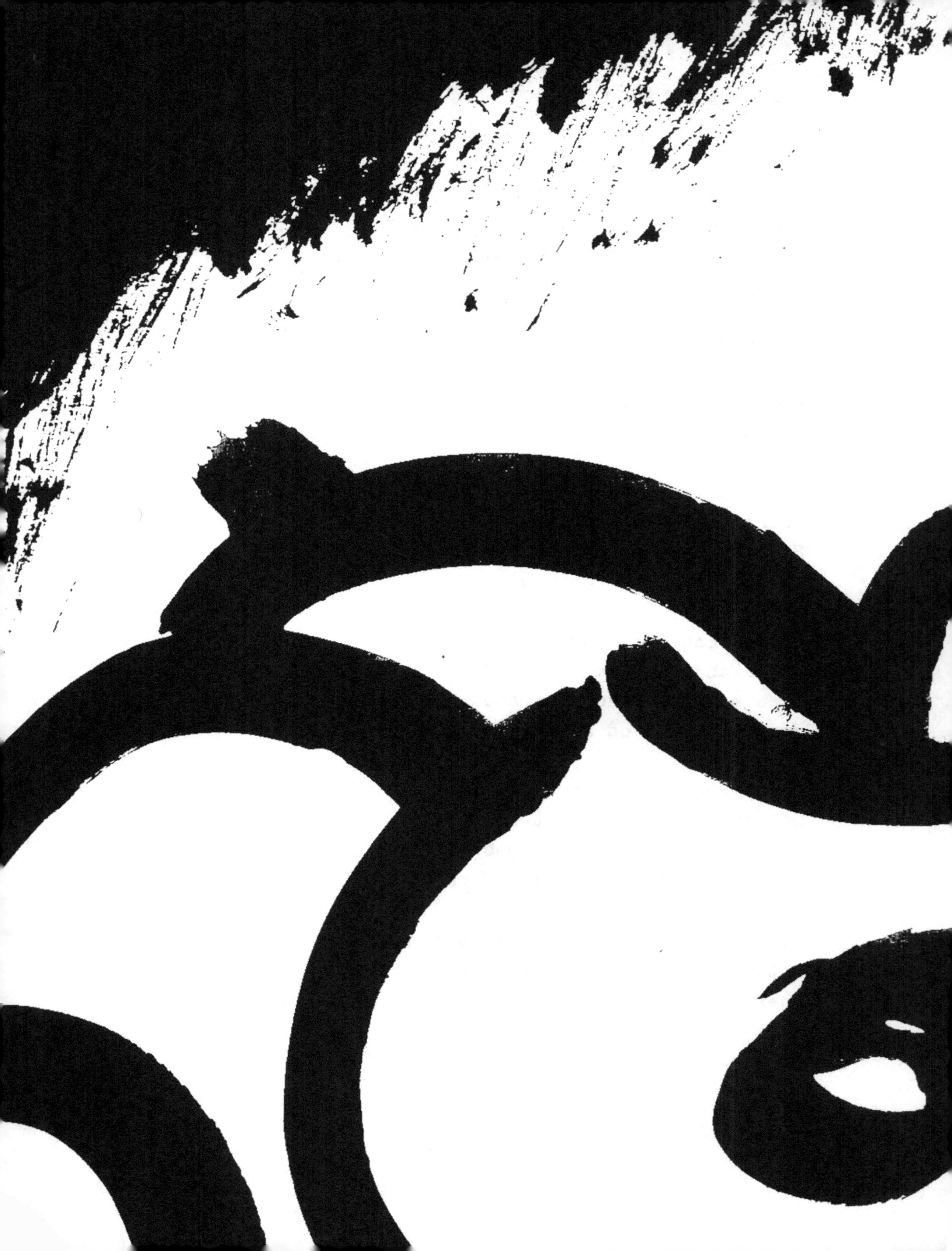

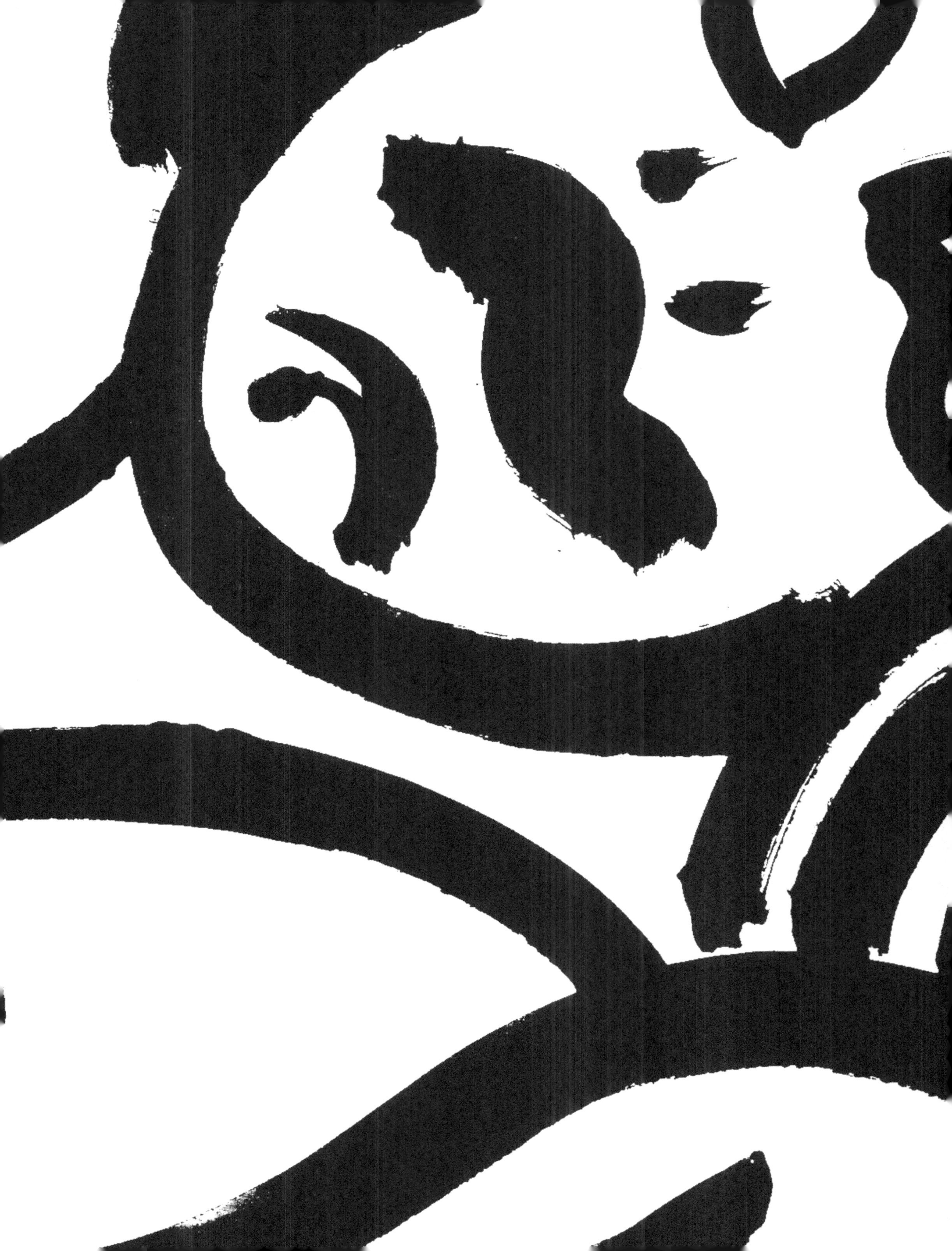

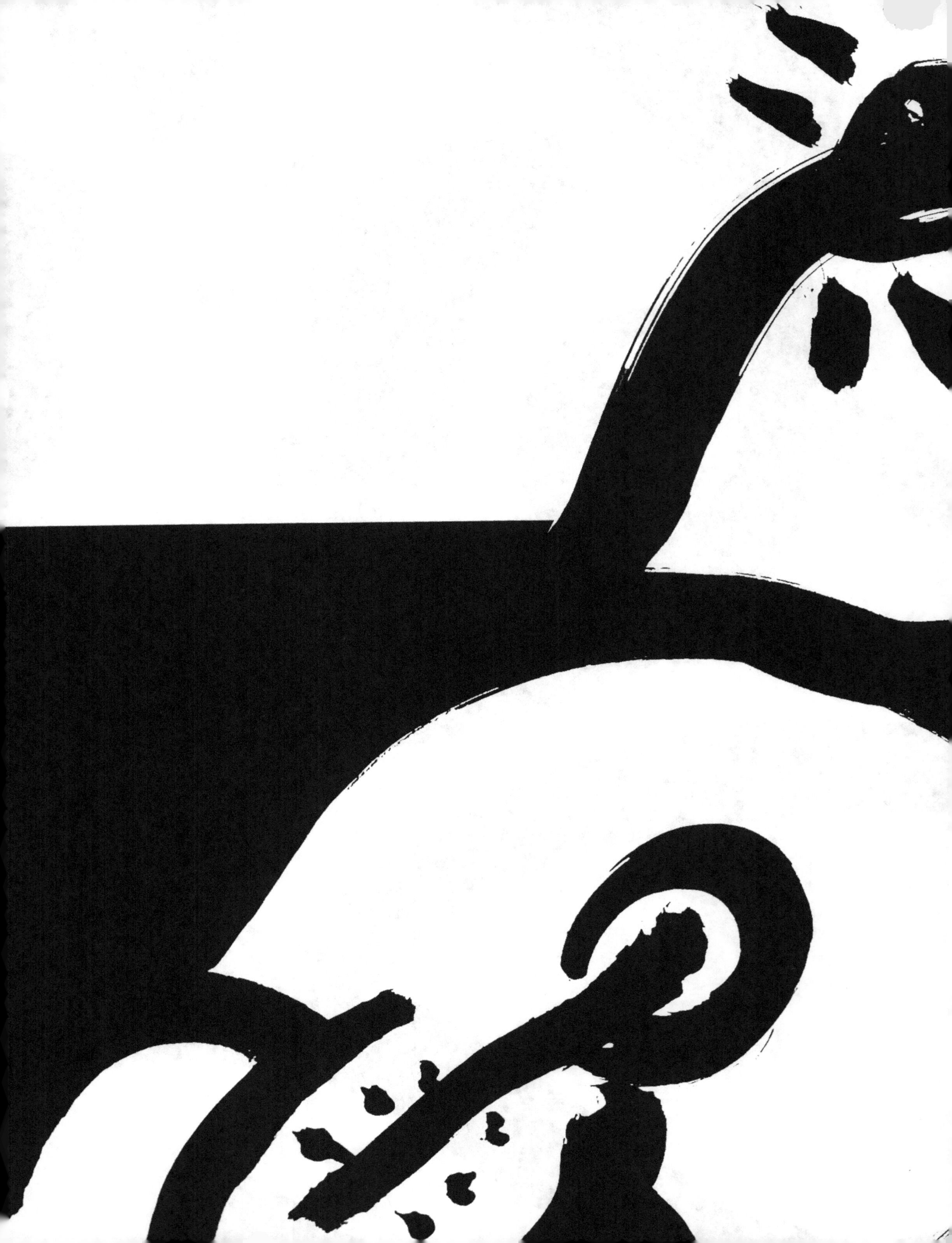

FORAGERS

In the estate of *The Drug Lord*
side-yard of this mansion-house
legend says curious treasure is buried
gold doused by torch and bright moon
enough to pay a thousand years rent
between the old well and mango tree
so -- watch the night

There were comings and goings
from the here and now
from dusk till dawn
day and night *The Foragers*
for some trifling reason
climbed the walls of the illusory

Like autumn leaves, green snake
they enter unlocked mansion gates
pillage the house, rifle rice sacks
until dirt features on a hundred hands
as though they sieved through the land, itself
to search for the imprudent year

There were other conspiracies of hierarchy
once distracted by a stranger's name
metal on four walls of the hiding place
also, disgorged lock-room, snowed cocaine

Starved on rice grass and artichoke tea
The Monk sat next to the mandrake tree
invited the drugged ones to search again

Pull up the golden curtain
I think of you, but you do not know it
And step out into the gilt-painted day.

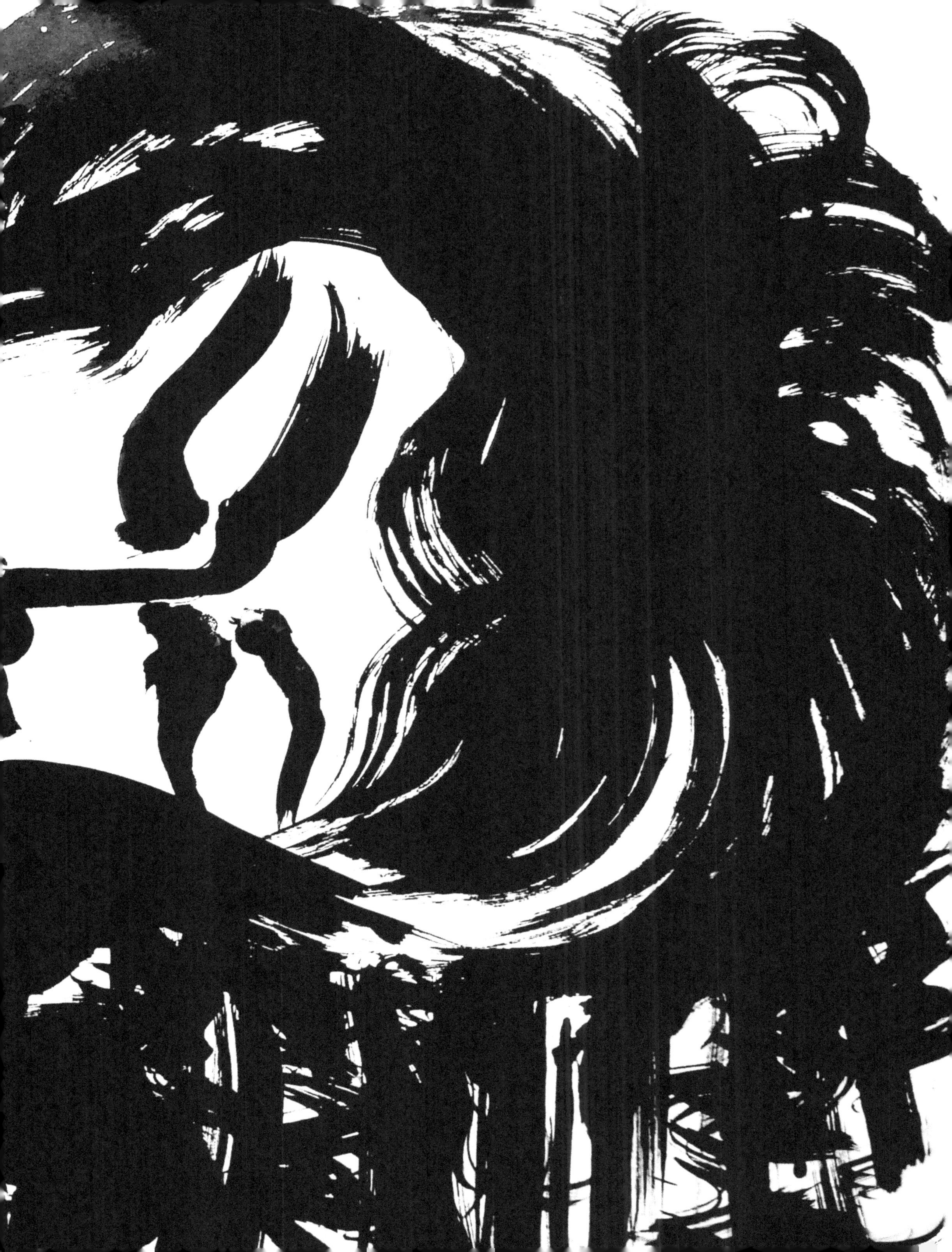

RICE FIRE

End of summer, mercury high
Along the hem of highway
Rice fires burn the rice fields
Gleams of flame reach red moon
Flying embers fall into the stars
Reach beyond histories firmament
It has always been this way
It is the custom to burn the fields
For the new rice cultivation
White egrets among sprouted grain
Insects in bamboo hedges
Ducks in the lake of catfish
Chickens inside harvest threshold
Pecking at empty husks
In the New Year following
Peach and apricot blossoms
In blue & white Japanned pots
Each branch hung with red or gold
Packets with new dollar notes
Nothing is old, for the luck
Nothing is worn, as the oracles deem
Then the sound of broken wood
Until the cooking fires are lit
Dig mud terraces, plant new rice
Tow the water buffalo and cart
The boy with a flute
The girl with a song
Riding on the buffalo's back
Where the water is deep, round ripples
And the fields of childhood, their golden pond.

LEAVE TAKING

Once, they tore up iron tram tracks
to make a million bullets

women burned valuable books
sold embroidered clothes for nothing

the rabbit caught in a trap with a tiger
but then, birds and cicadas tune up

fragrant incense rises like pencil marks
smoke uplifts from damp cooking fires

against the red silk sun, this firmament
see orchids, roses, as many weeping willow

knew streets older than the French names
white cursive script on blue tin signs
Ly Thuong Kiet Street, Da Tuong alley
everything pulls us back here.

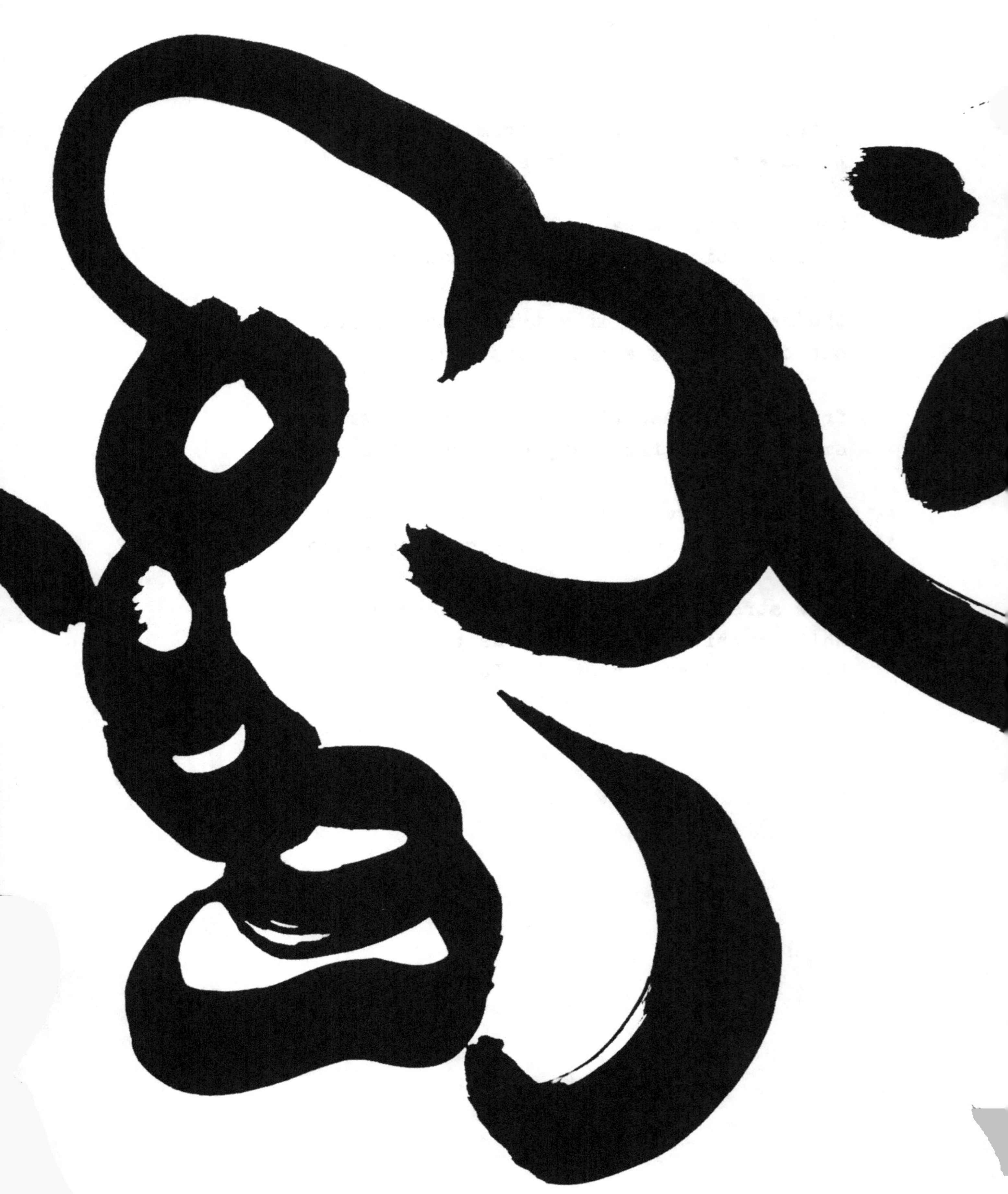

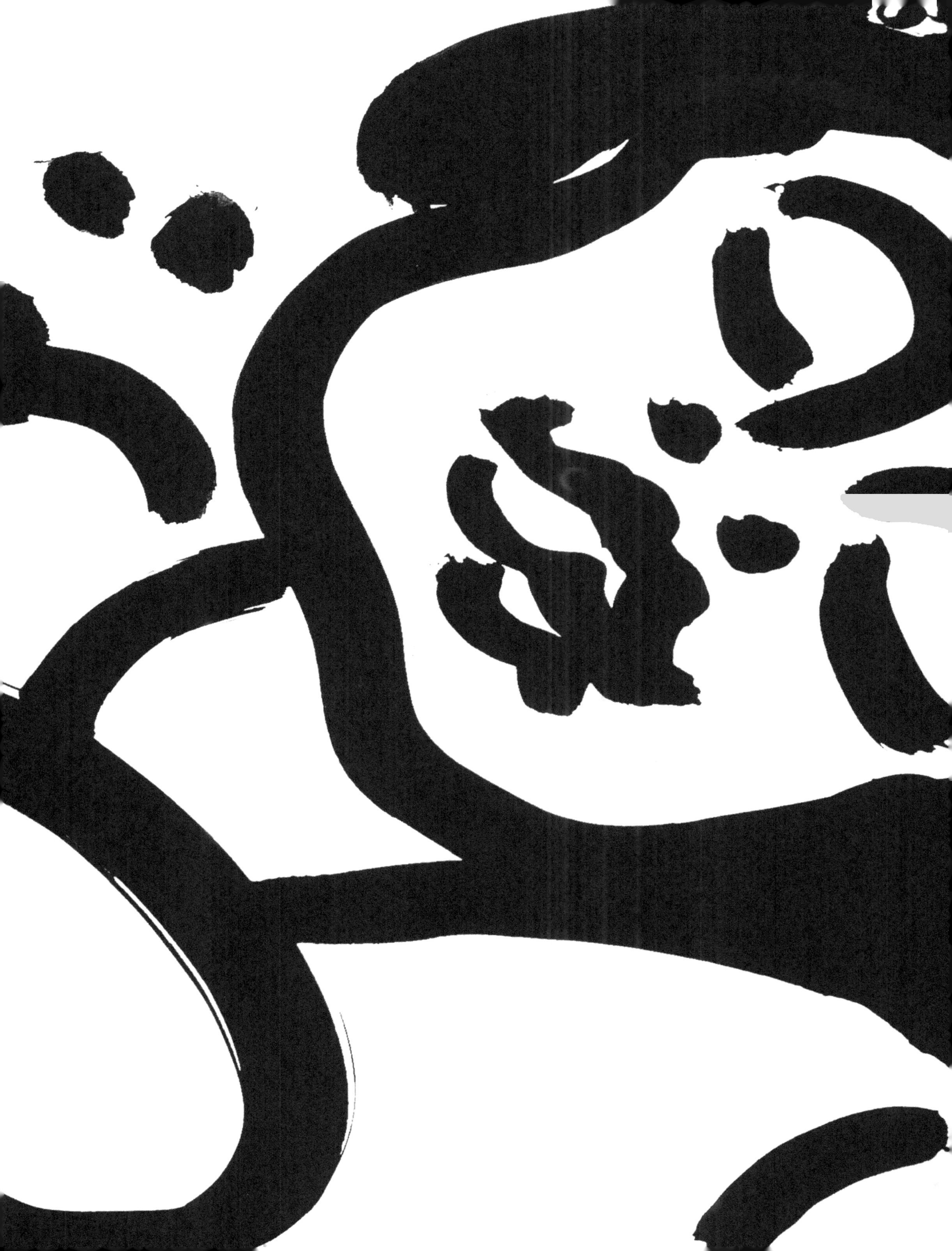

LOVERS' TREE

Some women are taken by the lovers' tree
with embroidered bower overhead
each wedding-crown and veil
even after, forever after
after candles are lit
after lipstick red kiss

Lovers use red, like spice
of all things beautiful, conspicuous
to you, to me, I know one thing
the kiss will taste like you again
will night wakes a thousand tomorrows
love you forever, as light fade away

after pearls given for luck
after rain falls with the day
some women are taken by the lovers' tree
near red roses in conservatory
doves ever gather in familial branches
what can they do on allegorical day
but listen to Medici's marriage choir

There is a moment, like a dream
and this was, soft echo of wedding shoes
across the flagstones to the long-gate
some women are taken by the lovers' tree
now the love-letters in the world are collected

A poet holds the richest pages
The Embroiderer of Names, love is found
after the writing, collecting, the gathering
all age-lasting letters of the lovers
until I saw the whole season in her arms

Now, marriage flowers all fallen and gone
the nests in the branches belong to love-bird
even a sparrow has found a home
and the swallow a nest for himself.

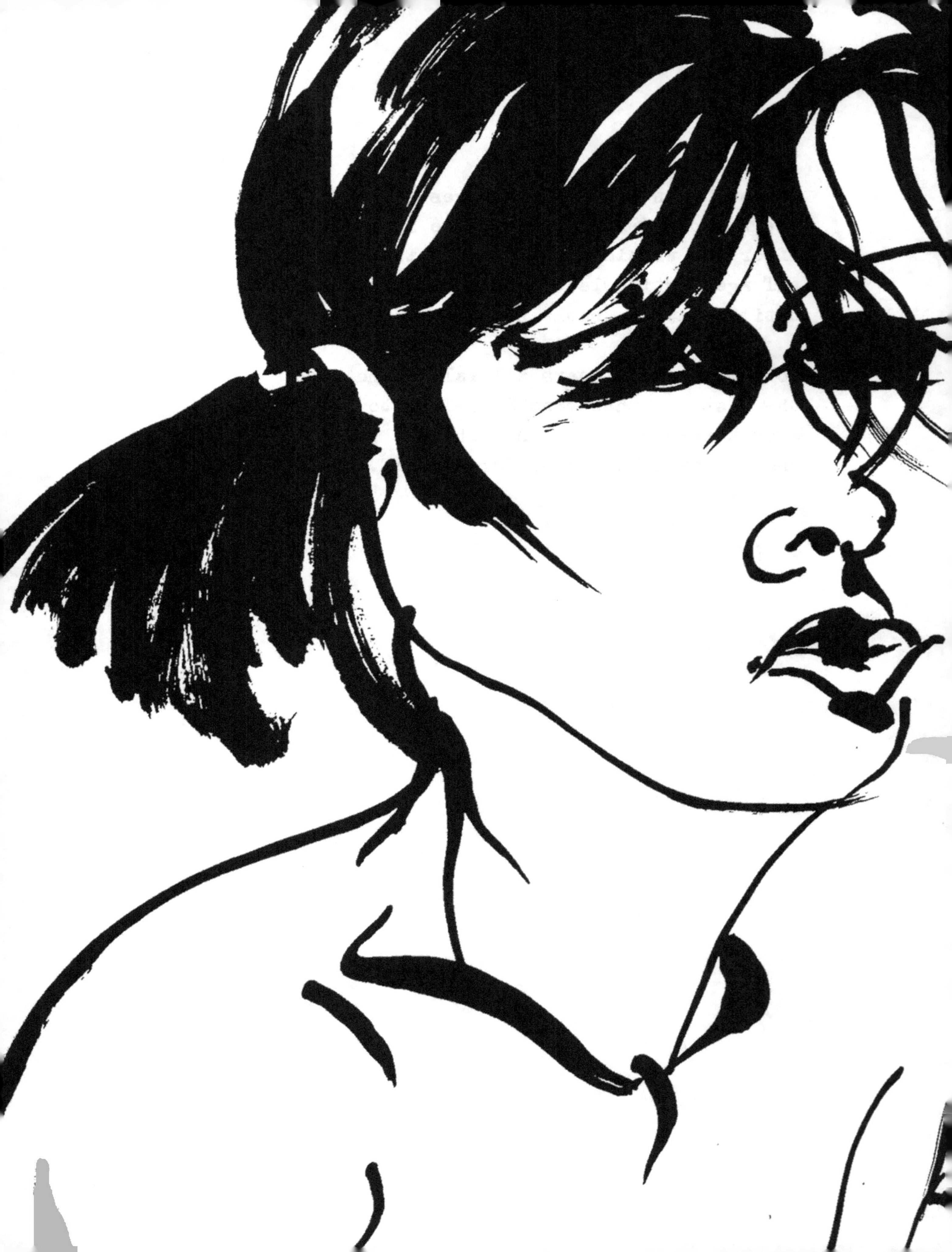

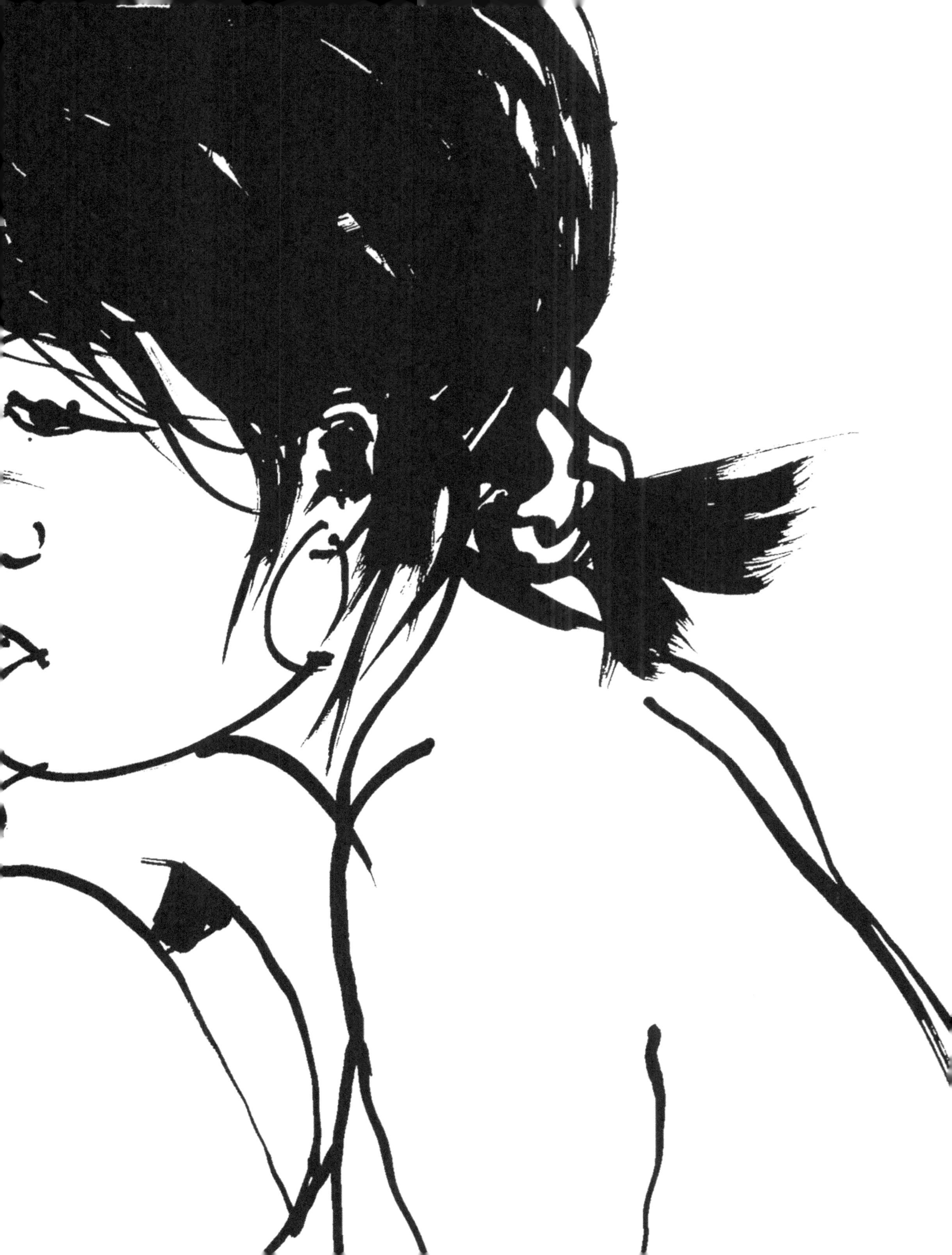

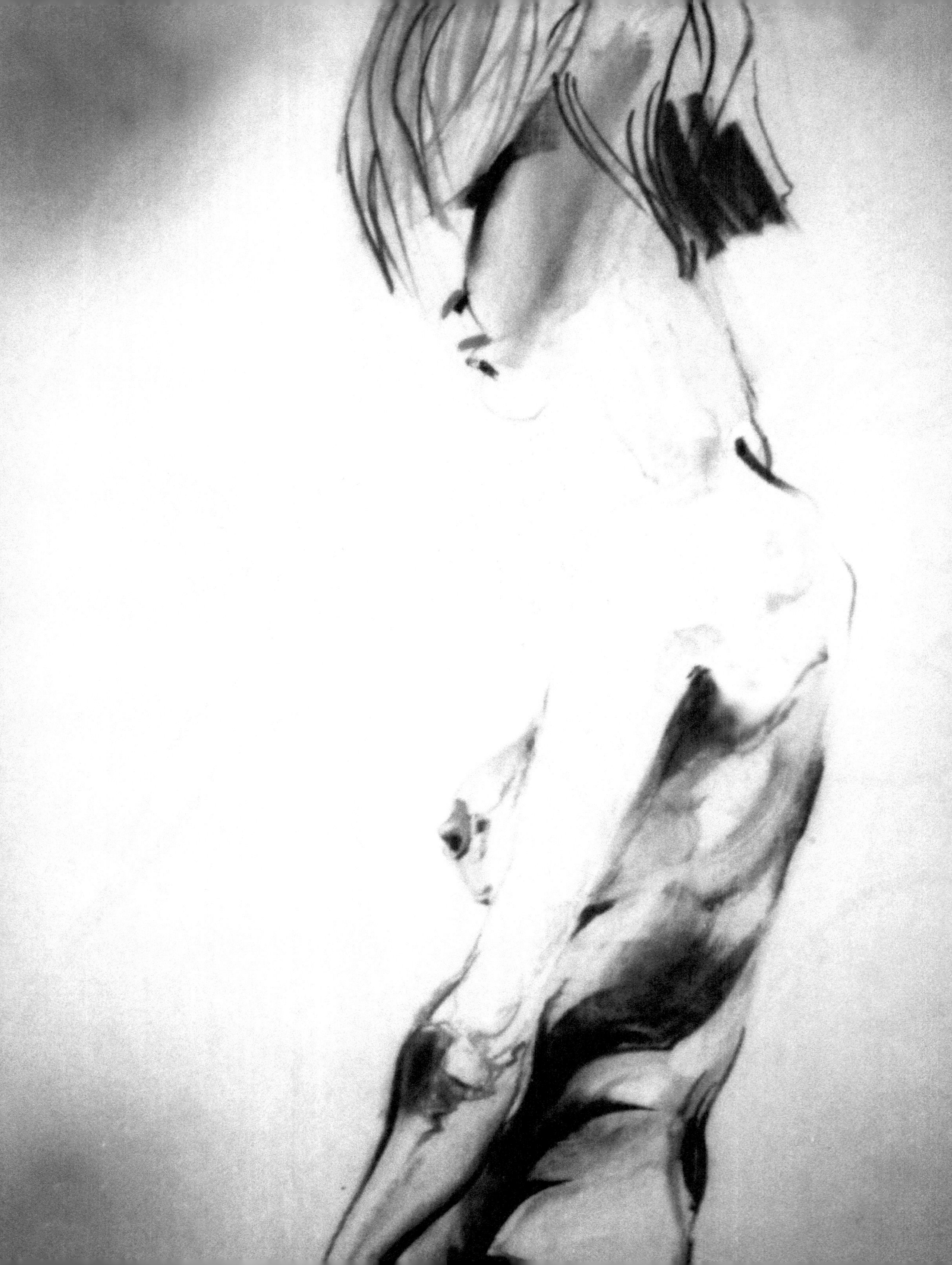

ORIENTATION

We arrive as strangers in a city
Hanoi introduces herself
Her never-ending bamboo flute

Too many occidental things that day
Silver, opium, jade and gold
The tempered heat of May

Red sun rising in a sky gone cold
But I did not meet
you, until late December

I met him in *The Crying Month*
Two lovers on a bridge to heaven
The falling down of tears

All along the street the dragon
Armored, sealed, tarnish, golden
World of pagodas and almond trees
With green, spring blossom after

Poems well hidden, secret notes
Inside the envelope of frozen leaves
Patriots messages, more than dangerous
And every so often, *read out loud*

Winter flood fast approaching
Corner cafe, cold coffee, wandered gaze
Take note of streets
Enter this disorientation.

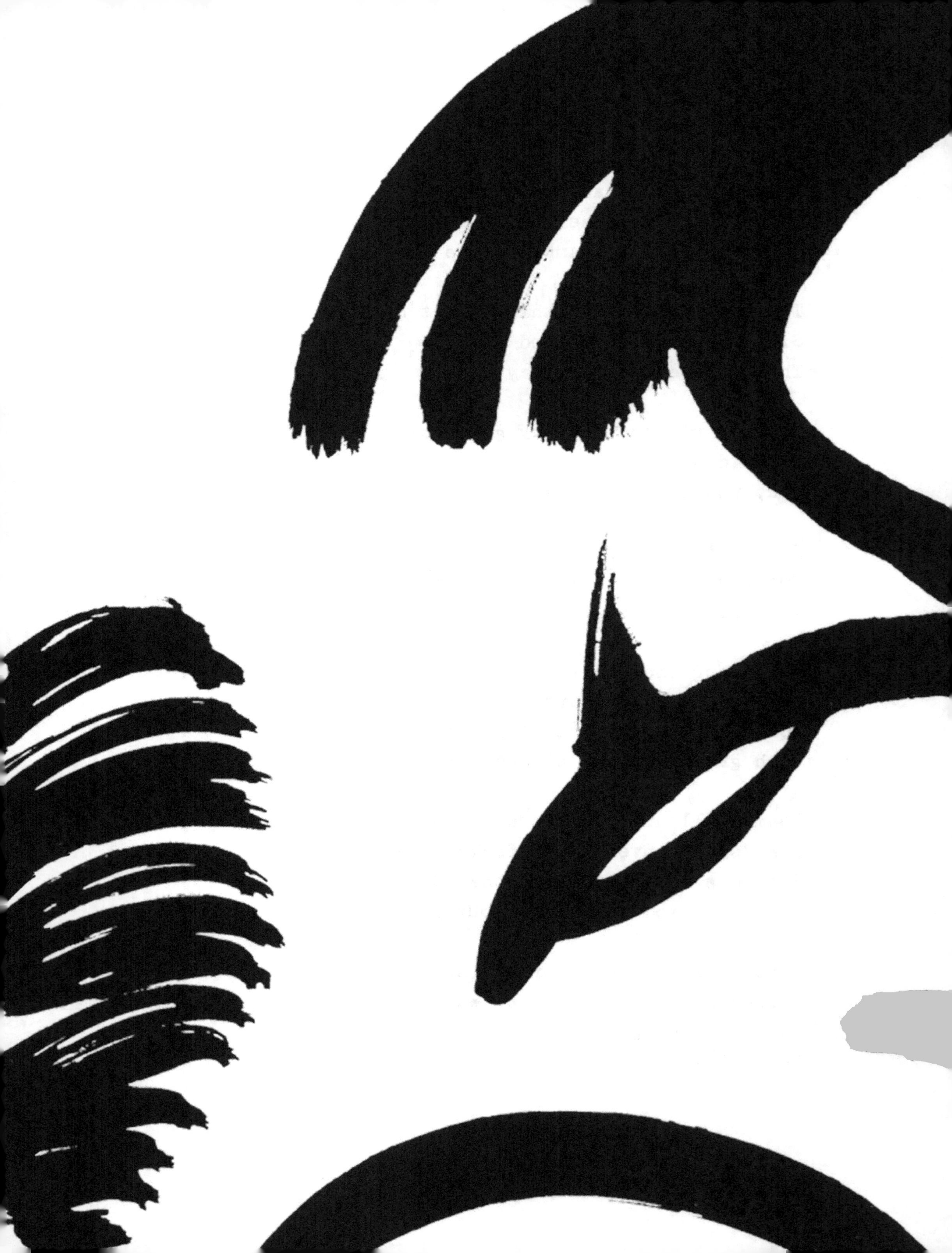

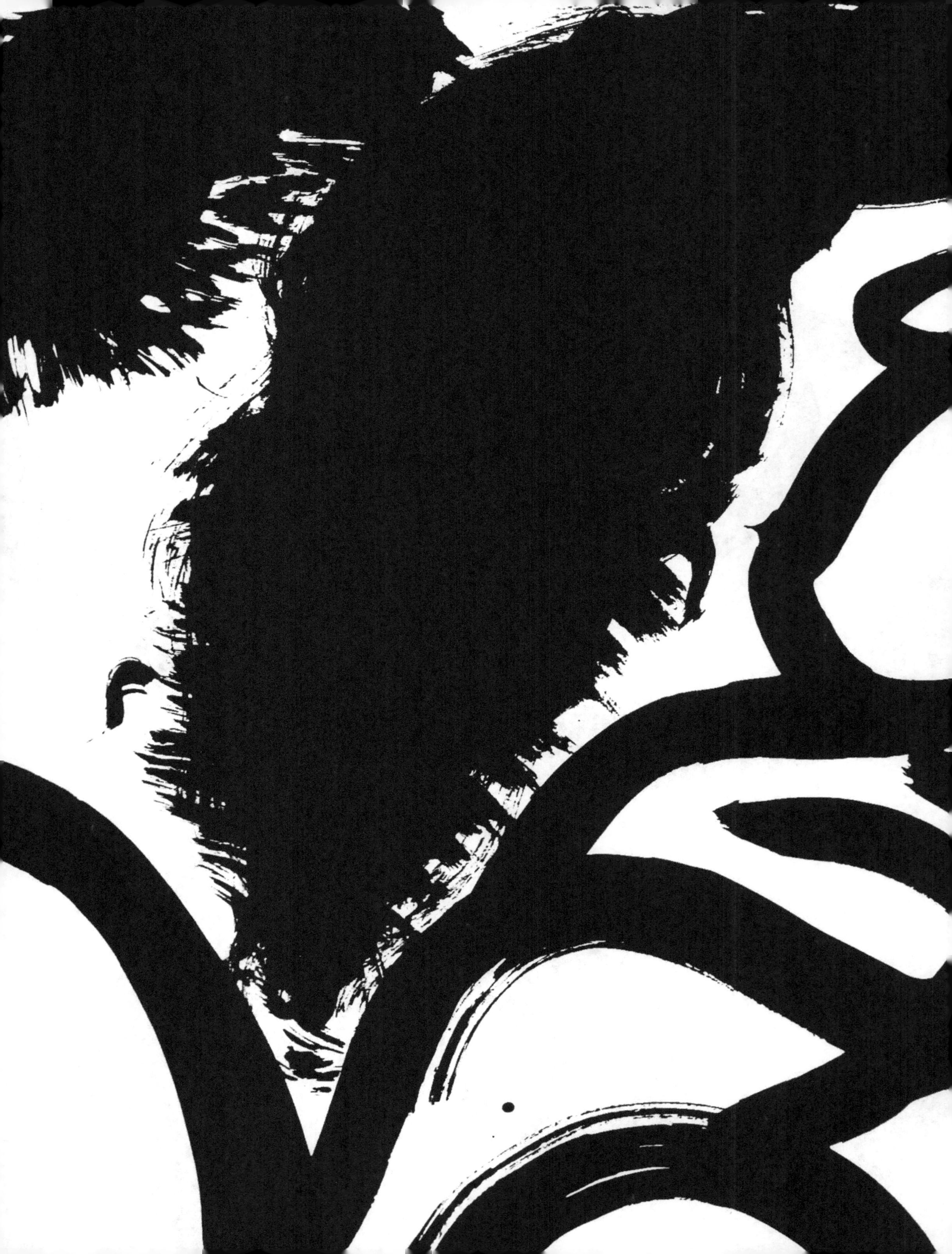

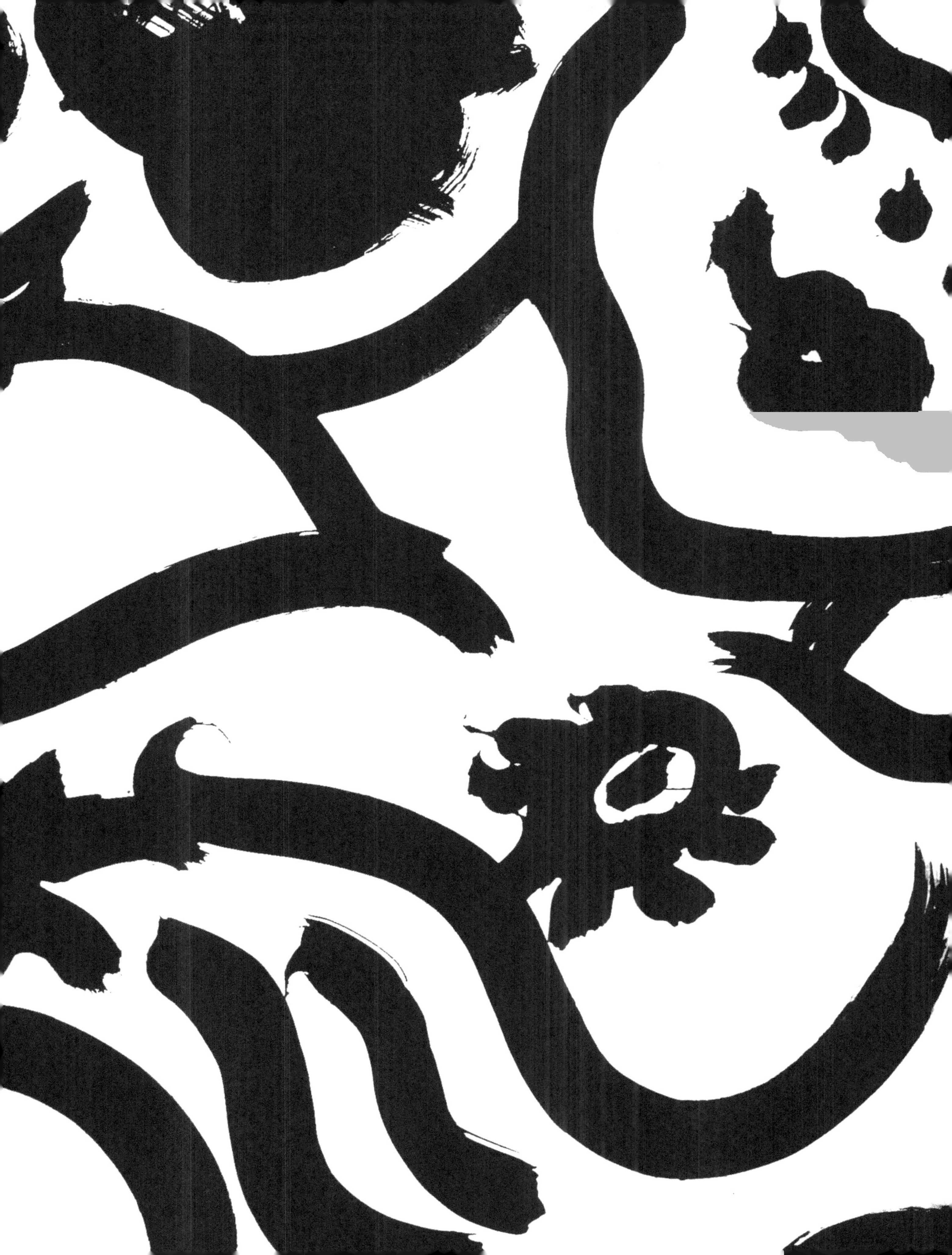

BLESSING

The English foreigners are leaving
Burn paper horses for their journey
Bring in the red crystal ball

So the Monks do come early
To perform numbered blessings
For borrowed, throwaway years

And a small carved plinth
On this, the divination sits
By the weight of its own weight

Position luck in our kitchen window
To realize how this is something
Of an anomaly, quiet reflection

From the lake, the sun catching
A bloody beam on the gate, *only then*
Something will matter, even red flowers
Rice thrown to invisible chickens

Those with tin eyes cannot see
In the courtyard they burn more
A horse, shoes, several hats

A bundle of money and worn jacket
Is it for the opposing dead
Those who have tin eyes
The Monk said

Paper and matches, or what?
To send a message, to guide a prayer
A sense of farewell's necessity
Alongside what we took, or left

See the incense smoke's godly path
Not black nor white either
Let it be a scent of dust and bone

It has a sense of purpose in the ether
Float in ink, float in wine
Let the bottle pour itself, with time

Because, back and forth, no place to be
But in *The Kingdom of Hereafter*
Not every river has a worldly bridge
But I would give you a thousand boats
To sail back home.

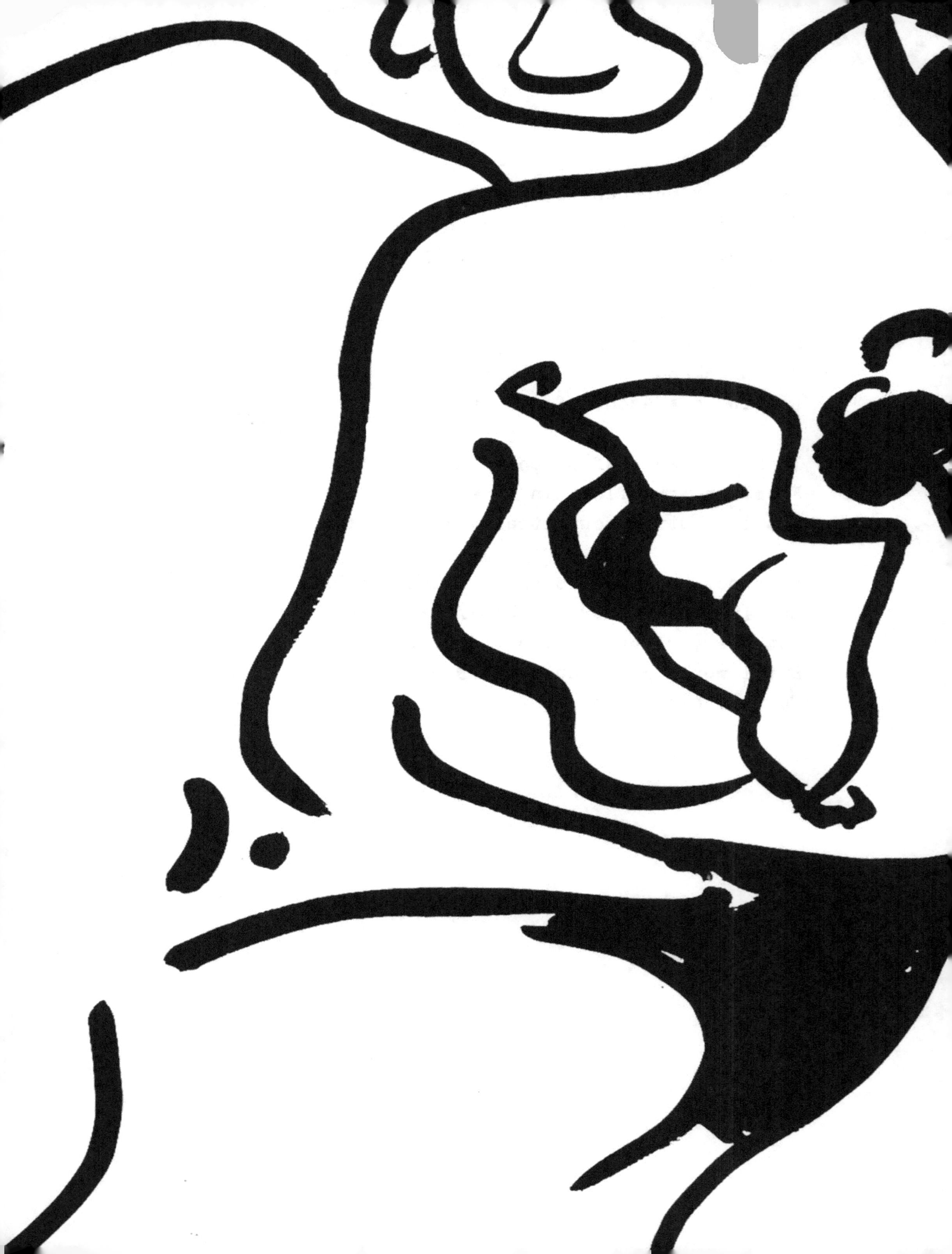

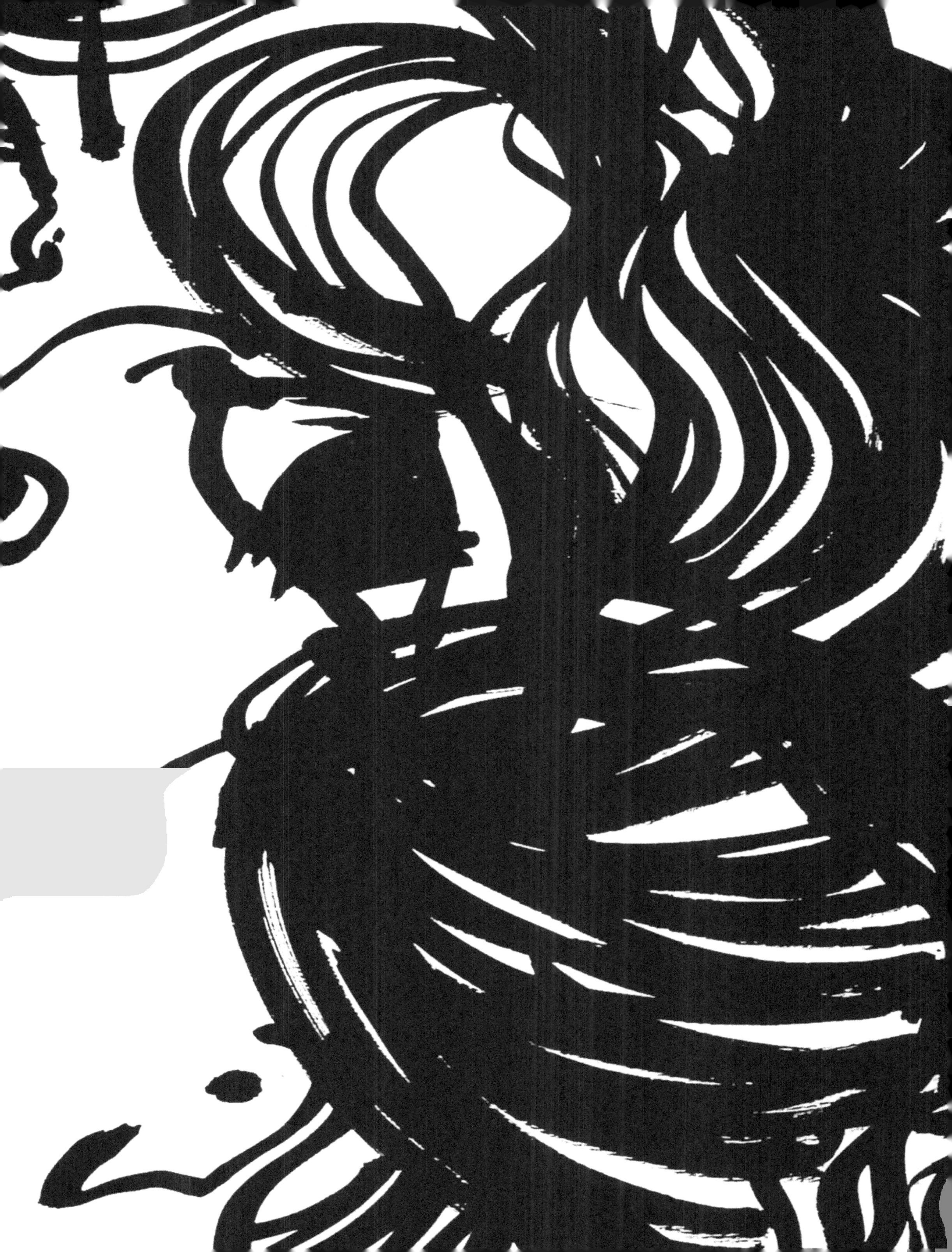

THE FRENCH QUARTER

All that woman wanted, men built
pounding, hammering overhead
narrow street, vertical stair case

there is a closeness to squalor
sight and sound to one other
intimate neighbors, sisters, brothers
put down a sedge mat and call it home

coiled and tangled, the roots of vine
betel vine grasps to hold old walls
trees-girdled in the storm drain
moss-bound crevices, tangled

heavy daub of voices, blot tranquility
balconies draped with wet laundry
rivet my thoughts of leaving
in the contemplation of place

some are forbidden to belong
anonymous transient
merely, passers-by on the way
to someplace else

invisible to the ones born here
families of ten or more
their glances skid over us
move, jostle, push aside
in a preoccupation to survive

all is heat and rain, insentient
trees-girdled in the storm drain
moss-bound crevices, tangled

betel vine grasp to hold old walls
tapestried properties and the bronze
bell of the temple, deep baying

there were monks and novices chanting
stir-up, song-lulled lotus world
sweet cassia, honeysuckle
punctuating immortal mornings

walking with the rain mist, stinging
eyes shaping vulture turrets
of colonial mansions on Ly Thuong Kiet

shadows on the road to winter
the city spreads orange clay-tile roofs
so many people; lost as we are

in a roomful of felicitous thought
silence then, silence slow
like a death, I have lost myself

open the shutters, wider, wider.

POEMS OF FISH

Early morning as I walked to the market
The sun was in my eyes, for a moment

I saw *The Madonna of the Abandoned*
Holding a dying man in her arms

But he was a dead fish
Every filament a small entanglement
The world a net, full of sharks

     The Black Madonna smiled
 And wiped her hands

Fish suffer away from water
Women say -- when you cut open fish
You find poems belonging to the dead.

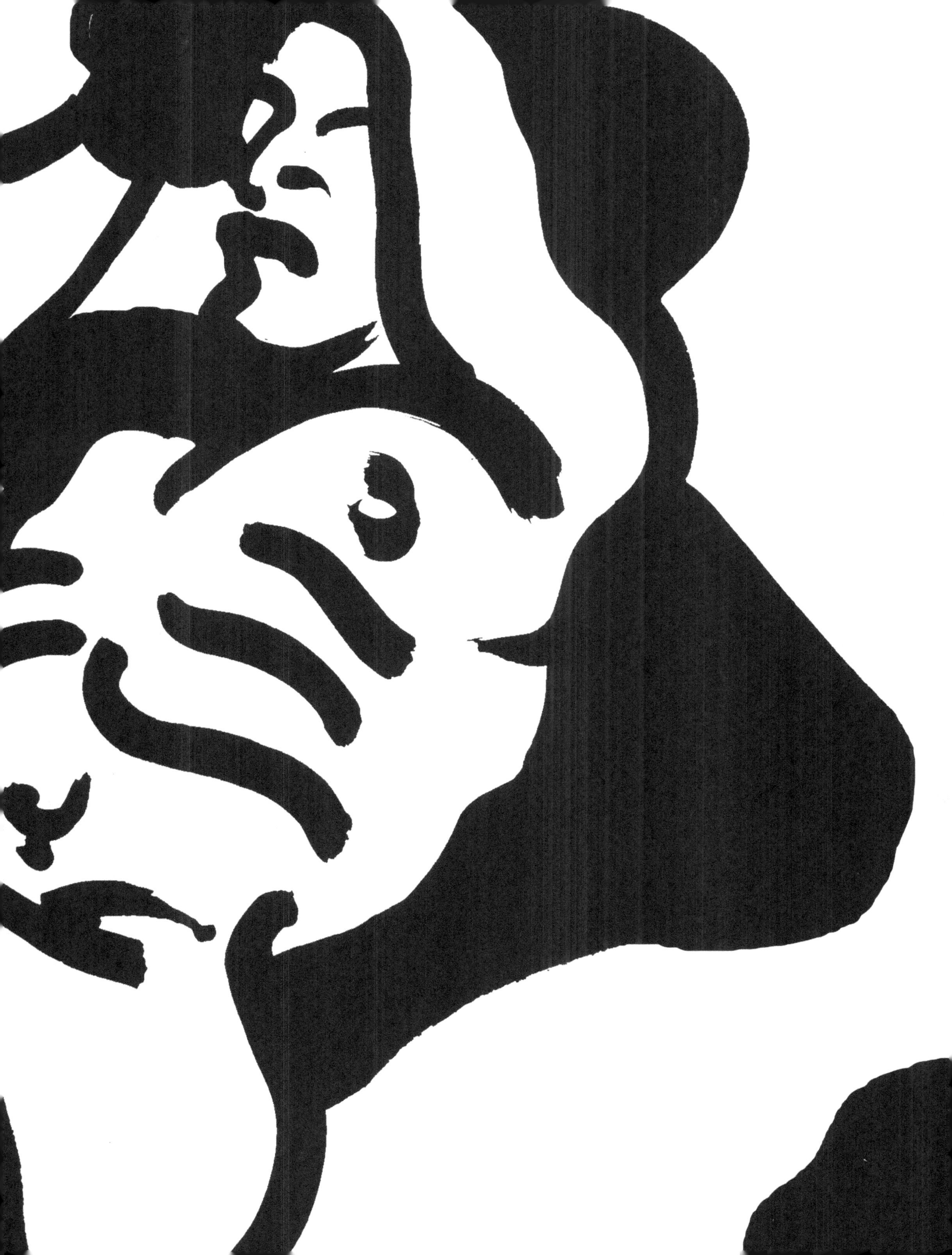

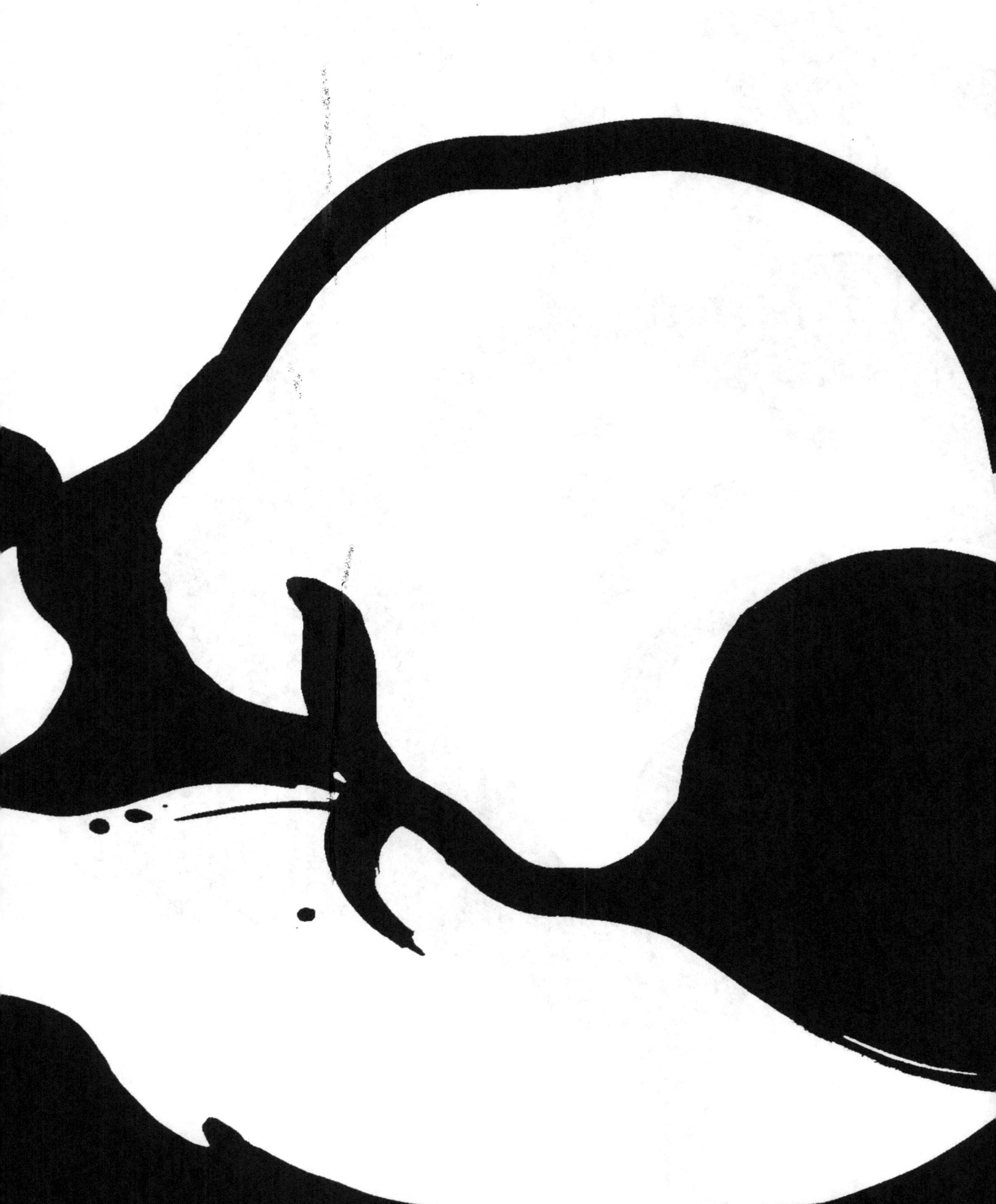

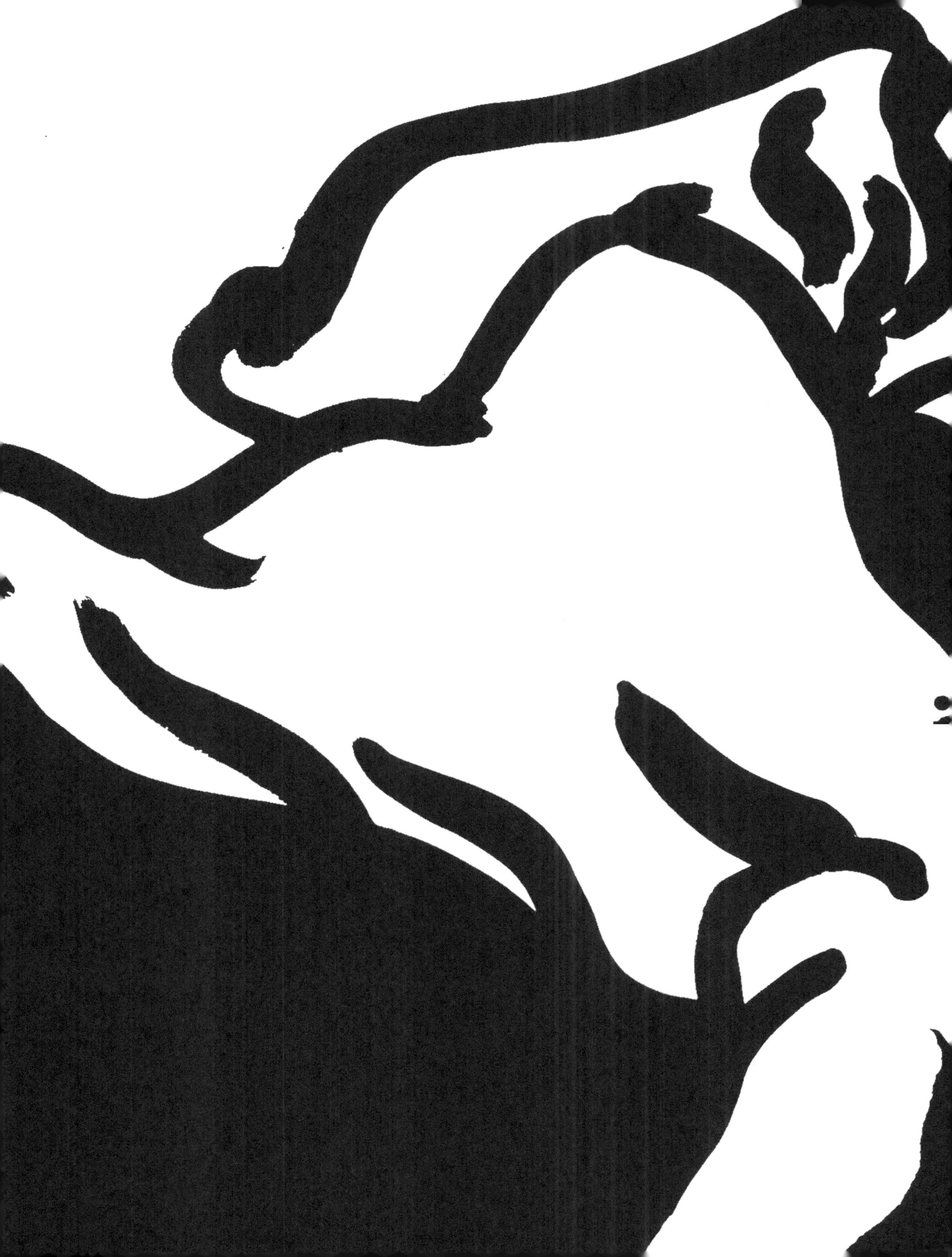

DA TUONG ALLEY

Night removed itself and morning came
Cluttered with fog, thick cold rain
A bean curd landscape they call it
When the fog and cloud lay in slabs
And the dawn and day meet each other

Crowds come into the alley
Like orchids, faces unfold and open
The women squatted down
In the vociferous din of the street
Shouting their way under round straw hats

Sitting there, same old place
Large baskets of garlic and ginger
Bitter cucumber, chives and taro
Holding cups of hot green tea
The rice is ripening in the field
Harvest is due soon

'Who is going to do it?'

Rice bowl and chopsticks in hand
I looked at their feet in the mud
And never said anything
On the eastern side of the alley
Old woman sits in the corner
Always a private smile on her face
An edge left for bitterness
Comes her grandiloquent statement
Voice bright, like neon lighting
Thoroughly she knows the answers
Still she asks, 'Why are you leaving?'

THE OFFERINGS

Fishing boats fall into the edge of horizon

Round boats lacquered in buffalo dung

We saw a dozen or more dolphins

Like a mighty gray congregation

Parrot-fish bright as morning rainbow

As sunrise turns the world to red

Disc of sunfish, fins catch fire

Children gathered up fish as silver

Like coins tossed for luck

Fish whose jade the sea resembles

On the cusp of sand

It is not Piha Beach

It is not Alexander Bay

But a collage of all the beaches in Asia

For a moment, think of nothing

But yellow chrysanthemums planted at low tide

Along the sand, offerings to the dead

Then the salt air tarnishes the petals

And sea-foam drags them under

Suffocated by it, washed out with talk.

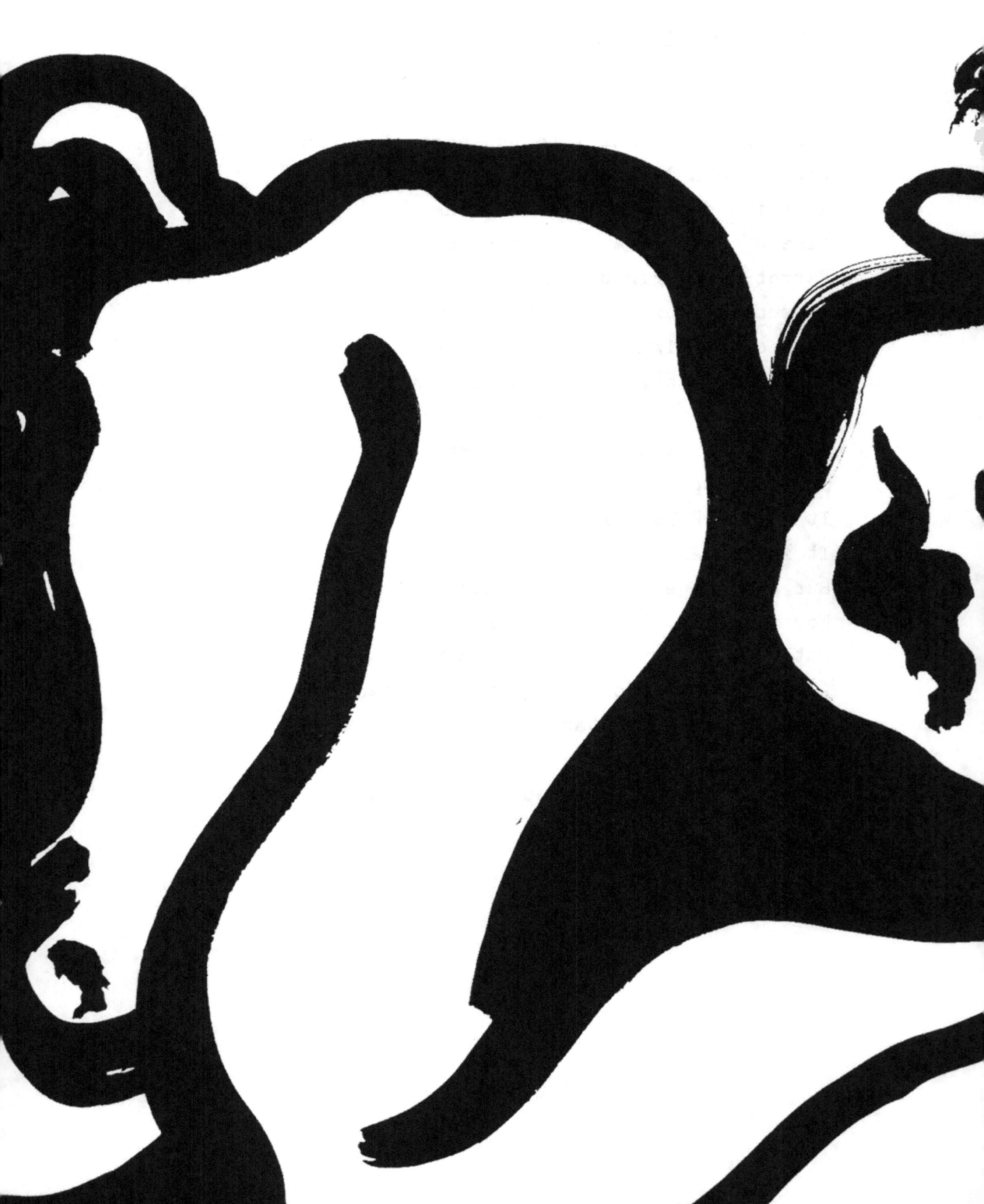

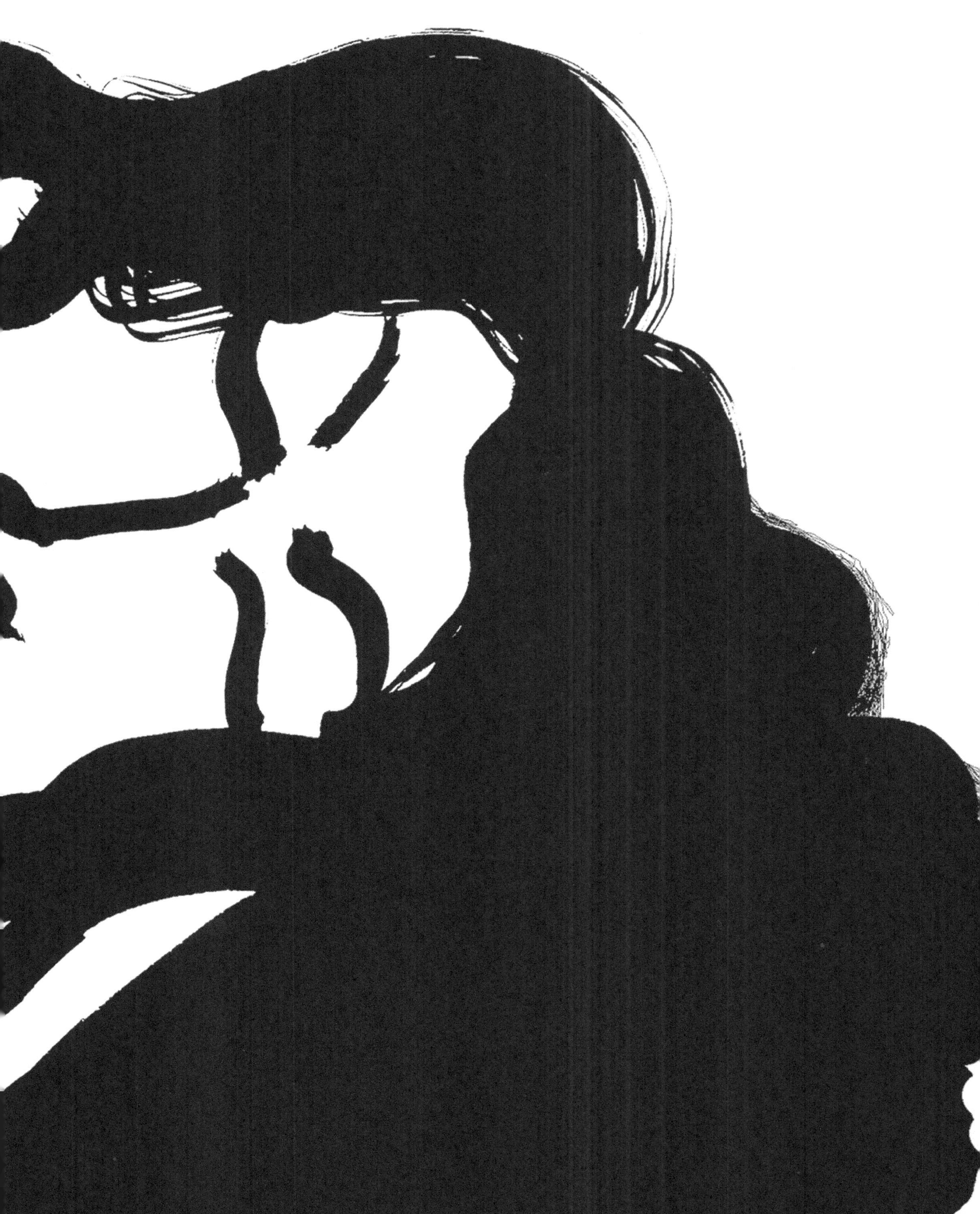

ANDAMAN

There is an old teak house
On the island of small elephants

Little drops of water, little drops of sand
Makes the ocean, makes the land

In a distance, no wave waits
Nor lei of frangipani around your neck

Moon in perfumed florescence
In the double-ness of things

A hundred colored prayer flags
Promise of a martyr, no cross, no crown

One bowl of green rice, was all the same
And on and on, this hungers refrain

Wood veranda, black dog marauds
Aftermath of monsoon, high tide ran its course
We have less, or part of it is gone

Night, the sun dips into sepals of horizon
Red as blood, divining iron mountain

So, we teach ourselves the otherness
Follow sunrise, one island to another

So little minutes make the days
For all who make waves, half our years gone

Soon what matters of the past
Of gold and silver, above and below

Break one old bridge to build another
However far you wander
Your dreams reach back home

In faraway room behind the shutters
Under lock and key's allegory
For what good is an island to me.

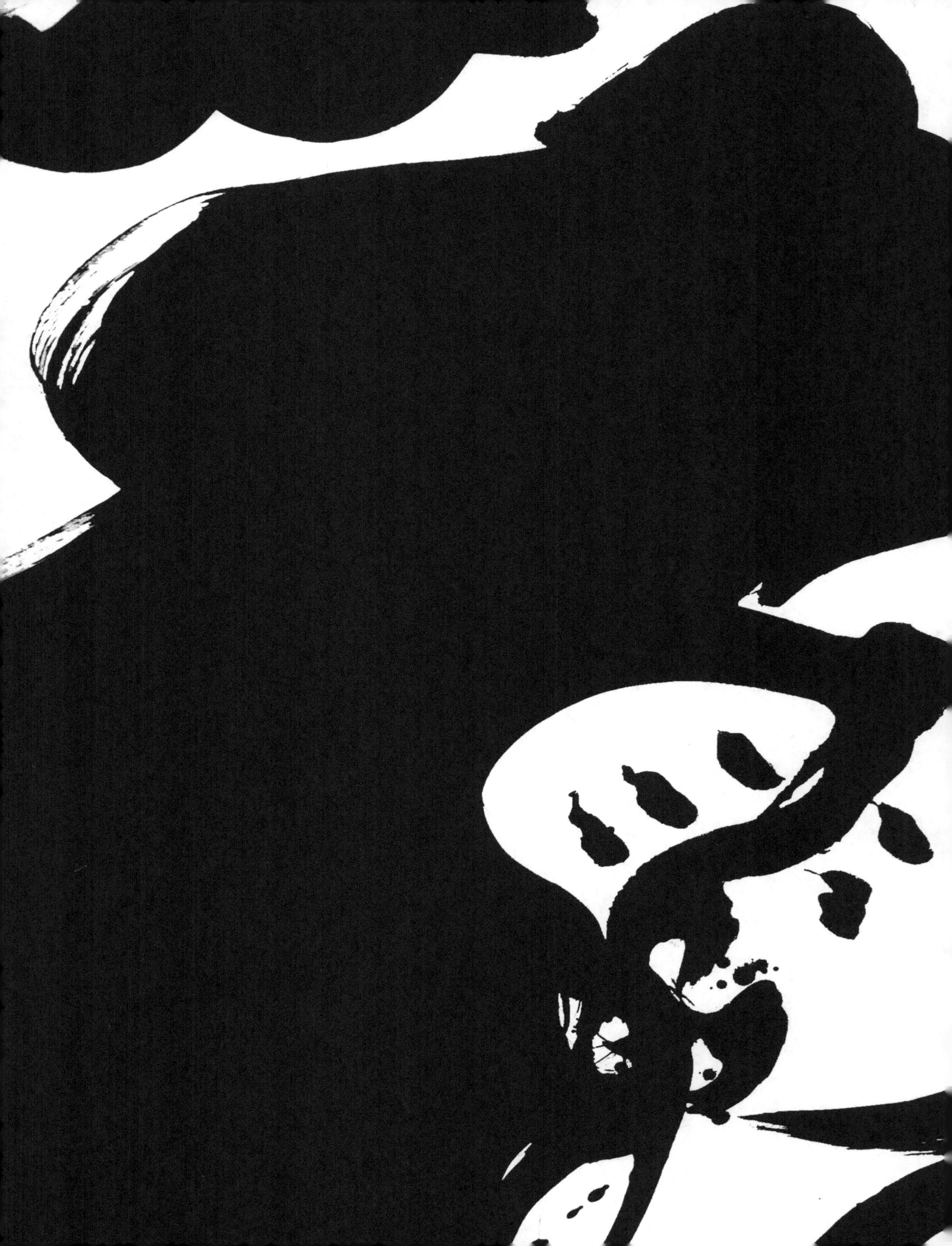

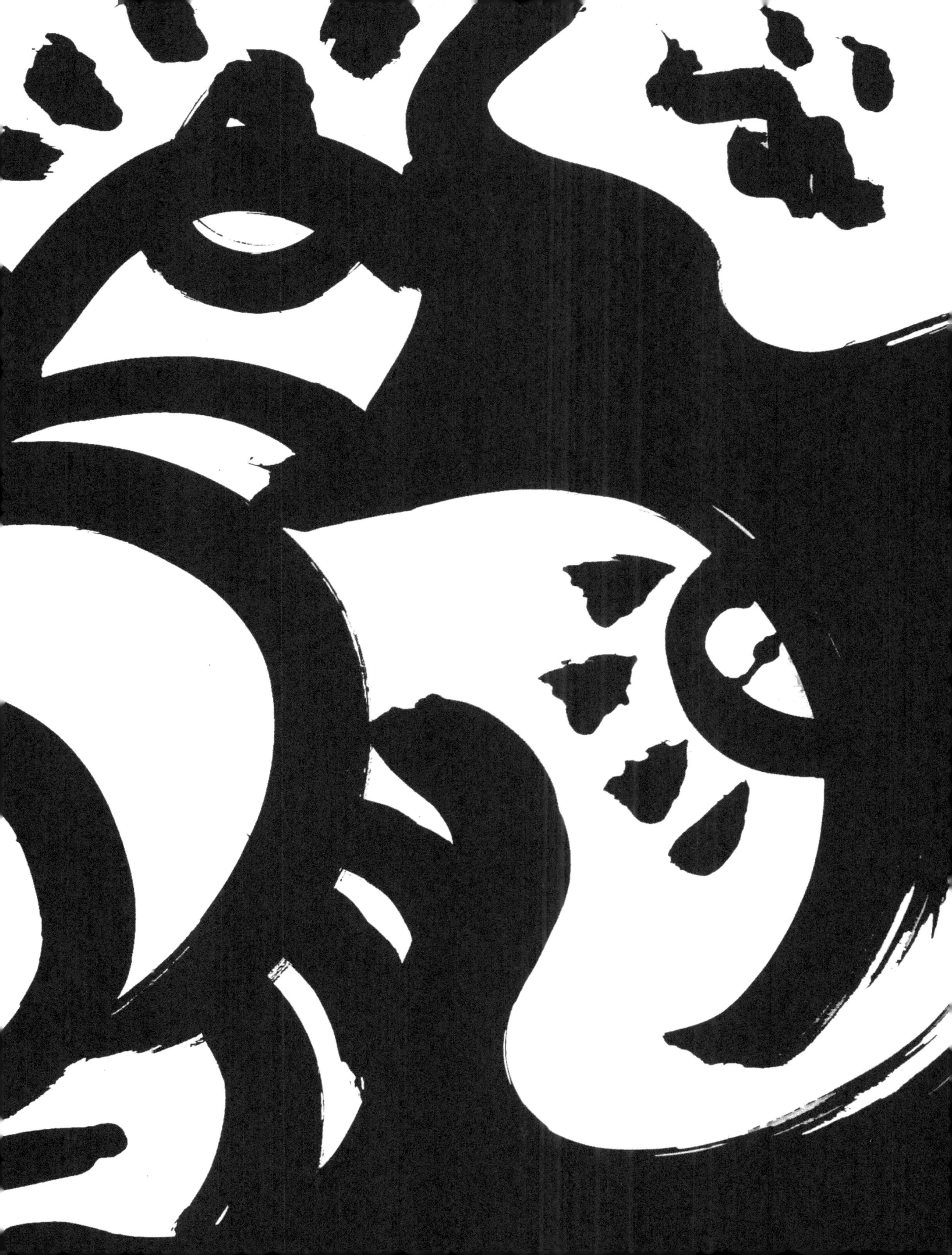

THE TEA SHOP

The window is open; dog barks
constantly, I have sat in the kitchen
beyond the homage of silence

while women with stone mallet
crush river crab shells for red soup
there was a strange taste, mercurial

there was a sudden dragonish eclipse
fishes fluttered like silver leaves
filigree net held unspoke secrets

now, you and I, share unsettled times
foreign words wrought our lips
as we mute language born to us

as the bamboo flute needs a breath
regardless of this time in exile
I shall exhume all memories

I found a lifelong taste for you
your voice filtered in my throat
my lungs fill with the breath of you
fossils of our time
a palace of glass-fish bones --

breaking in my heart

rain pressed down on bamboo branches
one moment, we drink the river's soup
one moment, pack our bags and are gone
some things presume change

there are old villages, hidden by rivers
but you are the one who knocks on my door
to give me a winter coat, with magician's sleeves
but that was a long time ago.

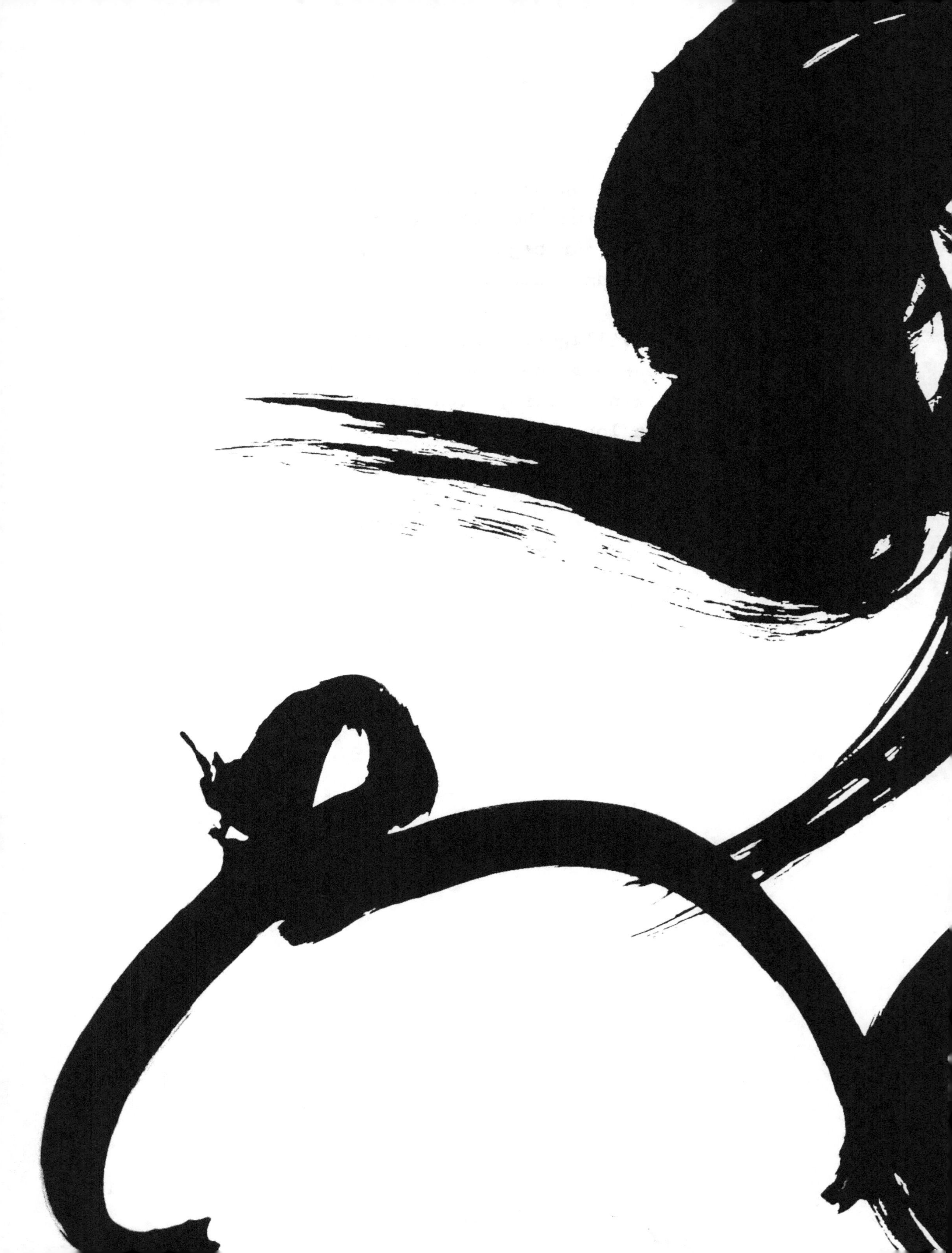

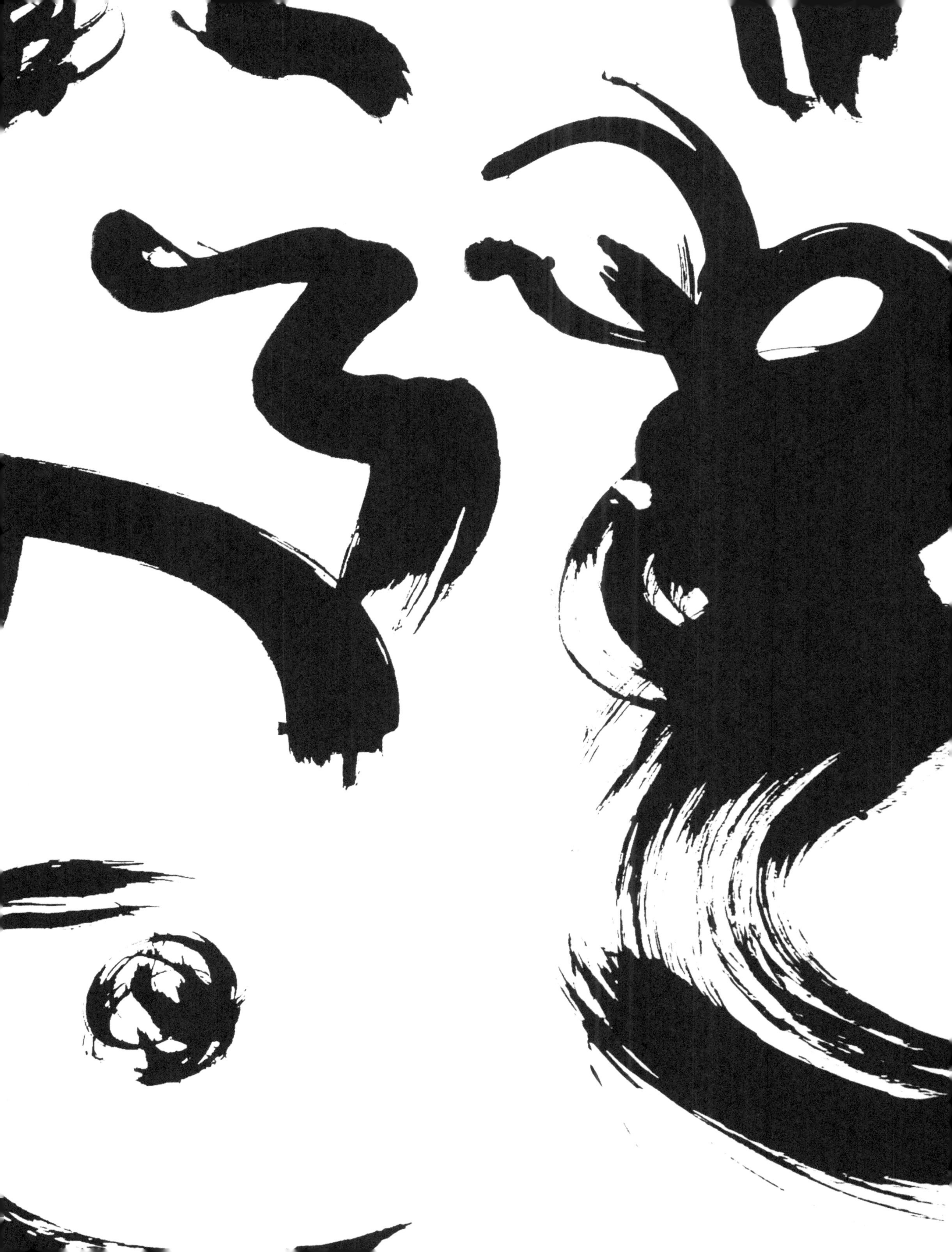

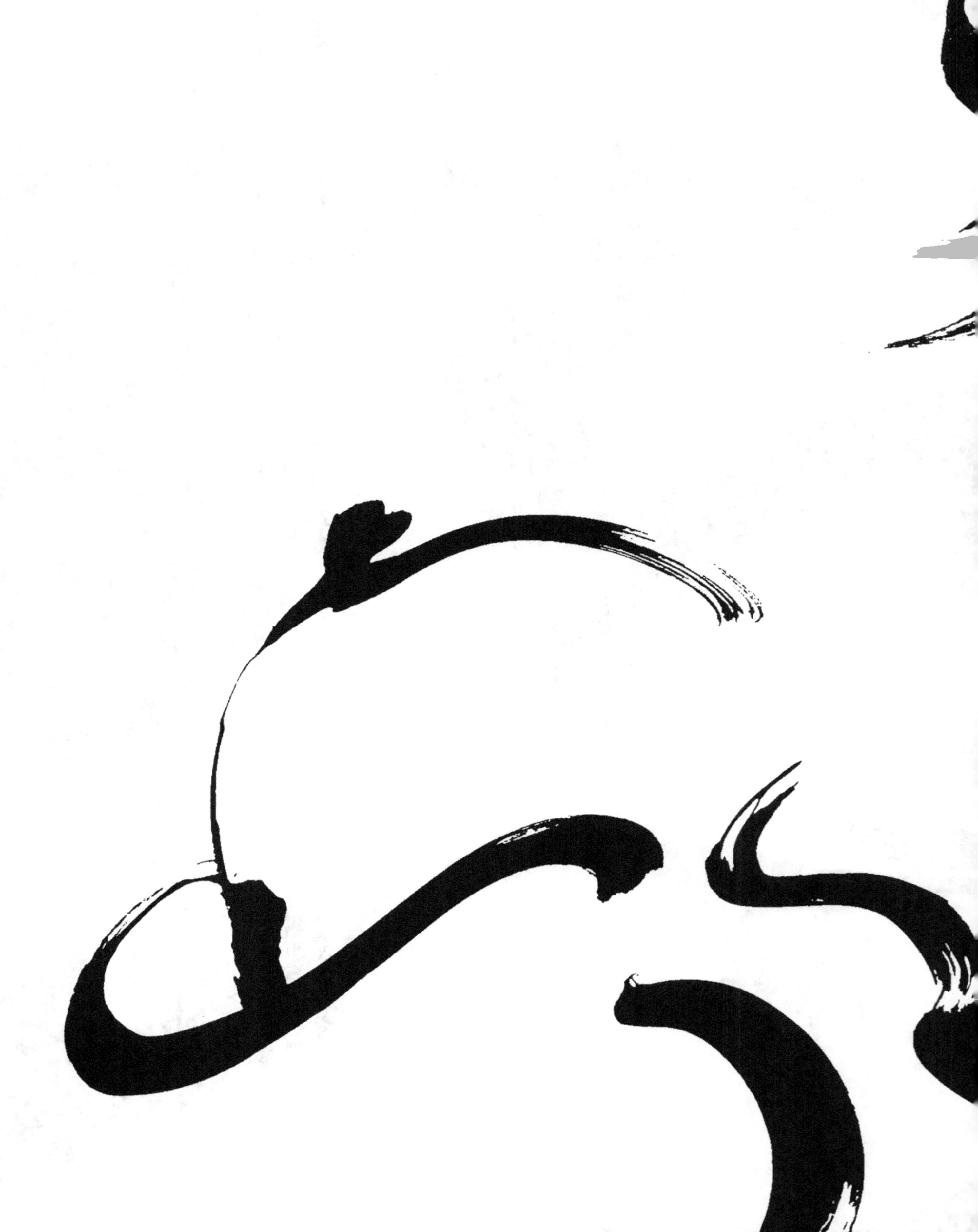

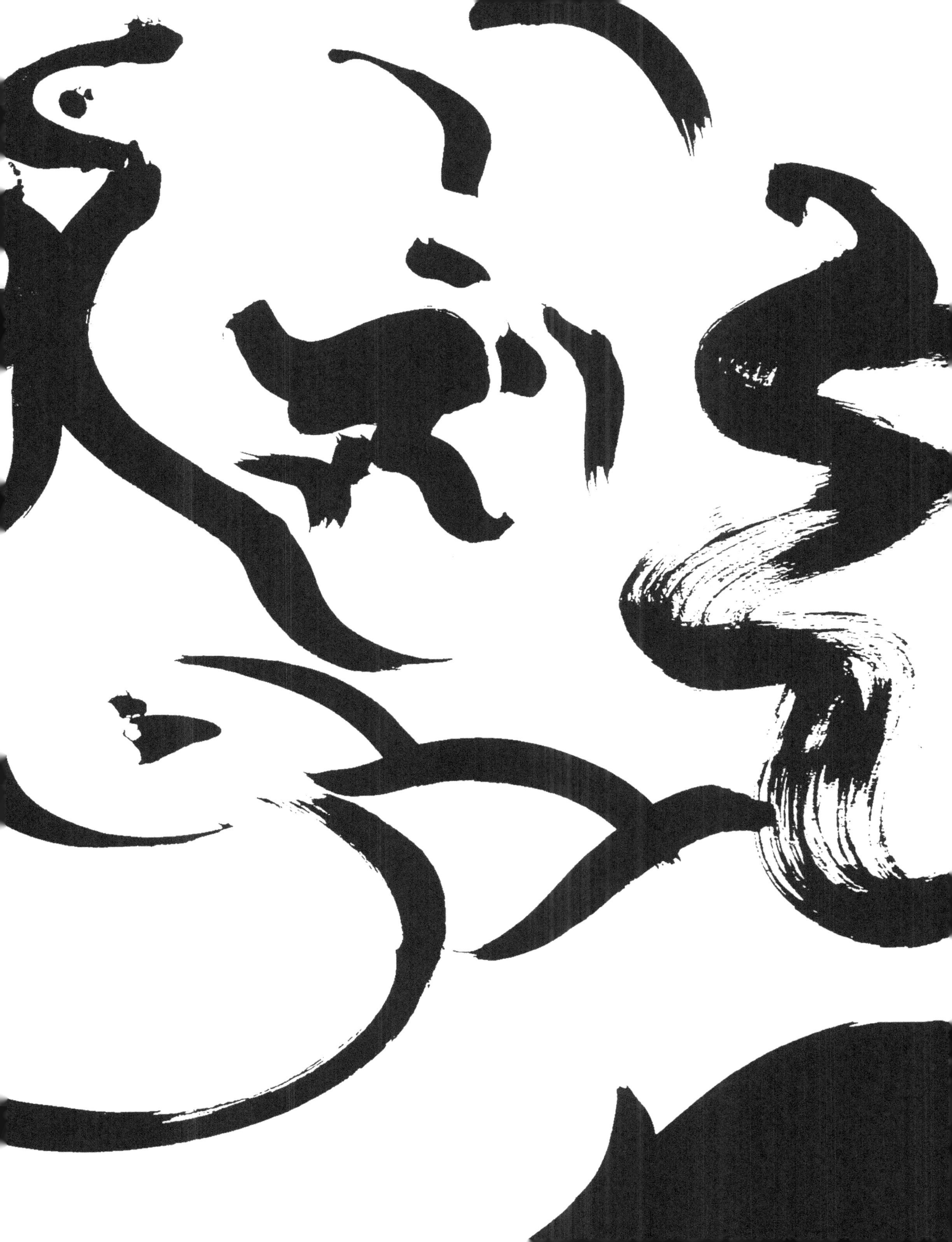

THE ALMOND TREE

Of the trees that came to be
In the courtyard of Maison Gaol
Through chinks of time -- in near past
Human or inhumanly, impossible
Some men are taken by the gallows tree
With chromatic leaves overhead
Even after, even after

After red lanterns are lit
After lipstick red kiss
After jade's perfect luck

Some men are taken by the gallows tree
Near lotus in the mudded lake
After rain fell with the night
After shadower of sorrow
Before night woke tomorrows
Birds will gather in familiar branches
What else to do on allegorical mornings
Not to embitter litanies of trouble
Who will take you as the worm is turning
As birdsong dies beside the dying

Now the birds in the tree have gone
One gardener rakes fallen leaves
The almond shell is in two halves to remember
The wood of the sacred cross
And the kernel -- food for a saint
After sweeping, collecting, the gathering
All age-lasting rust of the fallen
Until the whole season is in his arms.

H O U S E

The moon in equinox, rose the tide
It was the time for new life, bring word

Hardest of all was simple birthing

Against brittle wood, fire, smoke -- breathless
Moreover, ash and particulate in birthing room

Slip a mask on the newborn, while he is sleeping
Bitter bulletin of rice-fire season, smoke continues

More than that, everything known, will turn to dust
Indifferently, irreverent at this, fiery sarcophagus

The hollow-men, avarice bone-set
Cobbled wreath of maligned donations

Higher up, benevolence in black branches
Empty husks burst of energy

The savior saplings crush upwards
There and only there, all day long waiting
It's been twenty years already
Since you left, life will soon wear out.

ORCHARD SONG

Each apple you bite into
wears a shape of your mouth
red delicious, gala, granny smith
there is no such thing
as a bad apple between us
so we pick the worms from the pips
until the garden belongs to us
too late, said the snake, both will die
for imported apples are poisonous.

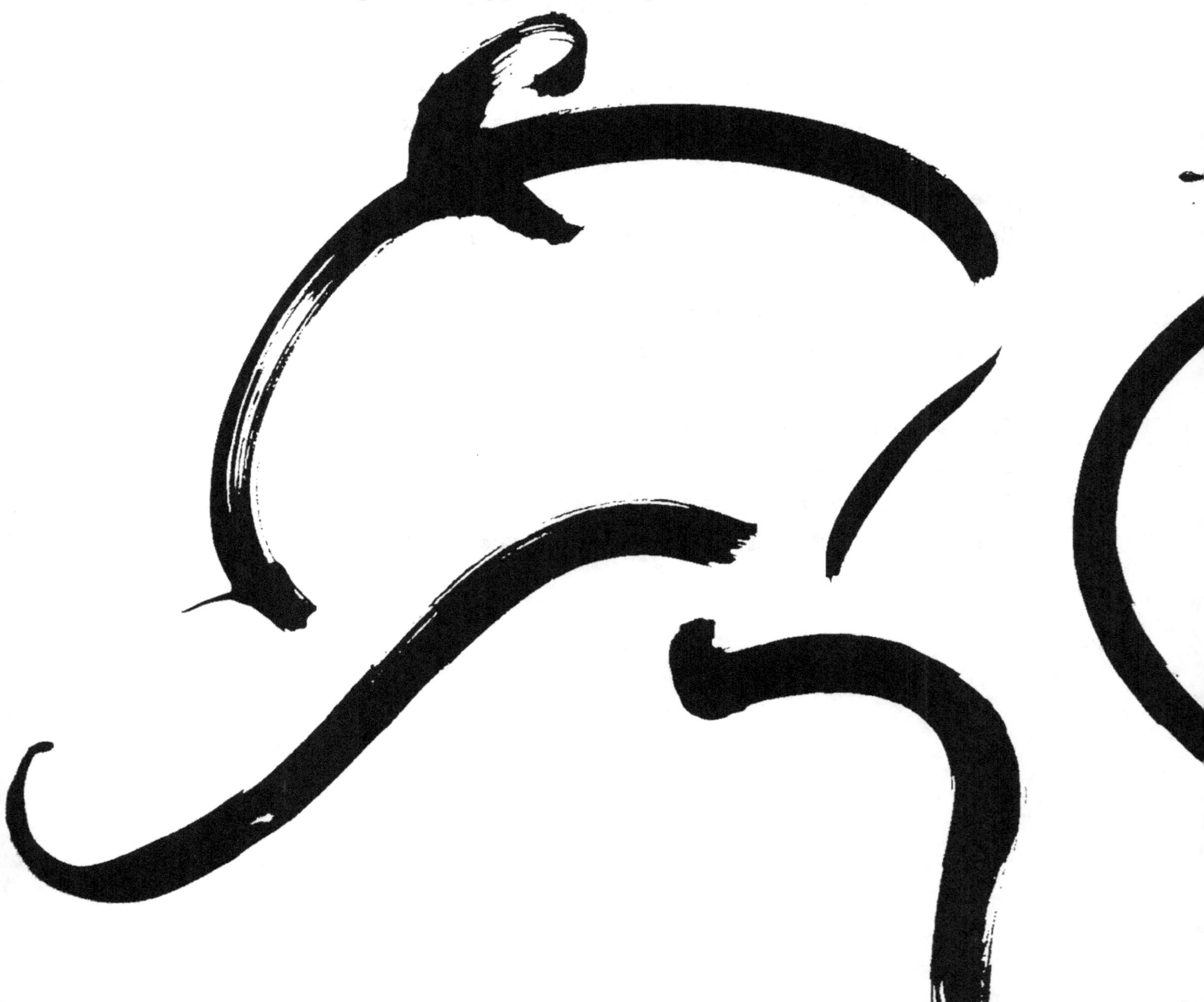

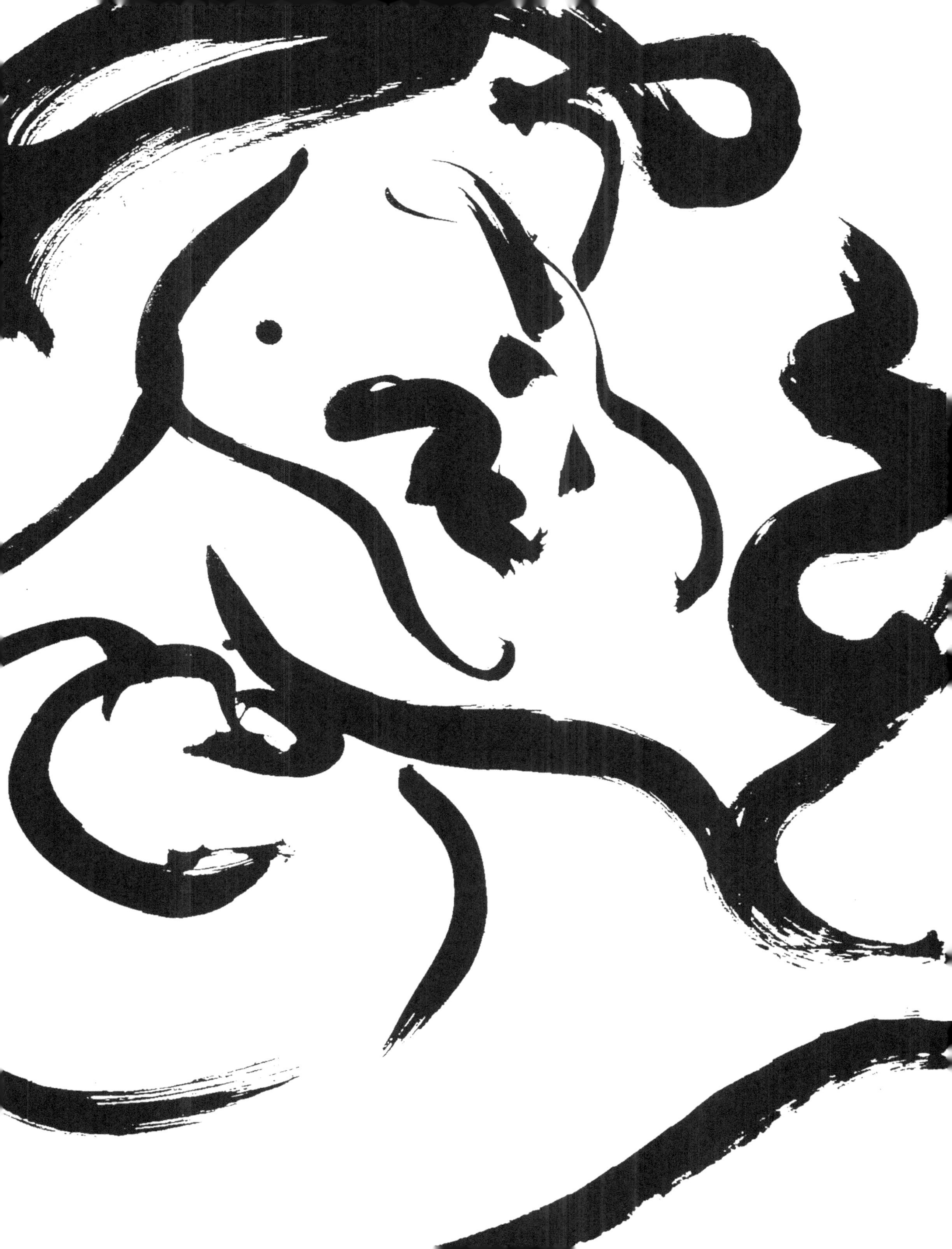

WRITTEN

In the old capital city
flood waters receded
after the storm of centuries

on the way back home
an unfamiliar journey
to sit beside *The Sword Lake*

there was a canopy of willow
reaching down to touch
the calabash of green water
for no reason, each fallen frond

thin mist floats in the wind
chanting of monks emerge
through quiet moments of rain

see a golden face
immersed in gold thought
a monk's pure countenance

there is a white temple in *Jade Lake*
spring in the winter
blood in the *Red River*

a new moon that cannot be found
a moment in the Cochin rain
a caged song-bird in the sky
a small song of bamboo pipe

blessed with luck
while fleeing from disaster
to succeed in a great moment
unseen, no more than so
such as when the blind man
touched my eyes -- somewhere
back in the Somerset countryside
to see a different world
through the same eyes.

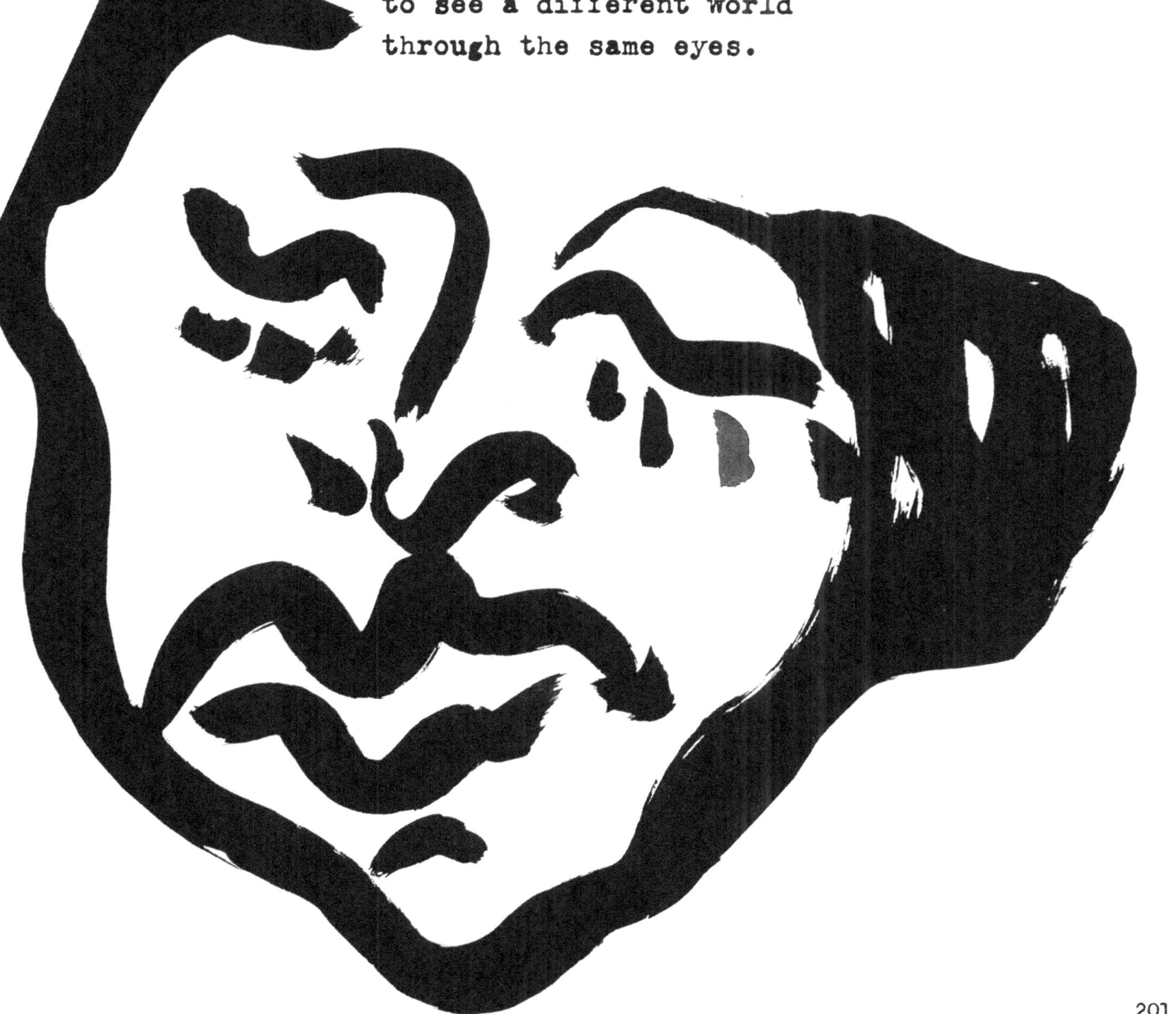

THE SOCIAL RULES

We learn Hanoi, her silk & hemp
Old houses, opium streets, the long way
Around, contemplate a nearby short-cut

There is a double vision of foreign land
The richer entire world, despite
The most dangerous avenues of fortune

But now the anchors, roots of reality
Independence and detachment mostly
People aware of one culture, one home

Exiles aware of at least two front doors
Room by room, mislaid objects
Some were dragons and opium pipes

Small scales for weighing red poppies
Held up a bunch of misguided keys
Most doors undeniably locked

Spent the entire time toing and froing
Street by street, around and in-between
Now the whole city revealed by lunchtime
Pungent lime and mint from communal plate
Another year in Hanoi -- is ending
All moments are taken
It was only us forgetting what was.

TO A FRIEND

You are where you have been

Thirty-five streets in the Old Quarter
Beyond that, white crane birds along the river
Young green rice, waiting for sickle or scythe

A riot of rain falling from common clouds
pattern of red lanterns on the wall inside
poems hidden in an almond tree

Elsewhere an outline of old man
As if foretelling the season for martyrs
Sharp corners on a tangerine wall

Broken wine bottles on top of the gaol
So the unknown, beautiful, dangerous
Stuff not to control or second guess

Or know more than a little, forceful thought
One by one, small hand gestures of place
Invisible, save for the warmth of your hand
On the small of my back,
Waiting for traffic lights to change
Noise and heat,
On Ly Thuong Kiet Street.

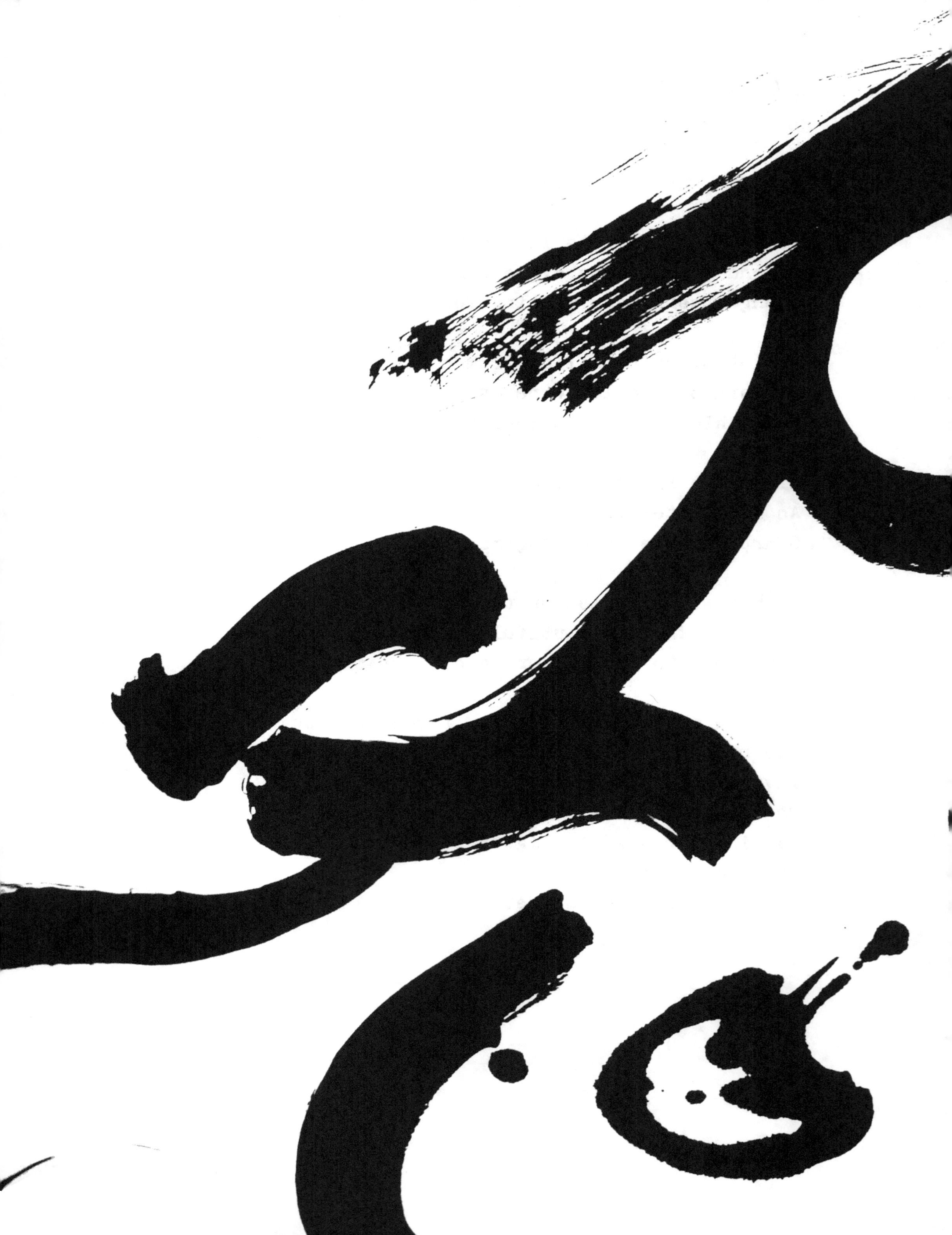

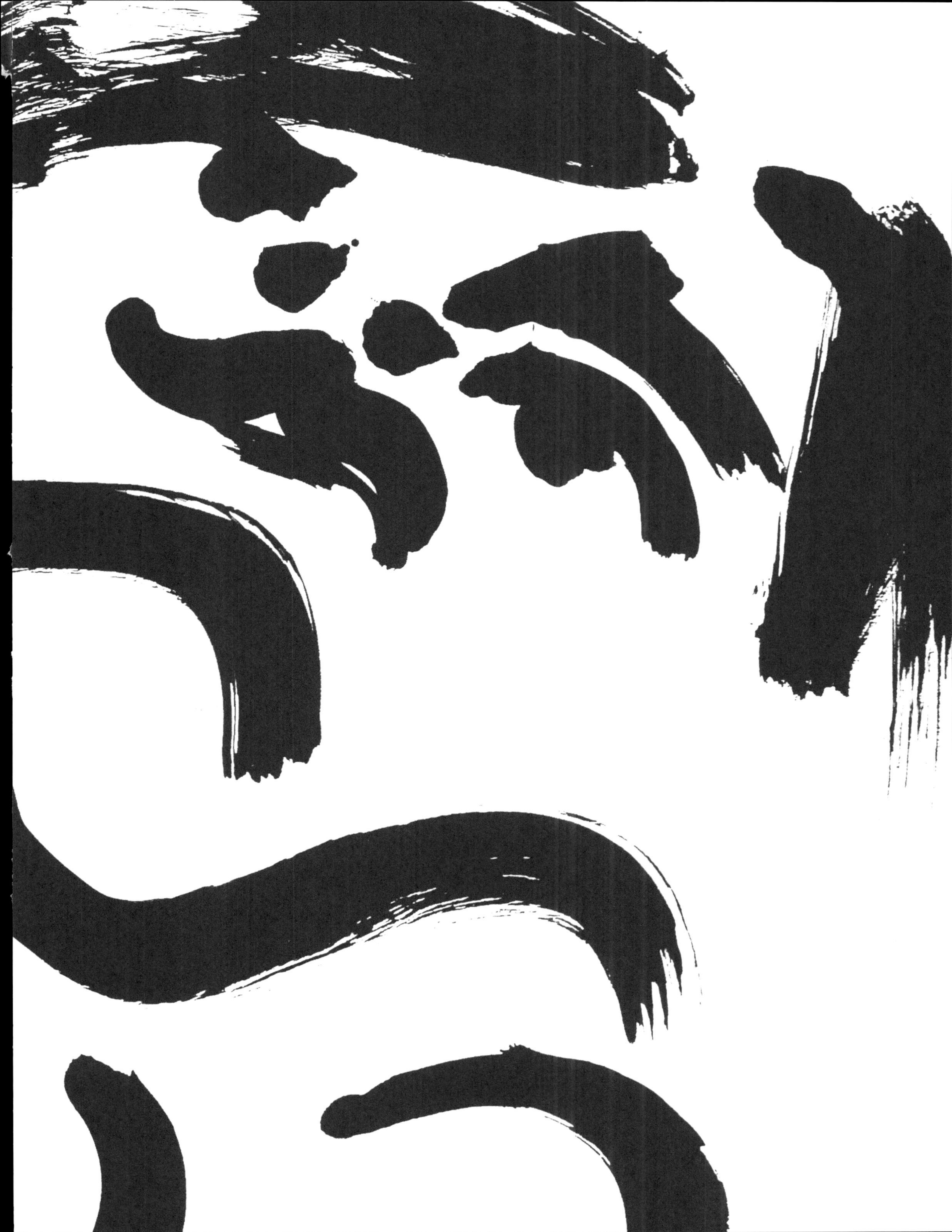

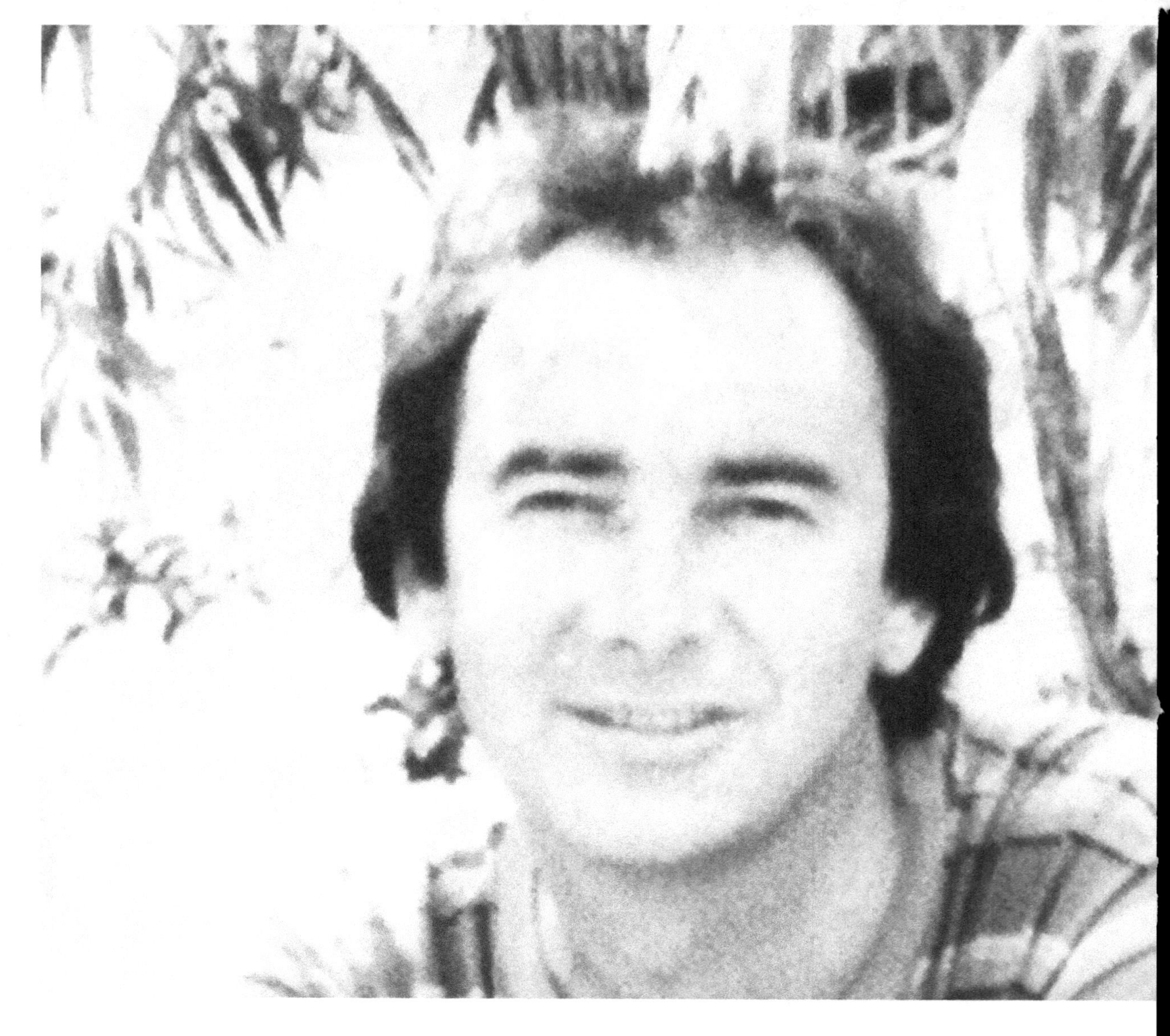

Bruce Blanshard

Born in Melbourne, Australia.
An award-winning Creative
Director, best-selling author,
designer, painter, and editor.

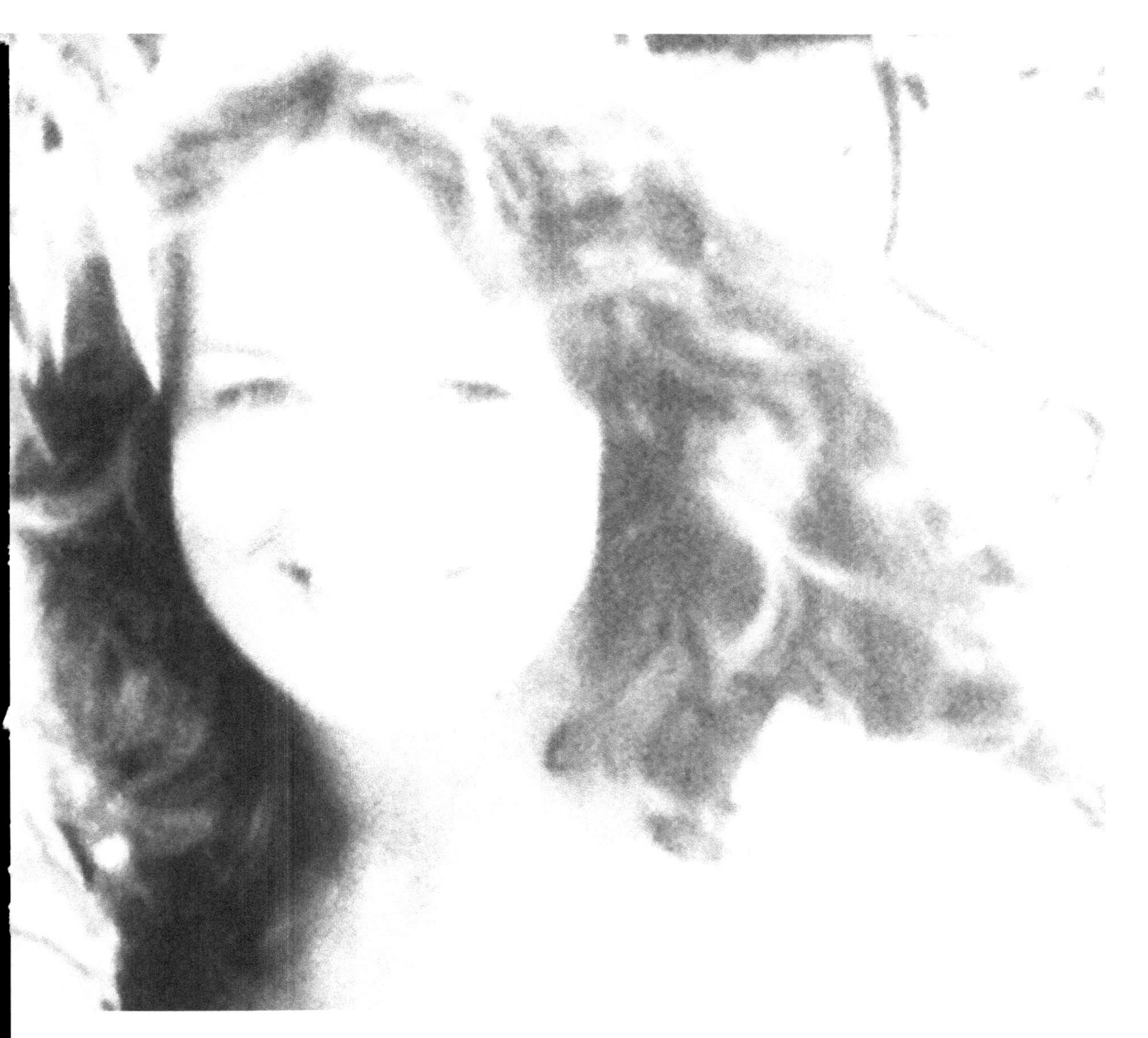

Susan Blanshard
Born in Hampshire, England.
An acclaimed poet,
essayist, prose writer,
novelist, and literary editor.

PAINTING HANOI

The Studio

After negotiating with university cultural directors', the Artist was given a security key to a large, private, upper floor studio in the historic Vietnam University of Fine Arts. Established under French colonial rule in 1925, it was called Ecole des Beaux Arts de l'Indochine, and founded by the French academic and painter Victor Tardieu, and the Vietnamese artist Nam Son.

Blanshard was the only foreign artist granted extended time to paint freely at the communist socialist university without interruption, or censorship. He painted alone, often while the models slept, under the drone of the ceiling fan through the forty degree heat of summers, through the humidity of monsoon rains, through the bitter winters where frozen winds blew down from the mountains to arrive under the French doors. In this way, brush stroke, by brush stroke, Blanshard amassed a great body of figurative work spanning a period of seven years.

The Paintings

The paintings are a selection from the Hanoi series of 800 works completed during the Artist's 'Black Madonna' period.

The Models

Local Vietnamese art models were authorized and approved by the University of Fine Art's administration authorities.

The Paper

The scale of the works cannot be measured by the inside pages of this book as the works are often larger than life. All paintings are black ink on white Xuan rice paper, 842 x 1189 mm or 33.1 x 46.8 inches

The Brushes

Chinese ink brushes have been dated back to 300 B.C. The ones used in the life paintings are from Huzhou in Zhejiang province, China. The main brush used by the artist to paint this series, is called a Jianhao—giant ink brush. The length of the handle and bristles combined make for a total of seventy-eight centimeters. The handles are of spotted bamboo, and the bristles are medium texture made from ox and rabbit hair. The Jianhao is made to hold a large amount of ink for long continuous strokes of both broad and fine detail.

The Charcoal

The artist uses only large fist sized irregular chunks of dense black charcoal.

The Ink

The black Chinese ink (mo) is made from soot and glue from animal hide.

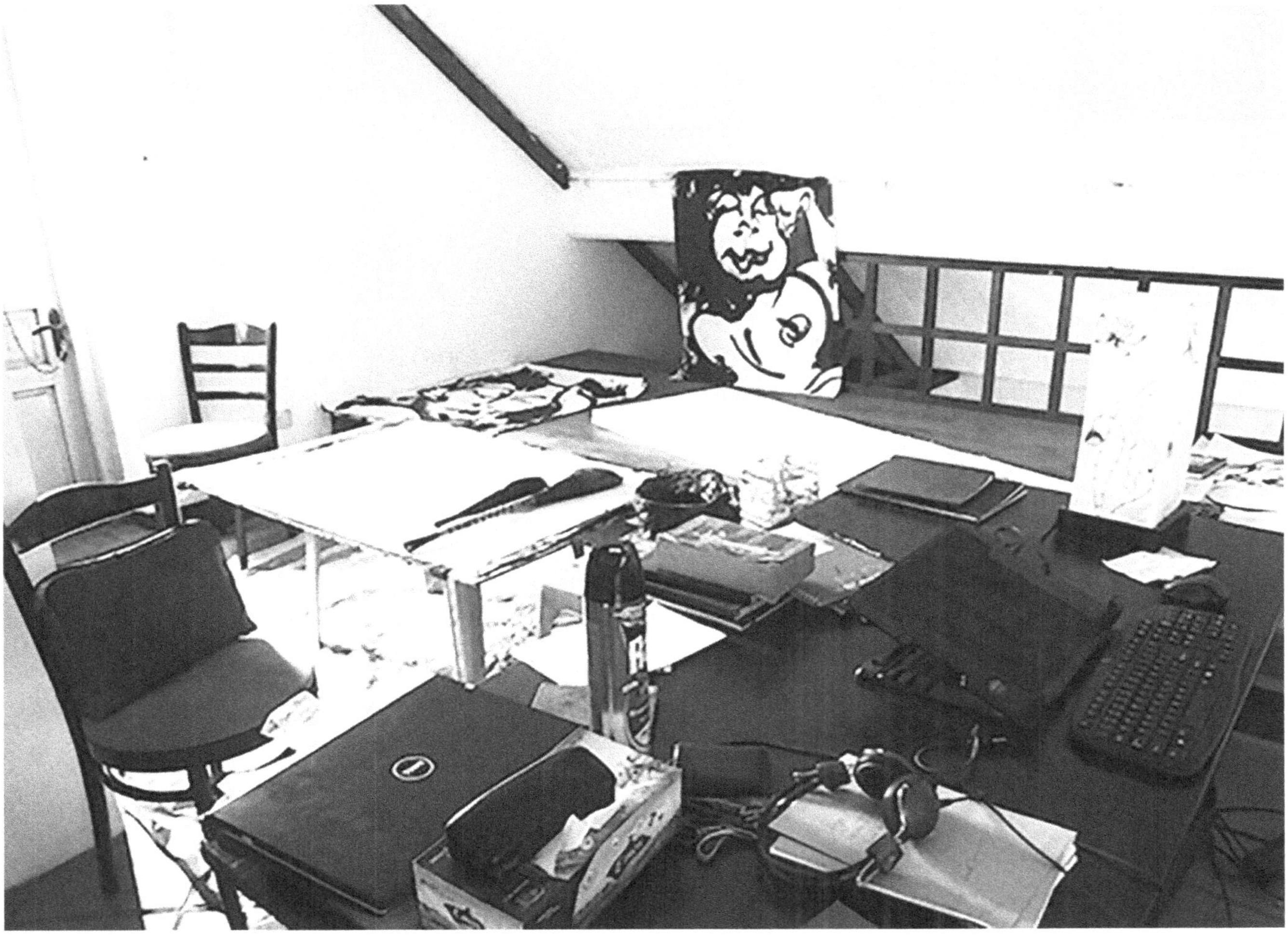

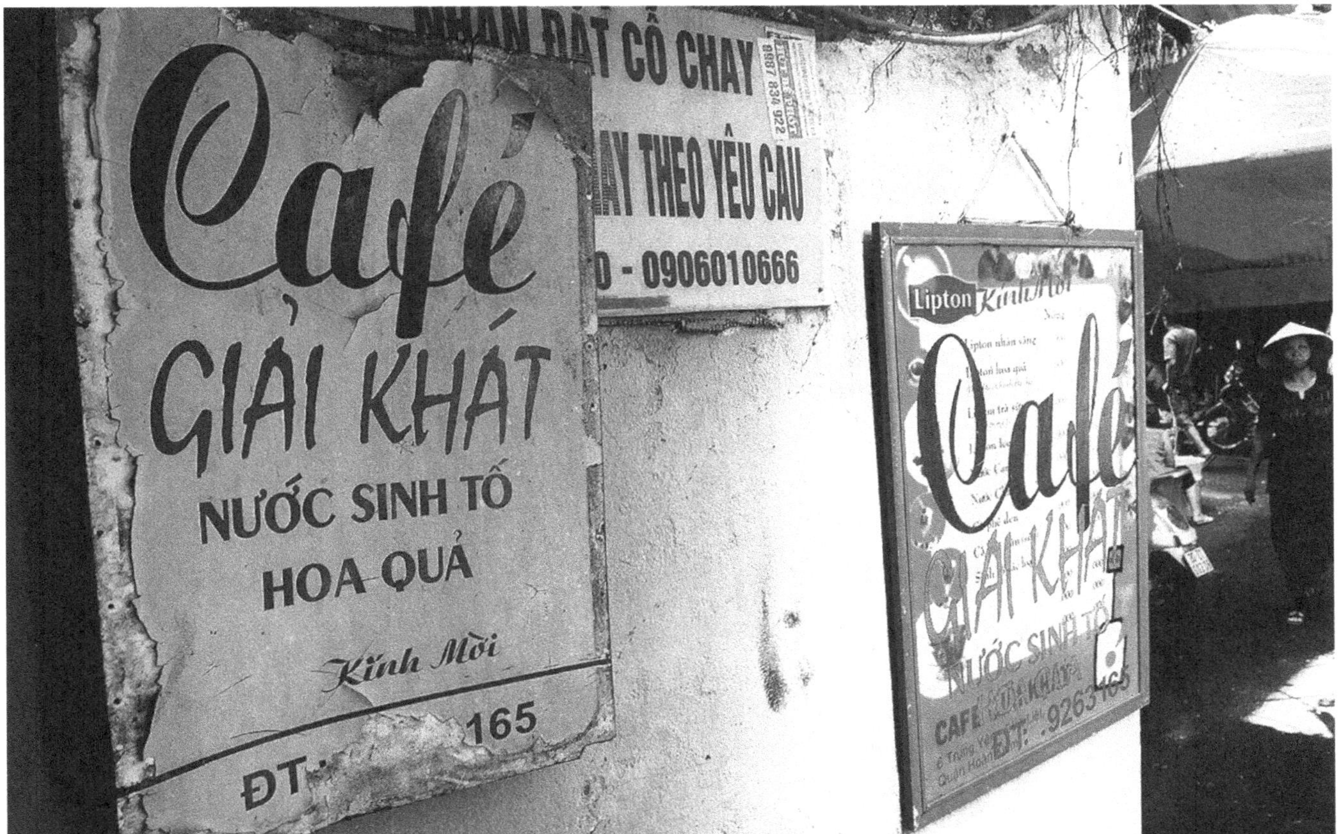

NHẬN ĐẶT CỖ CHAY
9897 834 922
MAY THEO YÊU CẦU
ĐD - 0906010666
Lipton
Cafe
GIẢI KHÁT
NƯỚC SINH TỐ
HOA QUẢ
Kính Mời
ĐT. 165
Cafe
GIẢI KHÁT
NƯỚC SINH TỐ
CAFE
ĐT. 9263165

POETRY HANOI

The Poet

Susan Blanshard's literary work is colored by her multicultural past and present.

She is an English revisionist poet and poetry editor for eighteen translated works: poetry, volumes of collected poems, literary critiques, including the poems for the 10th winner of the Cikada Prize, Sweden (the prestigious Nobel Prize for Asian poetry). She still continues to mentor and support South-East Asian poets and writers.

The Writing Rooms

From her writing rooms at Da Tuong Street, Bo De Lake house, and the colonial villa at Danang Beach, time spent in Vietnam inspired her international literary magazine submissions, and books of collected poems including: Fragments of the Human Heart, Honey in the Blood, Sleeping With the Artist, Poems From the Alley, and individual poems and prose found in later works, Quieter Histories, and Send the Raven.

The Vietnamese Projects

Whilst in Hanoi, she was invited to work on poetry projects for The Vietnamese Writers' Association. Susan was involved in the various international poetry festivals held in Vietnam, and The Vietnamese National Poetry Festivals held inside the walled gardens of The Temple of Literature.

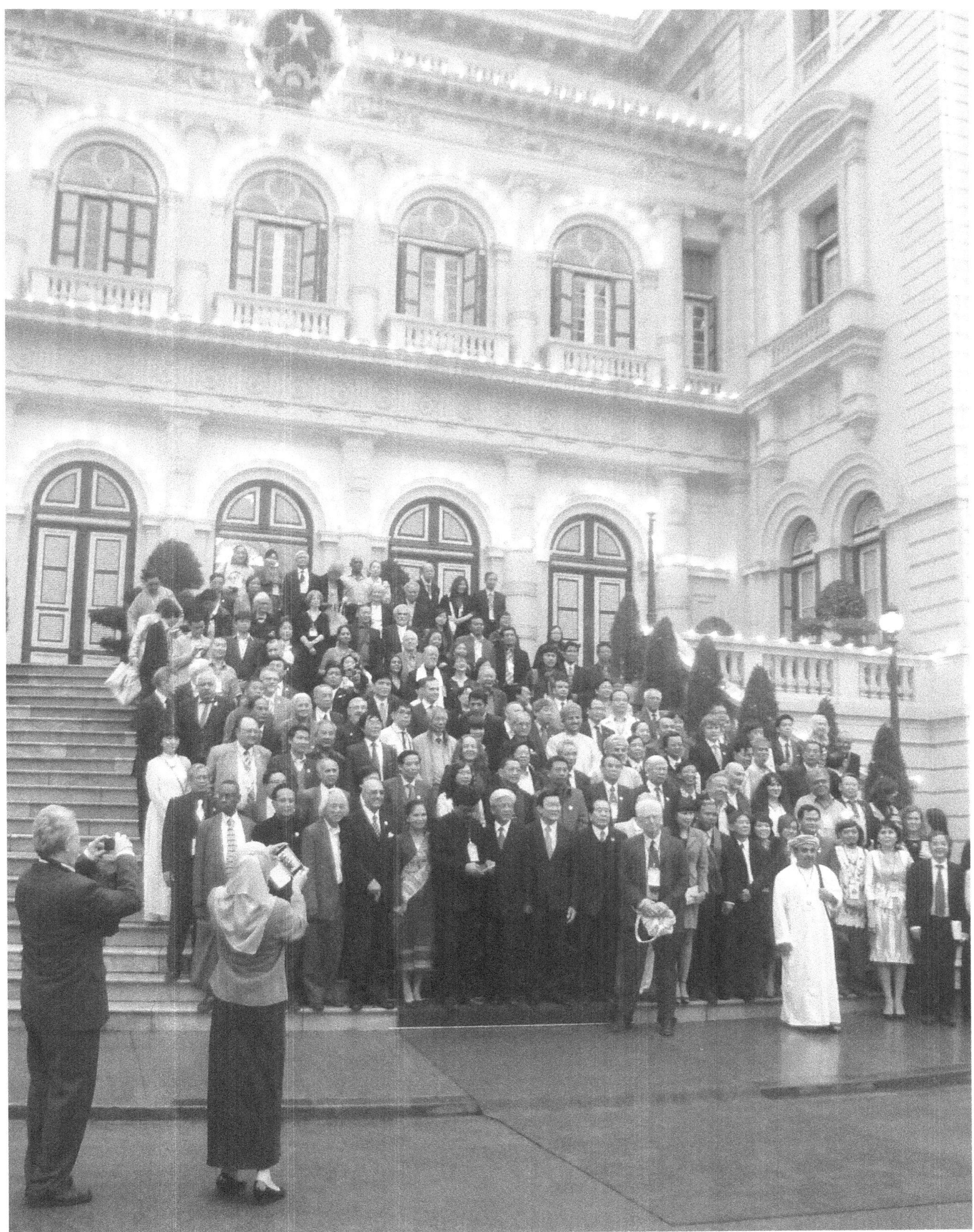